The
Sacred
Passage

The Sacred Passage

LIFE AND TIMES OF A SADISTIC GENTLEMAN

Mwana wa Musikavanhu

atmosphere press

Chapter 1

Lady Marunjeya never publicly displayed the exuberant nature of her internal joy. The recently announced election results had electrified her beyond her wildest dreams. She had called her friends and family several times over. Several press conferences and interviews she had participated in alongside Runobvepi, the Prime Minister-elect, had taken her breath away. A reserved, bat-eared representative of the former colonial master of the nation, a prince, was in the country to officially hand over power and cordially bury the hatchet. Going to celebrate on the streets was a near possibility for lady Marunjeya after having had dinner with this Prince. She could not believe her sudden elevation to the top of the world. A feedback session on how she had performed and appealed to the people was a necessity for her. A comment on her wardrobe and hairstyle was also not spared.

"How fidgety was I? Did I look uneasy? Did I look photogenic? Did I look like royalty or typical of a first lady?" She would ask several endless questions just to make sure she made the right moves for every moment. It was late in the night, and the expectation was for her to be in bed. Even her husband, Runobvepi, was still busy making corrections and additions to his independence eve speech, jotting down notes, planning and scheming for his first tenure in office. Their hotel suite offered them the peace and tranquility they needed to focus on the task ahead, and Runo was making maximum use of that opportunity. He had not shown any visible relief or the smiles of a winner. It all appeared normal for this former rebel and terrorist leader. He modestly handled the sudden transition from combat activism to governance. His former foes embraced him dramatically, turning back on their vile declarations against and characterisation of him. Several other dignitaries, besides the prince, were already in the nation, and several others were expected the following day. The Prime Minister-elect, Runobvepi, his deputy Simo and President designate, Professor Reverend Banner, were going to spend a greater part of the day welcoming visitors at the airport.

Runobvepi's image had been made into a standard portrait of a terrorist, his rebels – the axis of evil and the worst form of any genocidal machine. All this changed in an instant. This was the nature of Runo's relationship with his colleagues of the West, but surprisingly, never at any point had he stopped wining and dining with them. It was a very surprising fact. The news stations were awash with the analysis, reviews, and predictions of the future political and democratic path. Pronouncements made by Runo on rebel unity in governing the new nation were being applauded as a model for all but never as a deterrent to democratic growth. They reviewed possible economic growth projections but hastened to mention that the world was waiting with bated breath as to how stability would prevail before investors trekked to the new nation, scouting for investment opportunities.

In need of attention, Lady Marunjeya was already all over her genius. She knew that public attention would be on her as the First Lady. It did not matter how much thunder Runobvepi would command, provided she had her fair share of publicity. She distracted him from concentrating on his work. Lady Marunjeya hugged him from behind his chair and kissed him on the back of his head, whispering. Runobvepi continued with his work, knowing her usual don't forget me nag. She realised that, as usual, her critical ways were guaranteed to catch his attention. Runo, a past middle-aged man of close to medium height but denied the opportunity by the nature of his genes, was fragile underneath, full of cowardice, insecurity, vengefulness and temperamental, but would not hesitate to pack a ruthless punch at any slight opportunity. His thick-lensed spectacles were always used as a cover-up for his shyness or temper management as he moved them up or down or took them off for a quick cleaning regime. His lady was slightly shorter and slender too. Just as well they had no fruits of the womb; otherwise, he would have alienated himself from those children easily. Besides, the world had been saved, and not passing on his genome to the next generation seemed a welcome development. His greatest quality, however, was patience. He could wear out all his enemies by playing for time and utilising over-ambitious individuals to play his game.

"Imagine how they feel. You begged to join their movement after trekking through the length and breadth of this nation. Now they have to bow to you, a late entrant of the movement."

"It happens when one hesitates to grab opportunities. Politics is a game of chance and keeping the mind and eyes wide open. If you blink, you lose," Runobvepi proudly declared.

"Don't you feel threatened by how much you have betrayed them?"

"Betrayal?" He laughed sarcastically. "The games have not even begun, my dear."

"What else do you intend to do?" She smiled, nudging him on with pride.

"They have to get used to the reality that I am the ultimate authority and have to bow to me."

"It's only a matter of time before someone takes the Party leadership; therefore, you cannot overstep your authority."

"How will that happen?" He looked surprised.

"We are in a democratic republic now, and you have to exercise democracy from the Party level."

"If you remember well, the Party never exercised that democratic right to elect me. Why should they do so in future when there is a precedent?"

"There are too many seniors and mentors to let you run all over them?"

"That's why I have to reduce them to servants, begging me even for the air to breathe. The next time we have elections, there won't even be another Party in this nation except mine. Everyone shall vote for me. There are too many hungry faces after years of war, and this hunger shall bestow more power to me in search and exchange of favours," he answered with vigour, banging on his desk.

She almost clapped to the sound of his voice but flipped her hands continuously to conceal her intentions, although the secret was out in the open. Civilian life was not part of her plan during her life again, and the two seemed to have been cast from the same mould.

"There must be a political script somewhere or with someone. How do you intend to circumvent it?"

"It's only a matter of time. I already have my own set of rules, and soon my script will be complete."

"You forget that the task ahead is enormous. It might be impossible to achieve."

"Like what?"

"There is land to nationalise and redistribute, the economy to revitalise, grow and create employment, health services, education. You are inheriting a debt of nearly $1 billion, and the list is endless."

"Remember, mine is the power to safeguard, cement and consolidate. I never mentioned all those other castles in the air in my victory speech, and therefore, I cannot be held to account for that which I never promised. Power, therefore, shall be my only preoccupation."

"Do not be tempted to let things slide into an abyss because we could be exiled for gross negligence and incompetence."

"No, not at all. You see, my friends shall keep and run the economy while I deal with the politics. That is the trade-off."

"But I don't understand why you wanted to stick with the Bellyman (Only custom made apparel could fit this man. He was tall and bulky with a bulging stomach hence the nickname, Bellyman) in the first place and had to be persuaded to join the movement that rewarded you, eventually?"

"I don't blame you for not understanding because it was complicated."

"What was complicated about such a simple decision?"

"I couldn't leave my job."

"What job are you talking about?"

"To gather information on the Bellyman, sabotage, derail and destroy the movement. Remember when they appointed me Press Secretary, and I deserted them at the African Union international press conference, leaving them without a speech and representative? Bellyman had to conjure up a speech and excuses to save face."

"Oooh, I see. So, what programme do you have for the masses, Mr Prime Minister, besides consolidating political power?"

"Well, that is not a catastrophe because a lot of the 'don't forget us' aid has been pledged, or what's left of it after sifting the valuable precious gems, and will go towards clinics, a few token rural schools and roads to inspire them to do their development."

"How will you balance this friendship of yours?"

"The masses will be easier to manage, but my other friends need a lot of grovelling, negotiation and public insults to whip them into line."

"How are the masses easier to convince?"

"Tell me, my Lady Marunjeya, if, in this whole nation, you have heard of anyone who has graduated as many times as I did?"

"Nobody in the public space. Probably only Mudadi comes close."

"You see, my lady, I am as good as semi-divine to them. Half my work is done."

"What's your answer to Mudadi?"

"He is a novice in the struggle, and I will use hierarchy to keep him down while using education to prop him up as an elusive carrot in the open air. His flip-flops, missteps, blunders and excitable behaviour at the brokered agreement negotiations sealed his fate. Besides, he was vehemently opposed to the war in favour of retaining white privileges with improved recognition of the natives."

"Isn't that contradictory?"

"You only employ tactics that work. This boy has shown overzealousness already and could be an unmitigated political disaster if he goes unchecked."

"Exercise caution, Runo, my precious. He could bite you one day."

"Never. Never. One eye will be on the carrot and the other on the Party hierarchy, and any extra space will be to fight for personal enrichment. You add to those distractions such as vain pleasures, then I am completely assured of my complete stooge."

"Are you that sure?" she asked, full of relief.

"Watch this space," he assured her with a smile.

"I wonder if it was worthwhile to fight as splinter groups in the elections."

"No, it wasn't my lady."

"Why did you do it then?"

"Are you blind, my lady?"

"Blind to what?"

"Reality!"

"What reality?"

"Were we going to be in this privileged position if that had happened?"

"You were still going to beat them, Runo. I know you."

"You dream, my lady, because they voted for the Party, and many hardly knew me. It was Maggie's project that she sold to the Bellyman, intending to retain total control of our nation. Joe picked up the project knowing that he had lost out and was going to work under me."

"Why the Bellyman?"

"She had cut a deal with him and knew he was easy to manipulate. It's a shame that we appended our signatures to this watered-down pact for the continuation of colonisation. We have the burden of taking over all loans Douglas had been given to annihilate us and our kind."

"It's a sad development, but you have time to plan your revenge. Anyway, how was the project going to help Joe?"

"Our rebels covered almost three-quarters of this nation, and everyone only knew him since he was the commander. They composed songs about him and almost worshipped him. The rest of us were unknown quantities. I was better known to the international community than at home, and he wanted to utilise that opportunity to his advantage. Never mind the sincerity of the stillborn project, but I was going to be the biggest loser in the combined election project after the Bellyman. There is no doubt that Joe was going to take charge."

"That was extremely clever."

"Mudadi, too, knew that he would never get into the limelight and had to destroy the idea. That is the reason I snubbed the Bellyman on the project talks after our big agreement."

"You never cease to amaze me, especially when you refer to the failed agreement where the people of this nation were completely outwitted and outmanoeuvred by the leaders of this world. The mosquito had to get not only an insight into our malaria, but also to prescribe a non-negotiable non-antidote."

"You are welcome, my lady. The colonial masters' total lack of morality is unimaginable, especially when they mistake or consider our peace-loving nature for weakness and ineffective-ness. They, therefore, took it for failure that we didn't kill our own to disrupt Collarman (Despite having left his career as a Clergyman, he always sported the religious collar, and the public named him the Collarman) and Douglas' sham elec-tion."

"Everyone has always claimed to belong to the soil. Is hap-piness possible ...."

"It's all sorted already, my dear. Those who chickened out during the war have lost because their farms will be redis-tributed to a few after my colleagues have had a fair share. It should keep them happy for the next twenty years."

"The numbers are not sufficient, my darling."

"It's not about satisfying everyone's need but the spirit, the principle and drawing the heartfelt connection with the people. One white man, Jan Smuts, a former leader of our neighbouring nation, in his Rhodes Memorial lecture at Oxford University in November 1929, said that *Natives have the simplest of minds, understand only the simplest ideas or ideals and are almost animal-like in the simplicity of their minds and ways. They are happy-go-lucky, childlike with child psychology, good-tempered, care-free, love wine and song and have no desire to improve themselves.*"

"He was proved wrong by our taking up arms to fight his kind. You may need another option."

"We can always talk of compensation, and if all fails, I will direct anger at the incumbents who refuse to vacate people's territory. I will sacrifice them for my gain."

"Will that work?"

"It definitely will, especially with the sympathy and sup-port of the people."

"Your insufferable insolence and cold-blooded betrayal of your kind are unprecedented," she teased him with a finger on his lips.

"Thank you for the compliment, my lady."

She smiled and kissed him, getting ready to take a much-needed sleep in preparation for the independence eve festivities the following day. Her mind was still not settled on her outfit for the occasion as she wondered whether to charter a plane and look for another or force one of the leading departmental stores to open for business to satisfy her need. It looked too extravagant and unlike the etiquette expected of a first lady; therefore, she restrained herself. Though they may have been from different backgrounds, it was clear that *dzinofura nzivani*. However, her short and essential sleep did not happen. She was up periodically checking the time and on Runo. Lady Marunjeya took the opportunity to read through Runo's victory speech and see if there was anything she could have missed from Runo's intentions.

After gleaning through the speech, Lady Marunjeya quickly realised that Runo was non-committal on core issues that meaningfully changed people's lives. The biggest winner and favoured children were the incumbent oppressors after being accommodated and promised all they ever wanted and more. Their fears were allayed in reconciliation. The locals got nothing for their war scars and trauma. Their situation was never going to change except that they could sing freedom. The Bellyman's negotiation had already been undermined by the inclusion of the oppressor on the same table with, most probably entrenched rights and privileges. Any excuse for non-delivery was preempted by the call for patience. Many casualties were anticipated with the coalition, from all rebel teams, a sacrifice that Runo was prepared to make to please the oppressor. Besides, the coalition with Runo was a key element in limiting and suppressing the level of democracy in the nation. Everyone was supposed to have common interests and no dissenting voices. It dawned on her that her man was true to his word in their last conversation. It was already a closed chapter before anything had begun. It worried her, but she hoped to change his mind over time. She feared retribution, considering the courage, valour and selflessness they showed during the war. Runo was suddenly behaving as if he was the only significant man from the trenches of war and could dictate his will on his colleagues and the general public. The masses were not even privy to the agreement that Runo was so fond of referring to, which was a tragedy.

*

Runo had watched carefully as the press interviewed the Bellyman, his biggest political rival. He had taken his loss in stride and displayed a very mature image of himself. His score was only a third of what Runo had garnered, but he refused to be used by the media by being drawn into tribal politics or picking a fight with any of his opponents. "We have no tribes but a collection of groups who have been assigned certain tribal names by the colonial powers. It is therefore mischievous to create tribes when we have none," Bellyman correctly and rightfully responded.

"But Mr Bellyman, you seem to have support from only one section of the country. Isn't it fair to say your vote was tribal-based?"

"If that is the case, how do you account for the five seats our Party got from the other sections of the country?"

"Your point is noted, Mr Bellyman, so what demands are you going to make in the mooted coalition government?"

"It's not about making demands but negotiating. We have to come to a mutual agreement," Bellyman was very composed. He never complained about the problems with the electoral process, which was fraught with irregularities and Runo's untoward conduct. He knew he had lost his deal and Runo had pulled a fast one.

Runo knew he had a formidable opponent, though weakened by the election results. His opponent's ability to speak with a forked tongue was a reflection of political maturity and full acquisition of an essential politically deviant behaviour. Bellyman was particularly devastated by the results in his hometown, where Runo's Party lost but only by a small margin. He had expected a clean sweep with a very poor showing by others. Runo knew this man could be brewing something yet to fully mature with time. He particularly despised his careless choice of association, often communicating with Douglas, Maggie and even the hostile neighbour.

When he had been asked about merging the political Parties, Runo was very dodgy in his response. He had said, "While unity is vital there isn't a quick fix for crucial matters like merging two political parties. It takes time to achieve consensus". It was, therefore, justifiable to have an equally calculated response from the Bellyman. Refusal by the Bellyman to take a higher post, but in a ceremonial role of President, had forced Runo to appoint an unknown quantity in Professor Reverend Banner. From that point, Runo suspected that the Bellyman could be harbouring a sinister agenda. Bellyman also talked about political tolerance, referring to the pre-election violence where Bellyman's candidates were brutalised or denied access to the people. This was in the nation's eastern districts. Two of the Bellyman's candidates and eighteen party workers had been killed. Several were beaten up but survived. Again, this was against a backdrop of the colonial Governor having decided to postpone an election in those areas. Two weeks before the elections, to everyone's surprise and against all odds, the Governor then decided the elections would proceed. Runo did not take any of the Bellyman's suggestions kindly. The Bellyman, however, had explained that he wanted to assist in lawmaking and running of ministries. In addition, he wanted the repressive and restrictive colonial laws abolished. Still, Runo took it as an insult, and their love and hate, hide and seek history, was not ideal for trust. Runo had also escaped a few near misses during the election campaign period, and the first and usual suspect was the Bellyman, although there was a hostile neighbour and the outgoing oppressors also. His short-wired brain was not open to suggestions and advice, especially when not solicited or contrary to his expectations. It was only a matter of time before taking his revenge on the Bellyman. On other matters, Runo had done his part by encouraging all to stay and even invited those who had left to come back and rebuild the nation. The Prime Minister-elect was also taking part in a documentary to expose the brutality of the outgoing regime in a toned-down manner and reflect on his time in prison. Maximum positive publicity before any negative sentiment that could be expressed was his major scoring point, and he never wanted to miss the opportunity.

People were dancing and singing in the streets for a whole week leading to the declaration of independence. As he had suspected, his rule was going to be safe due to this celebratory mood. People were celebrating the departure of a racist and oppressive leader rather than a reasonable incoming leader. Freedom from restrictive laws and discriminatory actions was of paramount importance. With the new regime, it was clear a thief would be a thief irrespective of skin colour and, therefore, black lawmen had their job somewhat simplified. Blacks could now walk on pavements without the fear of having police dogs set on them. Any shop, restaurant or hotel presumably would be open for people from across the racial divide. Finally, blacks were going to be allowed to visit parks and other recreational facilities. Participating in pension plans and other company benefit schemes would be open to all. Visiting towns from the countryside was not going to require a *Pass* anymore. Those in the countryside had their fair share of celebrations, as they could sing and dance all night long. Curfews or any state of emergency were a thing of the past. They could afford to jump sky-high, proclaiming that independence had been achieved, finally. This was good news for Runo and a necessary distraction. It was going to take a long time for the mood to wear off, and by that time he would have consolidated his position.

Two clergymen who had performed dismally were very negative in their comments, but were not given a big platform to air all their views. They were perceived to be insignificant. Their views were, therefore, not important for the new nation. One clergyman, the Collar Man, who was a former ally of the colonial government, did not stop talking about the unfairness of the electoral process. He, however, was not aware of how people despised him for being a friend of Douglas, the leader of the oppressive regime. His truth, or the truth, was, therefore, not important at that stage. It was his army that was causing havoc during the election period. His inept and trigger-happy excuse for an army, the *Pfumo* band of bandits, terrorised villagers day and night while other normal army personnel were in demobilisation camps. A personal hate song denigrating Collar Man had been composed especially for him. During the election period, his helicopter-based campaigns and pamphlet handouts were never appreciated. People felt it was showing off after they did not accord him a platform when he personally visited the communities.

Only a handful of supporters, averaging about twenty people, mainly women from his church, attended his flopped rallies. To claim that his supporters were being intimidated was more than a double standard and a typical excuse for a religious character. His political career was put to bed by the election results, although he never wanted to accept and embrace reality. Mudadi quickly took care of Collar Man and showed his irrationality. He said of him, ".*Suffering from such a psychosis is expected when a leader unexpectedly loses power. He is in denial.*" The comment put to rest Collar Man's assertions. The other clergyman, the Stick Man (His Party symbol was a walking stick, and his campaign buzzwords were "Put your vote on the stick." So people called him the Stick Man), realised the futility of crying foul at this stage and held his peace. He knew the game had been lost, and chances of recovery were mathematical. His Party had been taken over by Runo, and his new Party had been handed a heavy defeat. It was best to think of other options than fighting a lost battle.

Runo was not going to overrun the oppressors and change laws at will because a deal had been made for the oppressive old regime to be accommodated in the new setting, having guaranteed constituencies and executive positions. This shocked most people, especially those in the countryside. Rumour had it that when the war ended, the colonial oppressors had surrendered unconditionally. When an election was announced, they could not comprehend why the rebel leadership had not assumed power and the oppressor was still running the nation's affairs.

The explanation given pushed the majority to vote and rid the nation of the oppressor, and the results were fully reflective of this anger. A transition was necessary, and the oppressor was overseeing that process until the people were able to run their affairs was the insinuation and rumoured response. It irked the rural people, especially after having borne the brunt of the war from the onset to the day it was concluded. Their views were divergent from the others. On top of their wish list was cleansing the whole nation of the colonial oppressor. That matter was not negotiable. Scepticism was now growing that the rebels they supported had its leadership now immersed in a loving relationship with that which they despised the most. Runo's pronouncements on forgiveness, reconciliation and working together would have been roundly condemned if most of these people had access to television and radio services or knew what it meant.

Douglas was the most reviled of the lot, and many believed he had one eye and a big horn on his forehead. Many, however, were surprised when pictures of him were circulating in the newspapers and magazines. However, the belief did not end, as people assumed that the pictures were being doctored for the public. How were these people – so ravaged by the war, oppression by Douglas and his kind, deprived of land, killed and maimed for crying freedom – ever going to be rehabilitated? Rehabilitated to learn that they and the oppressor were on par, not one above the other. To learn to love and live side by side as fellow citizens with those who once crushed and trampled on their rights with impunity and with no recourse for justice. Were they going to continue paying dearly to learn the oppressor's language? Was this new deal only artificial and for political convenience?

Chapter 2

That morning, on the eve of independence, she could have continued to interrogate him for her safety, security, and plans if there were no rehearsals. Her curiosity and excitement had to be bottled up until they were together again. Runo had to spend time at the airport receiving guests while she had to attend to other matters. The independence eve ceremony was held in a football stadium, with terraces on two sides and only a short fence on two sides. No roof had been constructed to shelter the people from the elements of weather. There were no chairs, so people had to make do with concrete terraces. A singer, leader of the rebel choir, led entertainment proceedings with his group. He performed from the heart, with all his might, soul and emotion, belting *Maruza*. Its chorus was repetitive but bolstered the message that the Colonial Wealth Plunderers were deceptive liars, coming from lands afar, had lost, were finished, and their time was up. A sweet message it was for the local people as they pointed at those of the colonial race in the stadium.

This was the stuff people wanted to sing along to and listen to all day. Douglas and his crew not only needed to get the message but to see first-hand how the people felt about them. If only they understood the local language or had bothered to make it official. Unfortunately, they did not care because they had made their deal. Their safety was guaranteed and leaving was a personal choice. The singer added another tune specifically for the bat-eared representative in *Mkoma Chari*, giving him a message for the ladybug about the excitement over the unshackling of colonial chains. The standing ovation, crowd uproar and electrifying moment in the stadium to the singing aroused Runo's envious anger. He never celebrated with the crowd, and Lady Marunjeya quickly noticed and returned to her seat. Runo was in his trademark tunics to continue identifying with the struggle and the people. He did not want to look extravagant at this stage to capture the hearts and minds of the people. His woolly, almost medium-grown hair appeared ages in the making but impossible to get to an Afro-hair trademark worn by most adult men of that time. Maybe it was due to some undesirable genes in his system. Lady Marunjeya was in traditional attire, capped with a scarf. She wore short African hair locks. The jet-black complexion of the pair made them seem as if they were cut for the moment.

"Why aren't you celebrating? This is our moment. Go with the crowd."

"This one is for the crowd and not for the leader." He showed a lot of apprehension and loathing.

"Yet the leader celebrates with his crowd and works according to their will."

"Not for me," he responded without any joy in his heart.

"I know you, Runo. Something is eating you. Say it."

"He sings as if he has conquered this nation when he is just a musician. He doesn't realise that he is just a little cog in my big wheel."

"Yet that little cog serves a huge task and purpose in the big wheel! Get over it, Runo. He will never threaten you in any way. You are so fragile and emotional."

"Let's focus on other issues and forget this one."

"I don't understand you. That song is an arsenal in your cache. It should serve you for a few years while you focus on other things. Are you going to react the same when the *Pidigori* man comes on stage?"

"That man knows my enemies, and that song shall get all the recognition it deserves until the people are tired of it or I get a better replacement."

"Explain, Runo."

"A song for one bolsters my position, not a generic or collective one. A collective one makes me a racist, and I should not have allowed it. Songs must be specific and not carry a group message."

"I see. You hate collective scorning. What a coincidence?"

"Exactly. It makes one lose the argument."

"Your will matters most, and other people's views are secondary or not welcome."

"Everyone must bend to my will."

"That's a discussion for another day, but isn't Nester your favourite?"

"Not in a thousand years! He is too enlightened and could ruin my future."

"Why did you invite him for this occasion from across the world, then?"

"To keep the crowd entertained and make this a memorable day in their hearts and minds. They think he is the world's finest. His consciousness is unparalleled, and that is reflected in many of his songs, especially the one he did for us."

"You have Buffalo Soldier, Redemption Song and many more that do not seem to support your point. Why did you agree to invite him, then?"

"Cliff Richard is my favourite and should have graced this occasion if it wasn't this pointless attempt in implementing democracy, not people who go against the grain like Nester. I guess I might have to use his message of hope amid oppression and the theme of a political campaign, which is inseparable from my advantage. You invoke that innate emotion in the people to rise to your cause because I have no choice."

"You contradict yourself a lot, and I never seem to follow your argument."

"Thank you."

"Look at the Bellyman over there feeling sorry for himself and waiting to report to you. The Collar Man and the Stick Man did not even attend the occasion."

"They are bad losers. The Collar Man assumed a miracle would descend the pulpit and save him, while the Stick Man thought Moses' magic would revitalise his stick and make him leader again. The Bellyman is my only credible opposition for now, but his poor results show that he is conquerable. His moves and tactics have become all too familiar. I should finish him off before the next election."

"The Collar Man once did good things for all government workers that they won't forget him."

"In every rural constituency I went to, they sing about him."

"That is surely not a good sign for you."

"Quite the opposite, my lady. The song likens his bottom to a grinding mill. Tougher than a mill, my lady, that it can crush undried millet."

"Eeish. I cannot imagine such a horrendous comparison and would want to quickly forget about it. Do you suspect anyone might revolt against you, considering all their preju-dices?"

"The mob rules, my lady. Once I stand to deliver my speech, hoist the flag and light the torch, everyone will go wild."

"Still, it doesn't address people's agendas."

"That power will deal a huge blow to the enemy. They shall wilt by my command of the crowd."

"How will you work with everyone going forward?"

"I work alone. That crowd shall be my weapon."

"How do you hope to achieve that?"

"A token gratitude tour is on the cards after this occasion across all provinces. If I cannot pull the crowds, I will fake them and bus them to ensure I send a devastating message to the enemy."

"How can you tell that it will work?"

"It's the post-independence trend. There is no rocket science. Remember, Jan Smuts said that Blacks are the most patient of animals, next to the ass. I shall exploit that psychology."

"For how long do you anticipate this support?" she was shocked.

"Maybe fifteen to twenty years. Piece of cake. The only dissent can be from the Party ranks."

"Provided people have jobs and incomes are sustainable, but if that does not hold, what will be your fallback position?"

"My lady, you worry too much. Save the stress for when I am dead. I told you that I am indispensable due to my qualifications. Mudadi will be the weapon in my bag of tricks. Considering his immaturity and over-ambition, my task is easy."

"For how long can you associate with Mudadi and any comrades not content with unfulfilled promises."

"Mudadi is a political freshman who thinks education gives him the right to lead. He has a short political shelf life. Mine was a decoy rather than an end in itself because I had all the time on my hands and friends to make everything happen."

Runo's moment came, and he carried himself like a gentleman. He spoke eloquently, endearing himself to every international ally he wanted to reach out to. Ziva, a key ally of Runo and the man who masterminded his rise to the helm of the rebel movement, was very hurt. He expected a smashing speech heralding a new beginning. This was the great betrayal he had never anticipated. The man he had assumed to be a passionate nationalist and patriot had turned out to be a chameleon. Ziva walked out of the proceedings in immense emotional pain just after the speech and impatiently craved to confront Runo before he led everyone astray. Runo's earlier suggestion that everyone should turn their swords into ploughshares and now talking about forgiving and forgetting, unity and reconciliation meant he was turning back on the people. Ziva was not amenable to the idea of sharing anything with the oppressor. He detested that idea and would not mince his words with the press. Ziva was candid but very temperamental, very impatient and had the energy of two men combined. He had piercing eyes and an imposing face complemented by a voice capable of tearing into one's heart and immediately instilling fear. It was very easy to identify him from afar because of his trademark brisk walk and his well-built body.

Lady Marunjeya memorised part of the speech and was disgusted by the rest. Their intentions should at least not have been made so apparent. She particularly found the praise on the Queen, her emissary and representative, nauseating, although she nearly worshipped them. For her, it was best to praise the collaborators of the struggle and make a diplomatic overture to the rest of the world in a toned-down manner. She had to hold her anger. Being in a public setting and at a key event, she had to display her best behaviour as Runo went on and on with his speech. It was time to listen so that she could interrogate him later.

In this instance, Lady Marunjeya just went with the crowd, but she was worried Runo could cost their stay at the helm. Ziva never bothered. He couldn't find a suitable alternative, and the timing was wrong. This was a loss he needed to accept and wait for an opportune moment.

Chapter 3

"Runo, I must congratulate you on the work you have done so far. It has been a tiring period for you."

"I appreciate that, but remember that I need to be on top of the situation. Success in itself isn't final; it's just the beginning of new obligations that must be achieved." Ziva was the last person he wanted to discuss this with. He never nodded in agreement with any ideas and was very defensive at times until he realised Ziva was not relenting.

"Last night was great for you, but the tone was not right for the people."

"Must we go through every concern, Ziva?"

"Every successful man needs advisers. Let me mould you into an ideal leader for the nation."

"What makes you think I am a failure already?"

"*Mazano marairanwa, Runo, mbimbindoga akasiya jira kumasese.* Give me a chance."

"What do you think I should have done better?"

"Your speech was too academic and dispossessing of our people. I had hoped you could do better."

"Explain it to me, Ziva."

"You were supposed to address the people, not your colonial masters. The Queen, her representative or that Lord emissary, they have nothing to do with our independence. It's ours; they cannot grant us that which belongs to us, yet you gave them acres of space in your speech. You overly expressed your gratitude to them above everyone else, yet they watched in the comfort of their homes as their colonial orphans were causing mayhem to our people. They never lifted a finger, yet you pay homage to them. To perpetuate their evilness, they even forced us to sign the pact for the continuation of slavery and colonisation. I expected that representative to offer an apology, not to walk tall and assume he was doing us a favour. How about a thank you to Marshal, Juli, Fidhe, Kenny and the others who helped us? Did our people die, suffer and sacrifice in vain? Over a hundred years of oppression, genocide and servitude, yet you call for forgiveness when we have to teach them a well-deserved lesson, push them against the wall and shoot them. You are very learned, Runo. How do you expect the people to suddenly forgive and forget because you said so? Is there going to be an appeasement? What do they get, Runo? Rehabilitation or financial assistance? I don't see you taking away anything from these Wealth Plunderers, yet our people continue to give the other cheek countless times. How does hatred turn into friendship overnight while the aggressors are still holding on to their source of oppression? I had never anticipated this twisted behaviour when I pushed you for leadership."

"Don't forget that it's Marshal, Kenny and Juli who pressured us to sign the pact of continuation of colonial privileges, on instructions from our oppressors. We were unprepared and were never given time to caucus when we were bundled onto that negotiating table at the behest of the world's leading nation. The brief disagreement break we got, the same guys prevailed upon us to immediately return to the table and sign that fraudulent document. Kenny was even more hostile to us all the way through that we failed to co-exist with him. Besides, you know our brothers to the south are still in shackles. If we take a hardline stance, they will never attain freedom."

"You know they are being used as ponies to delay our attainment of complete freedom. Let's push them out before they can be comfortable. We have the power, and no one can touch us."

"I do comprehend your extreme views, but leadership is about compromise."

"How do you compromise when you are losing what is rightfully yours? We don't owe them anything, and they never helped us in the war. We should, in fact, say thanks but no thanks. Time for you to pack your bags and go. What is ours only belongs to us."

"We don't want to start another war, Ziva. They will take a simple deviation from our agreement as a trigger for conflict. Our people need peace. Our nation is still fresh from birth. Enough of confrontation; we have to live side by side as friends and neighbours. There is enough for all of us."

"I have travelled the length and breadth of this nation. There is overcrowding in the rural areas and hardly any population in all the massive family estates for your newfound friends that you love so much. There is enough for your friends and nothing for our people. In the midst of plenty, there is hunger and starvation, and without crowding, the people have become overcrowded. The burden created by your friends, the biological warfare instruments used during the war, have turned into an epidemic. It will take months and years to contain the contaminated forests and rivers. Hospitals are filled with measles and smallpox sufferers. Dogs are being put down every day because of rabies, and cattle are not spared from anthrax and foot and mouth disease. You must hold them accountable and make them pay like we are now forced to pay for the debt they accumulated in an attempt to exterminate us."

"Business needs have to come first; otherwise unemployment will skyrocket. Let us live side by side as friends. You know very well that we cannot grab all the farms contrary to the willing seller willing buyer clause in our agreement."

"Our interests and needs are and will always be different. There is no way we can achieve a common goal. Let's not debate on such a straightforward subject. These scars (he lifted his shirt to show him bullet wounds) will not go away and will always be a reminder of your friends' brutality. Chase them away so we can run this nation on our own terms. Remember, its willing plunderer to willingly robbed situation we have cornered ourselves into. That narrative is not acceptable."

"I am still digesting," Runo was thoroughly unhappy due to the presumed pride and honour he thought he would earn by presiding over a white population. Chasing them and reigning over lesser native beings was for no legacy benefit to him. He wanted to be different from other states where the white population completely disappeared after independence. If it meant sacrificing his people to keep them, he was prepared to do it.

"There is nothing to think about. If they believe their origins are great, why don't they leave us alone? They can't because they are too comfortable at our expense and have come to love this nation to the extent that they forgot where they belong. We are going into this deal having lost already like we did at the brokered agreement to end war and go for elections. They made their deal; they own everything, we have nothing, and they want to stop us from using our newly acquired boot. After a while they will take away our boot indirectly. Be wary of them. They scarred us, murdered and dehumanised us, yet they talk civilisation. You, of all people, must know that. My assumption of your immunity to the cancer of a colonial mentality getting to the core of your soul was nothing but just my wild imagination. Now I know that education only brings out the arrogant nature of a human being instead of civilising him. I didn't realise you were only envious of Douglas' lifestyle, which you will assume and perfect as we have helped you dislodge him."

"I have heard you, Ziva, but I have to see how best we can co-exist and manoeuvre under the circumstances."

"You cannot co-exist with them. This is the reason their Marget Sanger, in her 1920 article 'The Need for Birth Control in America', said of us, *'The meaningless, aimless lives which cram this world of ours, hordes of people who are born, live, yet have absolutely nothing to advance the race one iota. Such human weeds clog the path, drain up the energies and resources of this little earth. We must clear the way for a better world, we must cultivate our garden.'* They colonised the whole world but never got along with anyone. They live and thrive off other people's misery and tears to satisfy their avarice. In fact, they crave to eliminate us so that they can live freely in our space. *Mapenzi anomwa muto vamwe vachida kuseva.* Not in our lifetime will they respect us. This is the reason they go everywhere, dig up graves and monuments without due regard for our values. Is it possible for us to do the same in their land?"

"That is true. Let me work on a plan, Ziva. Leave it to me."

"I am very disappointed, and you must know that's why they call me *Mafirakureva.*" Ziva left Runo's hotel suite knowing very well that he had backed the least suitable candidate for the job. It was too late, but he needed to fix it at the next Party congress. Runo, for his part, knew Ziva had to be tamed. A strategy to manage him out slowly needed to be in place without delay; otherwise he was going to derail Runo's plans.

In the following days, Runo announced his cabinet members. Two key portfolios were allocated to the former oppressors. It was an assurance that business, agricultural and farm interests were not going to be tampered with. The cabinet was one of the largest, not only in the history of the country but the world. At least it helped him to keep everyone in check. Runo even appointed some of his friends not affiliated with his Party or any other political Party. Surprisingly, some appointments were members of a defunct tribal political party formed during the struggle by Runo's relatives and friends.

These people were aggrieved by the low level of participation by members of their community in the war against Douglas. Unfortunately, their grievances were misplaced because participation in the war was voluntary. At least they could have mobilised their colleagues to join the war instead of starting a struggle within a struggle.

The public wondered how people with such divisive minds could be entrusted with the leadership of the nation. This move hinted at the possibility that Runo was the mastermind of the tribal political party. As for the excessive executive members, however, the public excuse was pinned not on incompetence but the need to accommodate everyone in a united government. Mudadi found it easy to explain once approached by the press. Runo picked the same mantra, and the issue was sealed. He seemed content and relieved that his subordinates were busy celebrating their appointments. It gave him the much-needed space to plan ahead of them. No one questioned why some notable names were left out, or key individuals banished completely. The only other person to interrogate him, after Ziva, was Lady Marunjeya.

"The Governor was watching while everyone was toiling and struggling to stay alive. Did you have to shower him and the Queen with so much praise, leaving nothing for your people?"

"Don't forget the gift the good Governor awarded me. How many friends will deny you the same opportunity?" Runo was calmer and more attentive, hoping to ensure he sold his vision successfully at home before attempting to do the same to others. He was occasionally nodding and looking down or sideways.

"What gift, Runo? And where is it?"

"You have a short memory. Remember he allowed a vote in the eastern districts where we had denied access to the Bellyman and his team in retaliation. It ensured a clean sweep for me, and the Queen never condemned the process, thereby giving our win perfect legitimacy."

"I understand, but aren't there supposed to be rules, rules that are foolproof to avoid such a situation?"

"No. You just have to take a gamble and hope no one will complain."

"It's a twisted world! Anyway, why did you dump the key security personnel and place them in some war zone or hotly contested strip in the world, opting to be served by the enemy?"

"It's payback time for the promises made."

"You could instead have used soldiers, not Intelligence men. Are you losing it, Runo?"

"I am the president now. At least you can call me, Mr President, RG or the Nob. Even Your Excellency will do, my lady."

"Don't divert, Runo. Why did you do it?"

"Those men were loyal to Joe and could have dumped me any day. I could not take that chance. Besides, they are from the wrong tribe. At least my old folks cannot let me down."

"What do you hope to accomplish by this non-mission you assigned them?"

"Nature will decide, and time will tell."

"What a horrible decision! They have become the new Uriahs, not worthy of any tears. If they make it, what will you do?"

"Their top jobs will be gone, and they will have to be content with the leftovers or languish outside the system if they so choose."

"You never cease to amaze me. On the one hand, you claim to be a dear friend and ally of Afar, but on the other hand, you collaborate with his worst enemies, the Easily Riled Pretenders."

"Political survival is essential. There are no rules of engagement on who can or cannot be your friend. You have to always keep an open mind."

"Will Ken serve you as well as you desire?"

"He knows his interests are protected and has all the time to decide on his next step."

"If he leaves soon, how will you cope? And has he severed

his ties with our hostile neighbour?"

"Don't forget the Great Crocodile is the most able among my team. Even Ken and everyone else in this country fears his name. He stopped the most irrational act by Peter that could have seen me lose this top job and possibly my head as well. I have promised not to interfere with the affairs of our hostile neighbours, and I hope they will understand my sincerity."

"You have agreed to have Maggie's and her allies' instructors and doctors for the army. Are you not afraid that they could be pushing for a sinister agenda?"

"Anything to stop her from supporting the Bellyman is welcome."

"Instructors, I can understand, but why doctors?"

"Our men were living in squalid conditions in the bush. It would do them some good if they were constantly subjected to medical tests, vaccinations and top-class treatment."

"You easily appointed the Sloppy Man for the army. Are you not afraid of him just as you are of Peter?" Sloppy Man was said to have been ruthless and unreasonable during the armed struggle. Runo felt that this was the right man to use for quashing any dissent. Besides, he felt safe with him because of his closed mind and hailing from a preferred tribe.

"Not at all. His name says it all. Even his appearance of a tired horse, a spent force and that unimpressive natural smile due to his short lips that cannot cover his teeth, almost giving him an overbite, makes him unappealing. At present, he is too much of a confidante, having delivered Joe's head on a platter. It was beyond my wildest dreams because I could never have ruled with Joe on my watch. That boy terrified me such that I wet my pants each time he disagreed with me, and the thought of having brown trousers on me for the rest of my life was not appealing. Owing to lady luck smiling on my side, that nightmare was turned into breakfast."

"You are so cold. Do you realise that many dreams and hopes were shattered by that death?"

"They will soon forget because of the celebrations, my lady, believe me."

"At least, will you assist his family?"

"The physician does not visit the sick, my lady. If she is content, so be it."

"He is the one single man who could send the enemy trembling every time and was an essential part of the struggle."

"He was, my lady, and we have opened a new chapter. Picks, shovels and labourers do not attend a field day, but the farmer does."

"You got your revenge, but the family has nothing to do with it."

"One day you will understand, but please stop being his family representative."

"Enough of your vengeance. As your wife, the First Lady, I also want all your consorts and or those that had or still have any interests in you out of your circle or the country."

"I thought I had already done that for you."

"Heli is still around, and you have elevated her when she cannot even write her own name."

"You have to understand that Joe was a big trophy, much bigger than the elections."

"I see. The dirty couple gets doubly rewarded and can ask for any favour from their Prime Minister. The lady gets bumped up war credentials, which she never achieved."

"You fail to understand some basic principles. Their hands get dirty, and they cannot push it back to me. If I want more, all I have to do is ask. The file can easily fall out of the closet, and they would be arrested for the most heinous murder of the decade if they refuse."

"Is it conceivable that at some point you might consider performance over allegiance?"

"I must be the only shining pebble on the beach, and therefore it is best to promote non-independent cadres."

"Am I the only one already waving goodbye to good economic and social policies for this nation?"

"They may join you long after your death. For the foreseeable future, no one will notice."

"Do you anticipate everyone to forgive and forget as you forced them to?"

"They have no option. That is the prize they get for giving me the mandate. Anyone who disagrees belongs in prison."

"Imagine all the comrades you did not incorporate in the army. They might revolt when they feel the poverty heat from some rural abode. All of Douglas' friends and volunteers are on good packages. Do you feel ashamed?"

"Not at all. I am looking at the big picture where all workers were not getting fairly remunerated. By uplifting their wages, it means they will be capable of helping their extended families and cut off those still thirsty to revolt or organise."

"It's a vicious circle because prices will be adjusted for inflation, and the change would have been in vain."

"It takes time. The mirage and illusion of a salary adjustment will be celebrated for a longer period to the extent that price adjustments in the short term will not be felt. However, I should be able to cross that bridge when we come to it."

"How can I make a nut job like you understand simple social and economic sense?"

"I will take that as a compliment."

Lady Marunjeya was frustrated because she needed a system that guaranteed her a lifetime as first lady, whereas Runo was immersed in his political gamesmanship.

Runo went on to proclaim the independence year as the year of the people's power. He praised the public for their unwavering support against the enemy. All possible epithets were coined to denigrate the enemy, giving the impression that Runo was nothing more than a god-sent saviour and a blessing to the nation. These were all in a local language, which he knew his friends did not understand. Runo had a nationwide tour where thousands voluntarily attended his meet-the-people rallies. It gave him time to assess any provinces that did not fancy him and where he had the greatest support. A perfect gift from Runo was going to be welcomed by those who did not fancy him, a gift of vengeance. It was only a matter of time. He made a good impression but needed his name ingrained on everyone's lips and minds. The best method was in song, and there were a lot of singers whose price allowed Runo to have his way. He wanted a complete replacement of the revolutionary war songs invoking the national spirits and unity with his wishfully immortal and infallible image. Everything traditional was to be slowly uprooted to weaken the people's power base and rallying point. Runo knew very well that culture is an instrument of power, personality and consciousness; therefore, suppressing it was his best bet.

Every school had to drop the songs and traditional practices. These were replaced by a religious and moral education subject to give an impression that morality was only synonymous with religion and not culture. To be moral meant being affiliated with some religion, especially in urban settings where there was no space for cultural and traditional practices. Religion had to be drilled into children's minds at a tender age, marking a new era of being grounded in suspended and theoretical beliefs. He knew that if children emulated, praised and looked up to someone who died crying, on his knees and praying, that would render them powerless. A hero who died fighting tooth and nail, trying to save himself and his people could jeopardise Runo's plans. He, therefore, relegated the role played by the veterans of the war through benign neglect .

After the tour, many hopeless Runo praise songs debuted on the scene. The people, in return, showered many praises on Runo, composed several praise social songs, and even wished him a long life. This wish became an introductory phrase at each political gathering and was later coined into a simple salutary tune: *Long live Runobvepi, Long live Runobvepi, Long live Runo.*

An idea was even foisted on to the people that Runo was

the godfather of all the educational programmes, health and economic development, if any. A song was composed and was played day in and day out on radio about how Runo had imparted knowledge to the people in schools, agriculture, industry, health sector and even during the war.

No one ever questioned how, in such a short time, he had managed to champion every cause, even in retrospect. How could he be credited with the results of something that was still being or was to be rolled out? Nobody ever asked.

One disappointing aspect of Runo's countrywide tours, which became a major and standing setback in his relations with chiefs, emanated from his family roots. Runo toured a well-known Runobvepi chieftainship for introductions and later a rally that afternoon. An assumption of linking his heritage to this chieftainship had catapulted him to the top. He knew it and thought he could establish some relationship of patronage with them. The paramount chief and his sub-chiefs were elated to welcome the head of state and a presumed family product. Runo was asked to confirm his totem and bloodline before they could proceed with their talks or welcome him back to the family. It turned out the Runobvepi chiefs had never heard of a Sacred Passage totem, neither had they ever heard of the family line he had talked about in the nation. Worse still, his family line had no link to the Runobvepi family line.

Runo's family line was several countries away from their nation, so they demanded to know how he ended up using the Runobvepi family name. A warm welcome and reception turned very hostile in a few exchanges, and the chiefs were thoroughly disappointed and became uncompromising towards the impersonator. Runo signalled that it was time to move on as he felt he owed them nothing. Some of his security detail were also displeased as they had assumed Runo was one of their own. Those loyal to Runo moved in quickly to assist him and whisked him out of the tense encounter. Great

Crocodile, back in the city, instructed them to quickly leave this province, his home province, knowing Runo was never going to make it out alive under the circumstances if there was going to be any delay.

The meet-the-people rally was abandoned and the presidential convoy headed back to the city. Before leaving the province, the convoy came under attack, with several members of the entourage sustaining serious injuries, and some cars were destroyed in the process. Their exit route was blockaded and an exchange of gunfire ensued. A few army helicopters were dispatched to diffuse the situation and rescue Runo. Runo was airlifted to avoid any possible further hostile encounters on the way. From that day on, Runo never toured the province and vowed never to appoint anyone from the province to a higher office. He was also looking for a solution to get rid of anyone from that province, but it was a difficult task because his Deputy, Simo, Mudadi, Dzinga, Great Crocodile, the army Deputy Commander, Head of the Army Air Defence team and a few key members were from that very same province.

It was also believed that Lady Marunjeya's family was from this region before emigrating to look for employment opportunities. She had taken up a different surname after her failed marriage, and no one could link her back to her roots. Runo later befriended a certain young man from an opposing clan living alongside the Runobvepi family. This young man and his family had just moved to the province to settle among relatives. While the young man was not a chief, Runo went on to install him and appointed him as the head of the National Chief's Council. All veterans from the war were ordered to surrender their weapons or face prosecution. He never again wanted to see a repeat of what had happened. In addition, he gave them an option. Either one had to join the army, get alternative employment or get a token of appreciation and not bother the government. For all the options, there was a need to register and have authenticity vetted. Many non-veterans benefitted from the registration exercise and were given high posts in the army ahead of true veterans. Some genuine vocal veterans were left out as impostors to punish them.

Youths in all centres were force-marched every evening to weed out enemies of Runo (dubbed enemies of the state) and promote Runo's political Party. There was a very thin line between Runo's Party and the state. To the majority, the two were the same. A women's branch was then formed to ensure that all women sang and danced in praise of Runo at all public gatherings. This group was given prime importance in the Party. Unfortunately, the regalia worn by these women had nothing to do with the political Party. It bore the image of Runo. The youths were given T-shirts with Runo's image as well. Runo's objective was to raise his image above that of the Party. He knew he needed to form a cult hero of himself in order for the people to believe that he was indispensable.

The youthful Great Crocodile, an intelligence supremo dating back to the war, executed his duties proficiently above expectations. One could spy on his friend and a friend on him, a soldier on his mate, and a lawman would do the same. He had even created a counter-intelligence unit within the Intelligence services. This unit consisted of all forms of professions: cleaners, drivers, vendors and many others to ensure that every negative sentiment was captured. Anything extreme would result in the ruthless termination of some lives. Runobvepi was over the moon at this development but was worried at its pace. He fretted over what the Great Crocodile could accomplish if left in that role. Things got even worse when Runo discovered that the Great Crocodile was even keeping surveillance on him. Runo quickly reduced his powers, moved him to another portfolio, and tried to limit his access to intelligence and military institutions.

However, many senior members of society and the Party who got too excited, assuming they were in a true democracy, were unfortunate. No one guaranteed their freedom after writing articles or after speaking. They were tortured or lost their privilege to exist among friends, family and on this earth. Some heavy metal-built army trucks were employed in freak accidents to justify natural deaths. At least people thought there was nothing better to expect from people who normally drive in the bush. In addition, it was rumoured that soldiers never went through normal driving lessons and tests. They only needed the courage to move a car. However, when the severity was worsening and people talked, the authorities slowed down on their games. This, however, did not change the public fear when confronting the state apparatus.

Runobvepi did not change the colonial repressive laws. The most notorious and horrendous ones were the Law and Order Maintenance Act, Unlawful Organisations Act and the Emergency Powers Act. Runo enjoyed and justified using them to deny his people that which they had fought and died to achieve. The Law and Order Maintenance Act, however, was the worst of the bunch. A state of emergency could be declared and justified in the most bizarre of circumstances. Once this happened, a wave of brutal and savage murders would be unleashed without any regard for humanitarian considerations.

Rebel parties and the army were called upon to integrate. There were, however, teething problems in the integration process. Some of Bellyman's rebels returned to combat after he failed to give them assurances. As head of homeland security, Bellyman never made arrests of his comrades. Even in the camps, some of his colleagues stabbed several fellow countrymen with knives, specifically those from Runo's camp. They had to sleep with one eye open to avoid being murdered. It seemed as if he was encouraging them because a trend was established.

Many institutions and nations came together to assist the new nation. They put together a package to help the nation offset some of its inherited debt and promote new ventures.

It was a gift to the government. Runo and his crew had total discretion over the funds. This project was highly publicised, and the well-wishers received endless praise. It was only until the funds were received. Then there was a looting frenzy culminating in the package not being able to meet any of its intended objectives. Mudadi was excited, Runo was content, and Simo, Runo's deputy, was overjoyed that he started making various investments around the country. It was a gift from the gods, as they were not accountable to anybody. Simo, though a Party elder and with executive powers, went along with everything Runo said or suggested. He never at any point disagreed with him. The public made all the silliest jokes about him. They joked that he thought Billy Ocean was an ocean, the g in champagne and Runobvepi's first name must be pronounced the same, there was no difference between a fan belt and a martial arts belt, he read his name as part of a speech (and his reading was bad), had no clue what would happen if his boss, Runo, passed on and wondered whom he would deputise. The public arena was just full of jokes about him. The public assumed that this man had very little knowledge, and Runo was out to take advantage of him. People felt very sympathetic to the man. They had a very strong connection with him. He was down to earth and could mingle with anyone in society. A vote for him was guaranteed in any election.

Schooling was made free as espoused by a new policy enacted by the Education Minister, Dzinga, to uplift the level of awareness and reduce the number of idle individuals on the streets. The policy was so subtle but softly criminalising illiteracy. Runo was hesitant to have the policy implemented. He feared being challenged by educated people. Dzinga, however, tried hard to convince him on the basis that there was a high likelihood of destabilisation when people had nothing to lose. He never quite agreed because of his reservations. A challenge to his rule was not welcome; this is exactly what he wanted to avoid, and he had to let it pass while he monitored its negative effects closely. Many of the school dropouts from the war era trekked back to school. Late teens were mingling in a class with under-ten-year-olds. The age matrix was just horrible, but somehow it worked because there was no option. Only one influence was overlooked. The behavioural aspect as many of the youths had already hooked themselves to drinking and smoking. It was not a good influence on young children, and the effects were never really scrutinised. It was just sad for those who fell through the cracks. Eventually, everyone ended up being able to read and write. Whether this policy helped uplift the nation did not matter because the literacy rate was high. This policy was attributed to Runo as the ultimate authority of the republic. A song was crafted to complement the policy and ensure its effectiveness. Its message was that the country had attained independence, and children could attend free education while parents could return to their daily chores.

In mocking the illiterate, there was an infant school-level song. The message was to force literacy and encourage all to attend school. If one is denied the chance to go to school, then one will die as an illiterate fool.

The literacy mantra even extended to gadgets. A complex gadget was termed *yakadzidza (sophisticated)*, while the simple and old fashion was termed *as* belonging to the Rhodes era, *ndezva* Rhodes, meaning it is ancient technology.

Parents were not going to pay tuition fees for primary schools. For secondary schools, nothing changed. However, parents still had to pay the building fund fees and a token fee for other daily expenses for the primary schools. This incorporated the school's maintenance fund, daily supplies and stationery. Whenever stationery was distributed, it was attributed to Runo's benevolence. In one extreme case, a school was close to an irrigation scheme, and funds were donated to supply piped water to the school and the workers at the irrigation scheme. It was discovered that there was a huge aquifer, and therefore water supplies could be extended to the surrounding villages. When the development was undertaken, everyone again attributed it to Runo. One old woman used to guard a water tap at her house from abuse by school children, and she had running battles with them all the time. The children would always tell her that it was Runo's water tap and therefore she had no right to chase them away. One day when school children were kicked out of school for non-payment of their building fund, she approached them nicely. Sympathetically, she asked,

"What happened to my grandchildren? Why are you going home so early?"

"We were kicked out of school for non-payment of fees!" the kids responded.

She smiled sarcastically and then laughed before responding, "Since you say this water tap is from Runo, why don't you get school fees assistance from this Runo?"

This was the very last time any schoolchild ever gave the old woman a hard time.

Donors contributed to the upgrading of roads and construction of rural health centres. Some roads were upgraded, and others remained in a sorry state. Donor funds to support the budgets had suddenly disappeared. Communities were asked to assist in rural health projects as local authorities provided medical supplies and employees. Members of each community had to mobilise funds, but the easiest way for the communities was to provide labour and materials for construction. Completion of the task became easier as the local authorities only had to provide the balance. Development never reached those communities that were not willing to make the sacrifice or take the lead. The public verdict still praised Runo's benevolence because of the lack of information. Those communities that did not participate did not benefit. There were very few secondary schools in all communities, and some parents decided to team up with their local authorities to build schools. This idea was replicated by many, and access to education improved dramatically. Some communities didn't embrace the idea, and children from those communities suffered. These less privileged schools were cheaper and, therefore, more affordable, giving a chance for more people to access high school education. Overall, the improved literacy rate for the nation was attributed to Runo's visionary leadership.

There was a devastating drought the following three years, and donors came through to assist in the construction of irrigation schemes and donation of food. Donor food was channelled through the government. The government, in turn, distributed the food and took credit for the food handouts. This programme design was very convenient as it was easy to hide the truth from the masses. Runo, who was opposed to the handouts initially, embraced the food distribution programme, realising it was a strategic campaign tool. Mudadi was instrumental in selling the idea to Runo. This legal mastermind was of Runo's presidential height, excessively pompous, felt he was on top of the world due to his educational qualifications and was inseparable from cigarettes. Cigarettes, to him, were a source of pride. To him, the nation was for him and Runo as the academic elites of the nation. Their conversation on the matter was brief, and the issue was settled.

"Mudadi, I assumed our freedom meant no close scrutiny from anyone on how we run our affairs. These people keep bothering us and monitoring our every move."

"They will always want to play the big brother role or schoolboy and headmaster relationship with us. Don't forget that some of our brothers are still paying for their colonisation as a condition of having been given independence without going to war. Their central banks are still managed remotely but directly by the colonial master from Europe."

"How do we deal with that?"

"Look the other way if you feel strong and ignore any

instructions they bark at you; otherwise it will never end. As you are aware, Joseph Conrad in his 1897 letter to R. B. C. Graham wrote, '*Human nature viewed in its crudest state among African savages is quite on the level with that of the brute and not to be compared with the noble character of the dog. There is neither gratitude, pity, love or self-denial, no idea of duty, no religion, nothing but covetousness, ingratitude, selfishness and cruelty.*' They have their never-ending prejudices and will always treat us with contempt."

"We still need to spend more from them; therefore, a diplomatic solution probably will resolve the matter."

"The more you depend on them, the more you fall into servitude. Maximise the opportunity to claim what's theirs to your advantage. We can even put laws in place for you."

"I see. This food is coming from a blessed hand is the message to the people. My infinite sympathy and sense of responsibility for the people have prompted this charitable act. My loving heart bleeds for the welfare of my people!"

"Exactly, Your Excellency, seize the opportunity."

"I am still worried about Maggie and our hostile neighbour. They also continue to interfere in the charting of our course to our destination."

"Don't rush; give it time until we gather enough evidence. These two nations could utterly destroy us."

"Thank you, Mudadi."

Runo later went on to introduce a drought relief tax on all workers to raise money to buy more food for the drought relief programme. The programme catered for rural communities only. None of these people knew of the drought relief tax, and Runo wanted to keep it that way. It was his beneficial secret. Most of the money raised, however, never served its intended purpose. Runo's crew helped itself to the spoils. Rural people were ecstatic that their benevolent leader, Runo, had come to their rescue with token food handouts and irrigation projects. It became an open secret that a vote for Runo would guarantee assistance in any disaster situation. Local political leadership from the grassroots started using it as a tool to coerce everyone to tow a one-party line. It was not uncommon to gather the people before any food distribution exercise and then ask for their political Party cards as a precondition to benefit. In other instances, people had to be subjected to Party campaigns and slogans before receiving their rations. Some donors started developing cold feet citing irregularities, abuse and politicisation of the programme. Whatever they decided to do did not matter to Runo because his name had been ingrained in people's hearts and minds early in his first term in office. Those who voiced against the abuse of aid and threatened to withdraw were condemned. Runo would tell the people it was his programme, and no one was supposed to interfere. He had the temerity to call their help neocolonial aid and mock any donor who dared challenge Runo's government.

Some local business people started emerging, who had close links with Runo and his Ministers. One such businessman was Powerman (he was corrupt and untouchable. The more deals he made, the more his standing became apparent to the public and that he could never be arrested. He was later nicknamed Powerman by the public). His notoriety preceded him. He had tasted neither prison nor handcuffs or even a simple call by any police station. It became apparent that the government offered him all the legal protection he needed. Kumbi, a Minister in Runo's government, a close ally and confidante of Runo, was always making deals with Powerman. He had been involved in a string of bank heists, but nobody laid a finger on him. Plans were afoot to start a Powerman Railway Company and an airline. The funds were abundant for him to do anything. During the drought period, Kumbi, as the Agriculture Minister, engaged the services of Powerman for grain distribution. His charges were so exorbitant it was difficult to conceal. More than 5% of the whole year's budget had been paid to one individual for transport services. Journalists started reporting on the issue in small print, and the leadership of Runo turned a deaf ear. The reports continued to grow until they became an embarrassment.

Ziva weighed in on the case and lambasted both Runo and Kumbi for complacency. He chided Runo for many unfulfilled promises. It prompted action. Powerman was arrested and hauled before the courts and convicted. He was then handed a part commuted fifteen-year sentence. Kumbi was absolved of any wrongdoing, and no one else became a casualty of the high-profile case. It became clear to a few that although Runo was not directly involved in corrupt activities, certain individuals may have been used as conduits to steal. Kumbi most likely was one such person.

A programme to resettle people on vacant farms deserted during the rebel insurrection was suspended. New qualification rules were imposed. The rules favoured the affluent with enough resources to run a farm. Rural people in need of land could not qualify under the new rules. All the senior officials wanted to ensure that each of their family members benefitted first before the available land ran out. Even their new-born babies were allocated entire farms when rural families had been allocated small pieces of land. Most of these farms were for display and privilege, not for production. They were a status symbol to show that they were the new "white men" in the nation.

Runo wanted a master farm of more than ten thousand hectares. His wish could not be accomplished because most farms that were within his preferred location belonged to his friends from Douglas' crew. Besides, he did not want people to believe he was a capitalist at this stage in his rule. He had to wait for an opportune moment. His young brother and sister, though, got a very good deal on a very fertile farm. They engaged the services of an experienced agronomist. Their project was a success. When Runo heard about it, the trio was summoned to Runo's palace and received a stern warning about their project. They were given strict instructions never to return to the farm again. Lady Marunjeya had no interest whatsoever in land, and she also convinced Runo to bury his appetite for land.

Journalists were not able to travel around the country to verify the land redistribution programme. The issue, therefore, went unreported and died a natural death. Bellyman, having bought his farms already, advised Runo against the qualification criteria. He offered free counsel to Runo to the effect that this qualification criterion was a horrible disaster as it did not improve the status quo or add value to the nation in any way. Runo never showed his disdain for the Bellyman's free advice. He was simply happy to see his colleagues benefit from their sacrifices in the war. He did not take Bellyman's advice kindly, though. The qualification criteria helped him to buy the allegiance he needed from his colleagues.

Runo felt the impact of sharing the political cake with subdued power and constant reminders to perform. The failure of the Bellyman to control some of his former rebels was frustrating. It was mind-boggling that he continued to plead innocent when his men were wreaking havoc. In addition, the Bellyman was pretending to be too keen to speed up development as well as to put viable and concrete policies in place as a diversion. For a while, Runo had been defending the Bellyman and making an impression that there was no sign of insurrection. When calls were mounting and footage of a five thousand-strong rebel army stationed by the Gwaai River leaked to the media, Runo watered down the rumours.

He said to one journalist, "After such a long and protracted war, there should be no zeal to fight. Everybody should be ready to disarm. If they don't then we will forcibly disarm anyone who still carries the war spirit."

One newspaper editor from the region affected by the insurrection did not relent in publishing articles on the bandit menace. He showed bravery in his push for the leadership to take action. He lived at the epicentre of the bandit menace and knew he would be targeted if he didn't act publicly to deter them. The articles he published became the only window through which the Nation could see the events in the region.

Runo wanted power, and as much as possible, and not a phased-out approach to all issues. Continuing to hold a need and dishing it out slowly or simply promising worked well for Runo as it guaranteed him power. He, therefore, decided it was time to change the status quo. Besides, he wanted to satisfy his ego and settle a score after Bellyman had continued to step on his toes. Runo felt it was in good order only if the Bellyman could apologise for giving advice and promise never to repeat that abominable behaviour. He, therefore, called Mudadi for a discussion late at night at his Palace.

"Mudadi, my partner, you did well in ensuring our democracy is supported by a fine constitution. No term limits and less burdensome on the responsibilities of the leader." He was very assuring and sincere.

"Thank you for the compliment, your Excellency."

"After me, you are the only one with the educational credentials worthy of a leader who can maintain my standard and legacy."

"Even my whole family, Your Excellency, bemoans the lack of recognition from the highest authority. My father did a splendid job. I don't mean to brag, but the other day we registered a law firm with all qualified family members as partners. It became a bore when the name Zinobo, Zinobo, Zinobo, Zinobo, Zinobo & Associates came up as is the practice in this country. We had to change it."

Runo felt not only challenged but embarrassed as he was the sole family member to graduate and would have dismissed Mudadi if he did not need his help. He swallowed his pride and continued but wanted his revenge one day.

"Before we digress, Mudadi, you want power and a clear

path is necessary. The road is littered with too much dead wood. In addition, the Bellyman and his crew add to the mess. We have not done anything but promote him in this arrangement. How do you see your way out?"

"You can frustrate him with meaningless and empty portfolios to force him out."

"I have tried. That is the reason I took away the homeland security portfolio from him. He had caused mayhem in law enforcement with his ethnic politics. You know he does not even have a portfolio as we speak, but he pretends to be keen to assist. I doubt his sincerity since he never wants to talk about the security situation in the nation. Even all the humanitarian and church institutions are awfully quiet about the dissident menace. What is your take, Mudadi?"

"Remind me, Your Excellency, did any of those institutions assist us during the war against Douglas?"

"They did not fight for our independence."

"What they stand for is, therefore, clear. Remember Father Bouts and Father Lavater with their phrenology fad that they used to justify our inferiority. Never trust a man who values a reward in some mythical place in the afterlife over life, a man who has faith but no reasoning capacity or a man who deals in fables over reality. We can only engage such a man and his religion for our benefit and to completely rule over our subjects."

"How shall we deal with the Bellyman? Maggie continues to work with him. She finds comfort in destabilising this nation through him as she is doing in Sri Lanka."

"This arrangement can end after the next election, and we will bypass him."

"What if he wins, considering his past glory and the disharmony he is creating in the government? The bandit menace is not even being blamed on him, and very soon it could be turned against me and used as a failure. With a few more moves by the Bellyman, then I will be history. He is such a great pretender, yet he is causing serious havoc. Besides, we need to rule alone, Mudadi. One Party, one supreme leader and one consolidated power-handling person. A 100% record at elections and no more serious and tiresome canvassing for votes. I cannot afford to have my people voting for other pointless opposition candidates. It is a luxury to indulge in the politics of opposition. The concept of setting up a Party merely to oppose and not assist the government is repugnant to me."

"He also wants the same, exactly what you want, Your Excellency, because all the people being terrorised by his men are being accused of voting for you."

"We are behind, very much behind in our plans, but let us use his tactics to give him a taste of his own medicine."

"In that case, we need him out and with dirty hands to finish him off in one scoop."

"I know he loves wealth, but there is no law that can help us put him behind bars for looting his Party's assets. However, what has happened in the law enforcement camps under his watch is unforgivable."

"Behind bars is not necessary at this stage since he may get sympathy and more support from being a criminal. Mess him up so that he loses his support and political relevance."

"How do you intend to achieve that, Mudadi?"

"Have you forgotten that they are receiving donated weapons and not handing them over to the government? Kenneth, our neighbour, is not helping by making the situation worse. He is still holding on to the weapons and refusing to hand them over to our government. Some of the Bellyman's wartime weapons have still not been fully integrated into the army; therefore, we have an ironclad case. In addition, tourist funds are drying up because these bandits have been targeting visitors. Homeland security camps are being bombed without any explanation, and we need to act."

"We intended to keep some of the information secret, never

get into the public arena. Are you suggesting we wash this dirty linen in public?"

"None of the weapons have been declared, and we will use that deviant behaviour to nail him. They have far superior weaponry than the nation at present. This is a man who is standing ready to accelerate the dissident menace at any given opportunity should we continue to give him an open cheque. We can accuse him of planning to topple you since he continues to deny acts of violence by his rank and file, but then again, will we be wrong? We have not been able to establish who exactly was behind all the attacks against you and our army positions. There is Maggie and her troops, our hostile neighbour, and now Bellyman's people making the situation complex. You earn the instant cult status of being invincible, and he becomes the proverbial villain if we expel him now."

"Excellent, Mudadi, that is a political bonanza, but if he accelerates the insurrection, what shall we do?"

"It helps our cause, Your Excellency. The accusation would have been vindicated. How do they continue to stand if no one is supporting them? The Bellyman must be a liar and a cheat. Too many parties must be acting in cahoots, the press is silent, the church is not on our side, Maggie continues to play games, and our hostile neighbour is most probably abating the conflict at a large scale. Your Intelligence man, Ken, needs to work harder."

"I agree, as I have been taught to make and wage relentless wars and exterminate enemies from the face of the earth. However, if we can't contain the insurgency as is happening now, what will be the fallback position?"

"Ask Maggie to leave our nation together with the hostile neighbour. She has done too much damage, and it is only a matter of time before they start knocking on your door. Your learned friend, the Great Crocodile, will also help you. He is the troubleshooter."

"Do you realise he has subtle ambitions and might take your rightful place? He is well aware that I mentioned to you the need to rotate the leadership with your province following next in line."

"I know you want me to watch him."

"Of course, Mudadi, that's a no-brainer."

"Don't worry. The manner in which he cleans up Bellyman will determine if he still has a future."

"A double-edged sword is good. We know he has no options. He shall succeed only to lose."

"That is his dilemma, your Excellency." They exchanged a clapping handshake. The sound produced reflected a high level of chemistry between the two. "Our work is done before we begin."

"The issue of religion you mentioned deserves more attention."

"From what perspective, your Excellency?"

"To control our subjects. Why not continue to criminalise tradition and promote religion to completely wipe out their reasoning capacity?"

"You have a point. While they close their eyes or focus on the Bible, praising and worshipping reciting the Jesus loves me mantra, begging for his blood like witches, we will be busy redirecting wealth to ourselves, changing laws and tightening our grip on power."

"Brilliant, Mudadi, let's drink to our future success (Runo had a glass of milk and Mudadi a glass of whiskey).

Chapter 4

The Bellyman and his crew were expelled from the government. They had no platform to respond or tell the story from their perspective. Bellyman's failure to fully account for the dissident activities to Runo resulted in the termination of the marriage of convenience. Their expulsion was not a formal process. A press conference was held where Runo announced that the Bellyman and his team had been sacked from the government. Bellyman and his crew were not accorded a decent exit or the courtesy of fellow countrymen and partners in a unity government. In a surprise move, Cowboy, a key member of Bellyman's team, was not expelled. Some rumours inferred that he was Runo's nephew, while others pointed to him being Runo's brother. The latter was more acceptable given the close resemblance between this man, Runo and Runo's son, who was working at the nation's television stations.

Songs to characterise and demean Bellyman were quickly composed and sung throughout the country. Only a fool plants weapons while others grow agricultural produce, was the message.

As expected, the intensity of the insurrection multiplied. Negative public sentiment grew, and the Bellyman's Party was weakened, but the fighting did not stop. Runo did not want the insurrection to be given credence. He suppressed the level of publicity to counter what the international press was doing. He also allocated a small army to attend to critical areas where, at times, curfews or a state of emergency were declared. Most of the army personnel were supposed to work as party agents, recruiting members forcibly. Bellyman's teams wanted to weed out those who were sympathetic to and had voted for Runo. He needed to amputate the cancer before it spread. Tiger rebels were being used as a perfect model by Maggie through the Bellyman. Meanwhile, Runo had the opportunity to use the discredited and archaic colonial legislation to suppress and oppress the people who had not voted for him, preferring the Bellyman instead. Bellyman had at one time recommended to Runo that these laws be repealed, but Runo refused. It could have been that the Bellyman wanted to take advantage of the freedoms to achieve a sinister agenda.

Owing to the presence of these archaic laws, Runo had seized the opportunity to liquidate and crush those who chose to remain independent, free or defiant and all elements that were unwelcome in Runo's nation. He wanted an electoral advantage by any means fair or foul, which, in this instance, meant that brutality was not out of reach. To justify to the public who was behind the insurrection, Bellyman was arrested without charges, harassed and inconvenienced several times. He was then put under house arrest. At one point he was accused of dealing in foreign currency, but the amount was too small to warrant being used against a prominent man like him. He was later accused of having precious minerals. Again, it did not work. His lieutenants were arrested and charged. One of those arrested was Dumi, a key strategist and military intelligence man for the Bellyman. Runo disliked his cool temperament and approach to issues, suspecting that he might have been silently protesting and plotting against him. Unfortunately, they were all acquitted, which was embarrassing to Runo. It was believed that while they were in detention, they received preferential treatment because Douglas' friends were still in charge. In addition, they were being coached in readiness for their trial. The same judges appointed by Douglas were in control and ruling in favour of their kinsmen's narrative. It turned out from Bellyman's inner circle that only a handful of people in his Party had full knowledge of the insurrection. Even Dumi, the key intelligence man, was left out of the insurrection mechanisms. He was not the plotting and scheming type as expected of his position.

All the colonial torturers who used to deal with Runo and Bellyman's rebels came in handy for Runo. It is alleged that Runo used them to torture some of Bellyman's men to force and extract confessions. The methods used were disgraceful, shameful and appalling, which was typical of a desperate man. There were cases of electric shocks, beatings, burning with cigarettes, suffocation using wet sacks and psychological torture. However, no scars could be shown as evidence. The Bellyman was left shell-shocked when the revelations came to light that one could consolidate the gains of independence through torture and oppression. He, however, realised that they were birds of a feather with Runo as he often did it to his membership that dared to oppose his views. He knew very well that he had sacrificed his men to protect a secret.

In his defence, however, this was a campaign of barbarism and terror by the government against its people. It was easy for him to articulate under the rare joys of non-incumbency. The same terror employed by Douglas had reared its ugly head yet again, he would say to the public. These victims were the same people, the patriots and nationalists who had suffered during the struggle to free their country. The same people were now caught in Runo and Bellyman's conflict. The conflict itself was a personal web forcibly spreading its tentacles to possibly create a one-party state. A one-party state that was not inconceivable given the fact that once the Bellyman was gone, then Runo could operate freely or the other way around. What puzzled Runo, in the absence of evidence linking some of the Bellyman's team members, was the level of funding for the dissidents. It was not clear how they were being funded and protected, yet they continued to cause untold mayhem. Whatever the case, Runo was behind in his planning.

An over-excited journalist once asked Runo;

"At Independence, you once promised that there shall never be any return to the state of armed conflict again. Why are you reneging on your promise, Mr Prime Minister?"

A frustrated Runo responded, "The Bellyman was trying to overthrow my government."

"Given how you formed the government of national unity, surely you could have talked over the issue and resolved it behind closed doors like statesmen. Don't you feel that is the ideal solution?"

"The Bellyman and his Party are like a cobra in the house. The only way to deal effectively with a snake is to strike and destroy its head." Runo put a lid on the session, and the journalist dared not proceed. He could sense that the man was furious.

For his efforts in pacifying the former oppressors and maintaining their privileges, Runo received worldwide praise. He became a model and an epitome of a gentleman to be used among formerly oppressed people. Had he followed Ziva's advice, vilification and derision would have been his reward. If his people had been at the top of his agenda, the whole world would have called for his ouster and head on a platter. Names such as despot, unrepentant terrorist or the butcher would not have been spared when referencing Runo. He perceived in advance whose side of the bread had to be buttered and made a personal choice. Runo declared that his nation would be part of the former oppressor's club of chihuahuas. Under this arrangement, relations would improve, goods would have free movement, and the wealth would be shared and common to all but skewed towards the oppressor.

To cap it all, his friends had to cement their position with a vital lesson. Runo was invited by a Queen, the former oppressor, and received one of the highest honours in her Kingdom.

This honour was only reserved for those who were part of the Kingdom, or an appendage. By accepting the honour, Runo admitted inferentially that his nation was not free and independent but still subject to the whims of the former oppressor. It was clear that the nation had lost the opportunity to chart its course and path as he had promised. Runo travelled for the much-publicised visit to receive the honour as the knight in shining armour for his people. He was inducted into the order and hall of fame for the Queen's empire. Gracefully, he accepted the honour, and it became a source of pride and personal achievement. Lady Marunjeya was excited to be by his side, receiving the honour and being officially hosted, but as poodles of the former oppressor. It was in the open that the relationship was not an equal partnership but where one was above the other. From this point on, Runo made sure that he made several visits to the Queen's land. If the press allegations were correct, labelling him as the visiting leader, he would hardly spend a month without visiting or passing through the Queen's kingdom. He made sure that his people had to watch a televised Queen's speech every year end. The people were made to believe that it was a privilege to be associated with this Queen.

Not to be outdone, institutions of higher learning followed suit. Runo received several honorary degrees from a cross-section of highly rated universities. He spent a lot of resources travelling to receive the personal crowns and used them to intimidate his people further. No one could challenge his position. Mudadi would just ask one simple question to any aspiring candidate gunning for Runo's job, "*Wakadzidza here?* Show us your academic record that is better than Runo's." The question signalled the death of the revolution. From freedom to schooling, the new leadership had fallen into the trap of supporting the very system that was oppressing them. They were reorienting the rather astute minds into robots. The curriculum remained very much unchanged and depicted the same oppressive kind as the major players, adventurers, discoverers, inventors and philosophers.

However, given the fact that most people had spent several years in the bush fighting the enemy or not having access to education because there were no schools, Mudadi's point went unchallenged. To ensure that very few people had access to higher education, Runo never considered adding tertiary educational institutions. He had several clashes and confrontations with Dzinga, his Education Minister, on the issue. The whole country had to rely on one university that was built by the oppressor for the oppressor's children. This institution had very limited places. Runo, therefore, often offered scholarships for selected individuals to go for further education outside of his nation. Some of the scholarships were awarded by other foreign governments. Most of the time, only top officials' children benefitted or received first preference. This led to the foreign governments withdrawing the facility or going directly to the people. While the idea was noble for Runo to offer scholarships, there wasn't a cost-benefit analysis. In many instances, the cost of awarding these wholesale scholarships was normally more than the construction of an additional university or more for the nation. Politically he was making a good decision to protect himself, but it was a very uneconomic decision. It did not matter to him and true to his word, his was the power to consolidate and politics to manage. For that, he was a man of his word and a very honourable person.

Ziva, in his usual style, had a confrontation with Runo. He tried to be diplomatic but was too generous with the truth, which defeated the diplomacy. An appointment had been made but there was no agenda. It was just an update during working hours at Runo's office.

"It has been a while since we had a personal or general conversation, and I thought it would be necessary to assure myself that His Excellency has not forgotten about me."

"We have travelled a long way together, Ziva. How on earth can you even imagine a gentleman like me forgetting who his friends are?"

"Your world keeps growing, Your Excellency, while my sphere of influence seems to have peaked. It is, therefore, not difficult to imagine the space or gap created each day between us."

"One nation, one people, a common objective and vision. That is what binds us together and to one another, Ziva," Runo was more assertive and on the lookout for any surprises from Ziva.

"Outside the political speeches, you still get the international recognition as an international statesman but also at an individual level."

"I know, Ziva, we have grown very close and have become personal friends with the Queen. It is such an honour to receive that recognition."

"You seem not to have forgotten our few in need of education and are helping them in every way you can."

"True, Ziva. I am a product of such programmes, having benefitted from his fund, the very founder of this modern-day nation, Rhodes. I cannot, therefore, turn my back on others," he declared proudly but was not sure what point Ziva wanted to make.

"Very thoughtful, I guess."

"What do you mean, I guess, Ziva?"

"Runo, just between us, what do you think of reviving the kingship in this nation?" Ziva blinked a few times and held his chin, pulling an "I caught you unaware" victory signal.

"Never, Ziva. It's an outdated model. We must move forward," he began feeling awkward and rested his back on the chair.

"Yet you receive what you think is the highest honour from some royal one in some faraway island kingdom."

"That's different, Ziva."

"How is it different when our King could bestow that

honour on you and still get the media coverage you need?"

"Let's not get too philosophical, Ziva, and talk about other matters."

"It's not a problem, Runo. Have you also considered the negative costs of your scholarship programme?"

"We need educated people to run this country."

"Is it wrong to educate them locally?"

"There are not enough facilities, and you know it, Ziva."

"Use the scholarship resources to build more facilities rather than donate the money to other nations."

"Nitpicking is not necessary. It takes time because we would need to make plans and then implement those plans."

"You can fast-track the matter and give directives. Before the end of the year, everything would be in place."

"Thank you for the advice. I will make a plan."

"You still have a whole judiciary bench full of Douglas' appointees. How can we rule freely when they can twist cases in favour of their kin?"

"In a democracy, you cannot bulldoze the Judiciary and make appointments that suit you. Each member of society must get an equal opportunity."

"You will regret that statement when they start making rulings in favour of their friends."

"Never. They gave me their word, and we have a very good working relationship."

"I am familiar with that statement, Runo, but I don't need to argue with you. On another matter, do you suppose you could spare some time and funds to collect all the dead bodies, skulls and skeletons littered across the nation neglected since the war ended?"

"I assumed the communities took care of the problem."

"On whose authority?"

"Surely people cannot coexist with dead bodies scattered on their land. They have to do something."

"As the Prime Minister, what initiatives have you put in

place to ensure that your people have a less traumatic existence in their land?"

"It shall be done without any delay, Ziva."

"Noted. There is an issue that we have always battled with as rebels, but we never seem to have found the smoking gun."

"What matter is that, Ziva?"

"Remember the endless female inspections owing to a potential threat of a biological weapon that we suspected was being planted in the ladies' privates?"

"I do, but that threat is history?"

"Have you considered the endless inoculations and medical experiments being carried out on our army by your foreign friends as a threat to our force and the nation? Is this not the birth of a pandemic that we could be witnessing? My force was in good health when we defeated Douglas."

"Ziva, we cannot be talking conspiracy theories at this stage. We are a free and independent nation. I could not deliberately let my people get in harm's way, and I can assure you, those are just routine medical checks."

"I hope you know what you are doing because routine medical checks don't make people sick or kill them. I know for sure that your friends believe that civilisation depends on race, and Francis Galton even stated that only fit people must reproduce. We could be wiped out if you are not careful."

"There is certainly no doubt about the purity of my intentions, be assured, my good friend."

"Enjoy yourself. *Mafirakureva's* job is done."

Ziva left wondering if Runo's brain or skull was entirely made from a coconut shell or some harder substance that made it difficult to knock sense into him. Runo seemed the most notorious of any personality he had come across. In future, it was going to be very difficult to deal with him, let alone approach him. This was not an outcome Ziva had expected. A nightmare was in the making. Just after the elections, he had been interviewed about their journey in the struggle and his friendship with Runo. Now, he regretted ever having said any positive thing about him.

"Runo was committed to working with his hero, the Bellyman," he had responded.

"What made him leave?"

"It was a tough negotiation to convince him that we were the Party of the future. Eventually he abandoned the Bellyman."

"How did he become the Party leader?"

" A new approach, fresh ideas and a cunning mind."

"Did you push for Runo's rise to power?"

"Indeed. While in solitary confinement I pushed for the motion and the rest is history."

"Is this a precedent?"

"Times have changed and democracy should take centre stage."

"Thank you, Ziva."

"You are most welcome."

✱

An exercise to gather all the remains of men who died on the battlefront and those who died in the crossfire was quickly implemented. The remains were collected and secretly buried in a huff in unmarked shallow graves in whatever forest they would have been found. There was no collaboration with local communities when the exercise was conducted and neither was there a proper census. Runo felt any census could affect the promise of immunity he had offered to Douglas and his kind. Those bodies in disused mine pits and wells were left for another day possibly in the future. People in local communities were at least relieved that they could go about their business without interfering with mortal remains at every turn. They had been haunted by scenes of the dead bodies, later by them decomposing and the skulls and bones greeting them each time they dared cut wood in forests, go cattle or goat herding or hunting. Ziva was the only man who could help his people or redirect Runo whenever he erred. Unbeknown to him, Runo was planning his downfall to avoid being questioned at every turn or reminded whenever he erred.

Despite Runo's efforts to downplay the conflict with the Bellyman, a scribe based in the Bellyman's hometown never stopped giving insights into the insurrection. Many tourists lost their lives, and the scribe never made it a secret. He instead gave detailed accounts of the events and the gruesome murders. Many farmers had abandoned their farms forcibly or to avoid a confrontation. Such farms were providing a perfect corridor for the dissidents. Ethnic fights also erupted in the suburbs of Bellyman's hometown, and some people had to run to save their lives. Such individuals had to sacrifice work and income for safety. The scribe enjoyed narrating the fiasco to the world. In one province, tribal conflicts were so fierce that communal people had to change their names and learn the Bellyman's language. This ensured total safety if any dissident came along. Ziva again was the one who confronted Runo.

"I know very well that I am the last person you want to see in your office, but I must talk to you."

"What kind of trouble do you want to start this time around, Ziva?" Runo was occasionally nodding, pretending to listen when he had no interest in the conversation.

"I am not a troublemaker but someone generous with the truth. You can only ignore me at your peril."

"Shoot, Ziva, in the interest of time."

"I told you to take care of your friends and not feed the dogs but let them go away. It has turned out that you have a penchant and a morbid desire to alienate friends while entertaining the enemy."

"Do we have different definitions of friends and enemies?"

"Come on, Runo. Must I show you my scarred body to define an enemy?"

"They were enemies but are now friends. Anyone who

goes against that ideal is an enemy."

"Benevolent slavery? That is where we differ, Runo. The Bellyman is one of us, and you cannot be treating him like a dog while the enemy is cheerleading. He is just being used by the enemy. Call him and educate him for the good of the nation."

"He chose the wrong path, Ziva. It's not your fault or mine."

"I prefer not to go along with such a political statement. I only deal with the truth. You and I know you are pretending."

"If he is clean, wouldn't he have appealed for peace or talks by now?"

"The question is, have you given him the opportunity?"

"The ball is in his court, Ziva."

"What have you done to make it easier for him?"

"I am waiting for an overture."

"This state of conflict is not good for our nation. Bring him back in the fold, and then we can talk of fighting our real enemies."

"I shall not open that door at this moment until such time he shows he is ready. How can he be used by the enemy?"

"Have you realised how much people are suffering from this dissident menace?"

"It's only a very localised conflict, Ziva, and, therefore, we should not give it prominence. Don't dramatise this insurrection."

"For a moment I thought I was talking to someone who has never been to this nation. Have you seen victims with mutilated faces? People that have lost their ears, noses and lips. People who have died because they associate with the wrong clan. Women who have had their wombs cut open because they had fallen in love with an army official or anyone termed an enemy. Do you realise that families cannot visit each other for fear of being caught in the crossfire, and it's a lived reality? A sister, brother, married or working in that region has to pretend to be a local or change a surname to avoid a guaranteed death. Must I mention the endless illegal roadblocks where motorists have lost their lives? When will you wake up? One scribe has even uncovered all this mess, yet you see and hear no evil."

"Thanks for the information. I have to act and do it quickly."

"I just hope this is not a political scheme?"

"Never will I deliberately put my people in harm's way. I am here to protect their interests."

"Do what you have to do then."

Chapter 5

A state of emergency was declared. Runo went on to increase the representation of the army in the conflict. An army unit was created to specifically deal with the insurrection. This unit was still outside the army structure and under Runo's party. It was a continuation of a training regime that had been established under a cooperation arrangement with Maggie. Maggie's instructors had been chased away because of their double-dealing. They were openly helping the elimination of Runo's men in favour of Bellyman's men aided by an unneighbourly neighbour. Other instructors from a more friendly nation were engaged to continue with the training programme. The scribe openly advocating for the quelling of the dissident menace was satisfied, and his articles stopped. Unfortunately for the civilians in the area, it wasn't all rosy. No man's life was safe. Arbitrary arrests, torture, murder of women and children, burning of houses, destruction of crops and livestock or long years of imprisonment became a daily dose of life for the villagers.

The dose of savagery, however, came from both sides of the warring parties. The dissidents who found the battlefront too hot to handle were forced into exile to preserve their lives. To gain political mileage, Party cards were forcibly sold to all villagers by their numbers. Reprisals were a gift readily available for any situation when the numbers did not tally with the party cards sold. Runo also had to maximise on this occasion. He created more units to crush with impunity. As in any war situation, disregard for human rights and enjoyment of freedom became scarce commodities. The people could not enjoy their hard-won independence. The Police Law and Order section was formed, and the Youth Brigade, among others. Everything was in the name of crushing those who wanted to subvert Runo's government. When approached for a comment at a political rally in the affected areas, Runo proudly declared, "Any dissident collaborators shall be eradicated." Meanwhile, the dissidents had their way of forcing allegiance in the form of language and surname. All residents of the affected regions had to adopt the dissidents' acceptable language and change surnames, replacing them with totems. The dissidents recorded a resounding victory in this respect.

Some clergymen went on a supposed fact-finding mission. On one side, they wanted to cover their tracks and those of their associates, including the unneighbourly neighbour, while on the other, be seen to be doing something. Their findings were negative, but they issued a statement anyway,

"The methods being used are appalling. We have genocide unfolding before our eyes. Hundreds have perished, innocent people to that matter and there are mountains of evidence to that effect. This brutality must end. The army must protect the people not terrorise the citizens. Our leaders have abdicated their duty to protect the people."

∗

Nate, Runo's Information and Publicity Minister and former member of a tribalist Party, had no kind words for the clergymen. This man was slow speaking with a boring, somewhat deep voice but not hoarse enough to catch people's attention. Nate was tall but very slow, probably because his muscles suffered from what could only be termed as a lifetime fatigue syndrome. Both his sitting and standing postures reflected a seemingly weak set of muscles and bones in his body. He called the clergymen's statement irresponsible, contrived propaganda. The problem was that, as a Party, they felt the church never lifted a finger during the war of liberation and was now trying to get involved because there was a black-led government. It was also believed that many of the church's shepherds in the affected areas were harbouring dissidents. The exercise to eliminate the dissidents had uncovered secret information, which was too damning for the church. These pastoral statements were, therefore, a cover-up exercise and a distraction to buy time to move their unwanted and unwarranted baggage out of the country. This was strategic to ensure that there would not be any evidence when the army finally sniffed them out.

In addition, they were seeking relevance and directing the story to a pre-concluded position. This position could not be tolerated. When the media tried to criticise Nate, Runo quickly sprang to the defence of his minister by saying, "These proselytes have no business poking their noses into a just cause of quashing an indiscriminate insurrection that's turning one of the country's regions into an atrocity zone. It is now clear who they represent and have no allegiance to the nation or interest of our people at heart."

Runo's utterances, while spot on, due to the world narrative, brought into question the peace-loving citizens, whether at all he had ever wanted peace and tranquillity, progress and development since he was promoting turmoil and instability to liquidate opposing views and justify imposing his will. The view was that he never looked back but continued on his vengeful path, rendering people's constitutional rights meaningless. Runo was most probably fighting a proxy war as many army positions outside the conflict zones were being bombed, and no trace could be established on the source of the hostility except to pin it on the Bellyman. There were certainly too many external parties with interests in this conflict. The Bellyman himself did not help matters by not explaining how his men were being funded. He further aggravated the situation by seeking shelter in Maggie's country, the Queen's land, getting assistance from their key businessmen. Runo concluded that, as had always been suspected, the Bellyman and Maggie were working together to cause mayhem.

While still holed up in exile, the Bellyman was interviewed on Runo's excesses, and he had no kind words for Runo. His words and advice, however, fell on deaf ears. Runo was not moved. He was livid at how the Bellyman was such a traitor.

Those fighting the rebels did not always have their way. Many deserted the army because they had been engaged in many hotly contested battles. It was reported that some of the rebels they encountered had far superior weaponry than the army possessed. In such situations, the dissidents had the upper hand and commanded the respect of the soldiers. It was, therefore, a foregone conclusion that under such circumstances, soldiers had to flee to avoid a one-sided exchange because the rebels displayed a winning arsenal. Before running, they had to shed off excess baggage in the form of food supplies to facilitate a better flight. In the process, the soldiers were feeding the enemy. One former soldier recounted how, on about ten occasions, bullets had narrowly burnt his ears. He feared that the next time a bullet might penetrate his skull, so he deserted his duties. Some deserted the army for different reasons. One had found the love of his life and was preparing to settle down comfortably. Her friends were jealous and informed the dissidents. She endured one of the most painful deaths after they cut open her womb to destroy a new life therein. The soldier could not contain the pain and also continue on duty. He deserted the army, looking for comfort far away from the battlefront.

Each successive year that Runo presided over the economy saw a dip in the nation's fortunes. People's expectations were slowly beginning to fade. Reality began to dawn in the public eye that their celebrations for the departure of an enemy from power would not translate into bread and butter. No visible new investment could be showcased for anyone to see. Affordable education was keeping people busy to achieve academic goals and not notice the war they were slowly losing. Health services had become free for the general public and everyone earning below the minimum wage. Queues were growing longer at the country's public health facilities, and the service started to deteriorate. Mudadi and his other friend Herbie, a very corrupt Minister of Health, had to visit one of the health institutions in disguise. The two received a very unwelcome reception and retaliated with whips after taking off their masks. It did not help improve the service, although the story made headlines in the newspapers. Runo used the incident to mark Mudadi down. Mudadi, however, did not stop; he even followed up on all cases where salaries had not been raised to the minimum wage. Whether on farms or in the industries, Mudadi made sure he left no stone unturned. When he was done, his reputation was badly damaged due to the nasty confrontations he'd had with business owners.

When Runo announced his five-year reform plan in his third year in office, the white business owners and former colonisers were thoroughly displeased as this had a significant impact on their business interests. They caucused and responded decisively to Runo and his government's future direction. Two major banks, the colonial banks, that held 70% of banking assets in the country, instituted an investment strike that crippled the economy. They had a major boost when the world's two leading financial institutions came to bolster their stance. A huge outflow of funds followed with disinvestments piling pressure on Runo and his government to change course.

The dissident menace increased with Maggie cheering them. She would even blame Runo for any violent incident in the unneighbourly neighbour's backyard. He was forced to adopt some economic stabilisation plans, which aided the freefall of the economy. The unneighbourly neighbour hardened its sanctions against Runo's nation. They pushed the expatriate head of the nation's steel plant to leave his job immediately and move with all skilled manpower to the unneighbourly neighbour. They knew it was a matter of time before the only steel plant failed. The company was saddled with colonial legacy debts, needed machinery upgrades and was now facing a skills shortage. Runo, overcome with anger, did not even think through this global war. Instead, he responded by making more social decisions to the detriment of the economy in addition to reversing his mooted five-year plan. They had crushed him before he had a backup plan. To turn back on the agreement to perpetuate colonial privileges, eject whites, and nationalise farms and companies meant their neighbour with unneighbourly leadership could never be independent. In addition, efforts to recolonise his nation were likely to be accelerated. He, therefore, had to take the loss on the chin and make peace with it until the time was right.

Although salaries for the local population in government had been raised to above the minimum wage, inflation was slowly eroding the purchasing power of that income. Further salary reviews were, therefore, necessary, creating a vicious circle and forcing Runo to chase his tail. It seemed Runo had lost the salary battle too. The salary increases had a very negative effect on the nation's budget. Salary adjustments coupled with affordable education, corruption and free healthcare incapacitated the government's ability to undertake any new projects. The war was getting costly for the government as well. An annual budget deficit became the norm. Whites slowly started leaving their government posts as the number of blacks increased. Some were even leaving the country.

Prominent people in Douglas' former cabinet, army and business circle had left the country soon after independence.

Most houses in the low-density areas became vacant, and blacks with money had the opportunity to finally move into the former whites-only suburbs. Companies were also closing and relocating to other nations. It would seem that the oppressors had bought themselves time to reorganise and relocate to favourable economies. Runo's call for all to stay was never intended in its literal meaning. He could have meant a safe passage, a sunset window, or an exit was to be allowed to all and, therefore, not cause despondency. The pact had set those conditions. Runo was not allowed to temper with the former oppressor's interests. No farmland could be expropriated since the oppressing royalty had vast interests, no natives could get justice for their past wrongs, whites would keep their privileges, and Runo could not renege on any agreements made by Douglas. The leadership still did not change their policy on education and health.

Ministers who had started with modest benefits and vehicles had their perks bumped up to rival rich private individuals. Mercedes Benz vehicles were introduced. Off-road vehicles were also introduced to cater for travels to the countryside. Friends of Runo were given top jobs in all parastatals. One man presumed or known to be his brother, popularly known as Cash Back (short form for his very long local name and his money-spinning games), was appointed head of the civil service medical fund. The performance of these institutions, though in monopoly positions, began to slide slowly and surely. The new parastatal leaders awarded themselves hefty salaries, probably incorporating a share for the appointing authority. The newly crowned leaders had no performance contracts or target profit margins. They, therefore, worked as they pleased. Runo never made an effort to reprimand them or whip them into line. The infrastructure of the parastatals began to deteriorate due to neglect, and their contribution to the Gross Domestic Product of the nation plummeted significantly each year. Still, Runo looked aside.

All members posted to foreign missions had to pay a certain percentage as security for their jobs through a responsible Minister. Such key ministries with financial potential had to be allocated only to close allies of Runo.

Unemployment began to make an impact, and everyone with a recognisable high school qualification had no option but to become a teacher. More schools meant more jobs for teachers but no jobs for those with production-oriented qualifications. At least this trend worked well for Runo. There was a scramble for teaching jobs by rural-based folks where most of the voters were based. Some remote areas continued to have a high demand for years because well-trained teachers shunned such places. The second most employing sector was the health sector due to the increase in health posts. Besides, some of the qualified health personnel were getting good opportunities abroad.

A command economy was adopted to control prices and the allocation of foreign currency. No economic policy accompanied the new way of managing the economy. All whites leaving the country or on pensions were given a right to get their pensions or assets in whatever currency or country they decided to settle in. The soft landing was too good to be true, but this was in line with the agreement for the continuation of colonial privileges. Those who had served in Douglas' army continued to receive their full benefits in contrast to those who served as rebels under Runo or the Bellyman. Runo protected the information, and the rights attached to it.

Each annual budget was punctuated by capped hikes in prices and salaries. All prices, from postage stamps to fuel, were determined at budgeting time, supposedly at the discretion of the minister. Retailers looked forward to national budget day. They made sure that they adjusted their prices as soon as the announcements took place. Unfortunately, from a national perspective, the budget had become a futile exercise. There was nothing attached to the budget except to consider increases and balance the numbers. It was devoid of any fiscal policy. Besides, it was no different from a dog chasing its tail. There were price hikes for inputs like fuel and corresponding or lower prices for the resultant product, leaving the profit margin the same or lower. Production was affected, and long queues marked the nation's retail shops for basic products like bread.

At independence, the prices of most goods and services were low and affordable to the working class. A loaf of bread was seven cents. After three years, that price had gone over fifty cents. At times the prices were reviewed without waiting for the budget, especially the price of fuel. The increases started modestly with a few cents but grew exponentially with time. The system was not working for the good of the public. It was easy to understand the position because those in leadership roles and parliament had priority or preferential treatment. They got priority on applying for foreign currency, paid no duty on imports, and the government paid for their children's education abroad. The local economy was for the majority to worry about because the leaders could take what they wanted as and when they had to. Slowly, the leadership started travelling abroad for medical services. It started as a status symbol but, in the end, contributed to the demise of the health service sector.

A metro bus service had its prices controlled as a parastatal but did not suffer greatly due to its monopoly position, but it could not generate cash for reinvestment in new buses and maintain an ageing fleet. The major problem was its inability to service the growing urban population. Queues for the morning shuttles would form as early as four o'clock just to ensure that one got to work on time. There were fewer and fewer buses servicing and plying all routes. Timetables had to be suspended. Political gatherings where buses would ferry people for free were given priority over commercial duties. Runo's rallies, national celebrations and funerals for senior officials were some of the priority areas where buses had to shore up at the expense of production.

Runo was aware that he did not command a huge following, and without the Party, opinions of him were very low. He, therefore, had to make up the huge crowds by any means necessary. The cost of these gatherings became an enormous burden to the company and weighed heavily on its operations as client companies and workers were forced to look for alternatives. Runo and his leadership did not only use the buses for free, but his policy extended to the national airline. Leaders, their families and relatives got free tickets. The airline staff and families also got free tickets even after retirement or resignation. At one point, a flight had less than 10% of paying passengers. Scheduled flights had to be cancelled if Runo arranged an emergency trip or tour, and paying customers would be stranded. It was a source of pride for Runo, but he never considered the commercial viability of his decisions. Every sector was equally affected, the railway service included.

The remaining white population concentrated their children in a few schools where their population could not be diluted. In cases where their numbers were in danger of falling to a 50% ratio, quick decisions were made to move an entire white population of schoolchildren to another school. In one instance, a whites-only boarding school ended up enrolling black children in the spirit of independence, until the ratio of the whites dropped to 60% and the black staff ratio had gone up to 70%. To worsen the situation, a black headmaster had been appointed. At the beginning of the next school term, all the white children failed to report for school. A strategic decision had been made to move them. To delay the race dilution in schools, whites often introduced barriers to entry, such as promoting an equestrian culture, knowing that natives didn't have the luxury of owning horses, let alone buying one for a child. Whites also moved to a few suburbs to keep contact among themselves. Their shopping malls were exclusive. Salaries in many private companies, however, remained unequal in favour of the white population. A two-payroll system remained very much in use, and Runo had promised not to interfere in the running of businesses. Some of the businesses complained when price controls affected their operations. To keep the people happy, Runo did not adjust the prices. Instead, he introduced a government subsidy for each product affected by price controls. This measure worsened the budget deficit.

All the notes in circulation from Douglas' reign were phased out, and new notes were introduced. A dollar, which used to be a note, was introduced in coin form, and a ten-dollar note took the red colour of the former two-dollar note. People missed the dollar to the extent that they coined the phrase *warova sechumi yepepa*, referring to a person not seen in a long time. The phrase *uchaona nhamo tsvuku inenge pondo* disappeared because there were no two-dollar red notes any longer. As more and more people attended schools, the local terminology for monetary denominations and their sum totals disappeared slowly. For instance, *shereni* became ten cents, *tuubhobho* became twenty cents, *koroni* was replaced by a quarter dollar, *chishanu* became fifty cents, *chumi* became a dollar, *chumi nechishanu* a dollar fifty cents and so on. These new notes quickly lost value, and the general public wondered why Runo had introduced a worthless currency instead of keeping Douglas' money. Not only financial terms were affected but the entire spectrum. Riddles and puzzles in the colonial language became more acceptable as affluent, while the local *zvirahwe (riddles)* and *ngano (folk tales)* were associated with the shallow-minded, irrespective of their depth and content.

The price changes affected everyone, and the rural population was affected the most. Some products which could be acquired cheaply and easily for daily consumption, such as vegetables and tomatoes, had their prices adjusted too. It put a strain on many families as the income earning capacity had not changed. However, there was no time to complain because there were several political meetings and gatherings where people were threatened for not attending. The number of meetings in the initial years of Runo's rule was so disruptive that even a workday could be disrupted by political agendas. Voluntary meetings were seldom and probably only for the executive committees where the general public was not supposed to be privy to the discussions. Ad-hoc meetings became the norm, and the public hoped it was just a passing phase. Unfortunately, the phase was taking too long to pass. It became clear that the paradise the people were dreaming of during the struggle had vanished into thin air. The torture by Douglas' regime had been repackaged by Runo into indoctrinating meetings, intimidation and coercive activities. You had to be either on Runo's side or with the enemy, but being against him had serious consequences. Some free-spirited individuals would escape from the villages or pretend to be going on journeys once a meeting was called to be safe from Runo's Party bullies.

At one point, Douglas was worried about the direction the economy was taking and the level or lack of economic acumen among Runo's team. He was interviewed and gave free advice to Runo and his team:

"Mr Douglas, we understand that you are thoroughly unhappy about the state of our economy. Why? Is it a case of sour grapes that you have now lost your privilege?"

"I wouldn't, never will I ever consider running a country on this basis if you pay me to. Everyone is now running on gravel roads with many potholes. Thank goodness we don't need to travel to rivers and dams for fishing any more owing to countless road dams you prefer to call potholes. "

"Your system was very iniquitous and never served the needs of the majority. You made sure it only served a limited number of people to keep a false impression that everything was going well."

"Yet none queued for bread or milk. Milk was delivered to each house-

hold, and now you have to travel to the shops. One needed a few coins to buy bread, and in a few years, you now need ten times the amount. Tell me, who is better?"

"It was delivered to a few who could afford yet you never did anything to uplift the lives of the majority. The excellent economy you talk about was only on paper or in the press at best, your kith and kin's press, to be precise, just to glorify your rule when there was nothing tangible in reality. Real unemployment was over 50% and less than 5% for the white population. The debt inherited by President Runo's government is strangling and choking the economy, and this is one of the reasons we are where we are today."

"I don't see any new investment. Your leadership is busy destroying what I built. No economic deals are being made for the future of this nation. Obsolete machinery is not being replaced, yet you want to blame me."

"Don't you think the colonial government must pay for leaving obsolete machinery, the scars of a gruesome war, reparations for colonialism, for impoverishing the local population, loans to purchase weapons to kill our folk, leaving us with a billion dollar debt yet we are being asked to pay for things we never benefitted from?"

"We brought civilisation, and for that, we need to be appreciated."

"Given the chance, what questions would you ask the leadership?"

"If you wanted me to change the name of the nation and the currency, why didn't you just say so?"

"Would you have complied, Mr Douglas? Besides, you did most of the killing to keep your grip on power and white privileges?"

"With the benefit of hindsight, I would have said yes. Other than those two, there is no progressive change that has taken place in this nation."

"I know everyone is clever in hindsight, but thank you, Mr Douglas, for your time."

"You are most welcome."

The reporter for the only television network lost her job for giving Douglas the platform to speak critically of Runo. All forms of hate speech were formulated to silence Douglas and blame him for the war and oppression. Mudadi was very emotional about how Douglas' regime was extremely oppressive, making them take up arms to fight him. The leadership claimed to have taught Douglas democracy, which enabled him to get the platform to speak and walk freely despite his crimes. Douglas was labelled an unrepentant racist despite Runo having extended the hand of peace and reconciliation. They wanted him to apologise for his unbecoming behaviour. Douglas decided to keep his comments to himself and not offer any consultation or free advice to Runo and his crew.

Owing to the economic decline, recurrent droughts and increasing unemployment, the family and societal hierarchy was adversely affected. The moral values were not spared either. Those with the capacity to generate income could dictate and influence family as well as societal decisions. Elderly respect slowly waned as the rich and famous earned praise and worship. Sex outside marriage became common as those with money shaped the future values and what was to be expected and accepted.

Runo himself slowly imposed himself on the power structures of the nation. Power devolution was removed in favour of centralisation where Runo could influence decisions. The posts of District Administrators became ceremonial as they had no control over finances and decisions for their districts. Governors too lost all their power except for what Runo would have tasked them to do. Parastatals were forced to centralise their finances at their respective Head Offices and had all financial decisions taken from a central point, giving Runo access to all the money he needed.

Chapter 6

Lady Marunjeya was thoroughly unhappy that people talked less and less about her as her publicity levels were dropping. It was not her intention to just become an appendage to Runo but also to build her reputation. It had been four years since her husband assumed office, and his Party was due to have an elective congress. She was worried again that Runo might be sidetracked and a succession plan incorporating all former rebel contributors put in place. Lady Marunjeya kept her fingers crossed that everything would work according to his plans. A quick in and out of fame was a very unwelcome nightmare for her. If only Runo was not temperamental, she would have assisted in coming up with the plan.

One day she officiated at a newly formed organisation promoting the rights of children. The publicity drove her crazy, as the founder of the organisation was never mentioned. She came out as the philanthropist and kind-hearted mother of the nation. It gave her ideas. After a few weeks, the owner also thought it was a good idea to work with Lady Marunjeya. The owner started courting her for a partnership. Meanwhile, Lady Marunjeya thought it would be good to take over the organisation. She went under cover of darkness to negotiate the takeover. The owner refused and kept the partnership offer on the table. This was the last time he was ever seen alive. Those who cared to talk shared stories, but Lady

Marunjeya never cared. Lady Marunjeya, however, did not get the organisational policies, plans and vision. It did not matter to her as she went everywhere with this new project, getting all the attention. It was only the publicity that mattered to her. Lady Marunjeya became a darling of the nation. She would later arm twist Runo to avail funding for the organisation to boost her profile. Lady Marunjeya, however, still felt empty to have publicity without any corresponding power. She wanted something bigger and to command more respect. First, she wanted to be referred to as the Mother of the Nation. Quick implementation of the protocol took effect. It, therefore, became taboo to call her Lady Marunjeya. To the public, she became Lady Amai Marunjeya Runobvepi. Privately, people would question why she wanted the title when she did not have any children. It boggled the minds of many, but they had to comply.

Fewer and fewer urban women were chanting the Party slogans as their men felt jealous. It was unprecedented to have one's wife displaying an image of another man on her chest or bosom. Many women were, therefore, threatened with divorce for promoting Runo over their husbands. Some stopped, but others continued depending on their source of income. Lady Amai Marunjeya had never been seen doing the same, and this was another source of contention. It was talked about, and the press had its fair share but with restraint. Nothing changed as the Runo train kept gathering momentum.

Lady Amai Marunjeya yearned to dance with the Party leadership and gave Runo sleepless nights. Runo thought it was a good opportunity. He approached Mudadi for a dry run of his idea.

"Mudadi, my partner, the energy from our women is subdued so early into our rule and needs to be revitalised."

"It's upsetting, Your Excellency, that your people are not grateful for our liberating this nation for them. All the sacrifices we made cannot be in vain."

"Any suggestion, Mudadi?"

"The First Lady has exhibited a lot of energy with her project. Imagine if we incorporate her in the Party."

"Our Party congress is not far off. Are we not late to start this project?"

"You give the instruction, and I will whip everyone into line. You know me by now. I don't expect a challenge from some individuals who lack academic discipline."

"Well done, partner. I shall set everything in motion."

✻

Runo was quick to implement the idea because he had other plans unbeknown to Mudadi. He ensured that Lady Amai Marunjeya had been accommodated in the Party hierarchy. A few leaders in the capital were delighted to be invited to the president's office. They were very happy to comply and do a favour to their beloved leader. There was no negative expectation from people who revered their leader except to thank him for having given an instruction or command. Runo then delivered the good news to his lady Amai.

"My lady, congratulations are in order for landing your future post as the head of the women's wing of the Party," Runo sounded like a gentleman in command.

"I am not part of the political Party hierarchy. How is that possible?"

"You are now as we speak, and the women are preparing to endorse your nomination as well as your sole candidature for the congress."

"Well done, Runo. You are my Knight in shining armour."

"Don't mention it, my lady."

"Hold on, Runo. I know you. Why did you do it?"

"For the good of the Republic, my lady," he pretended to look indifferent.

"You are selfish, only faithful to yourself and never looking out for anyone's interests. Tell me what you have up your sleeve."

"Do I have to bring all my plans in the open when your wish has been granted?"

"I can just turn down your offer and spoil everything for you." She did not mean it but wanted her man to be open.

"Listen, my lady. The congress is coming up and I want a dry run of my plans."

"What plans, Runo?"

"If they can accept you without proper congress protocol, then our stay in this Palace is guaranteed."

"How is that conceivable?"

"I can also declare that there is no vacancy in the praesidium, and no one can question it."

"There are others who may have had plans. How will you deal with them?"

"Too many are contemplating taking that route. They must fight against each other and not me. Mudadi will then finish them off, or whoever will still be standing. As the women's leader, you shall throw your weight behind me. A new youth leader, with my blessing, will be elected. He shall support me with his life. Our third force is the former fighters, who are very comfortable with me at this stage because I have recently become their patron. I shall leave the congress unscathed."

"Do you understand that you may never win any Party reelection in future with such a level of deception?"

"Who intends to have it, anyway?"

"I see. Once this goes through, then the fate of the Party is sealed."

"You could not have said it better, my lady."

"Next year is election time. Don't you expect some retribution from your Party?"

"It's early days, and ours is a popular movement. My election is guaranteed and, therefore, I have to work on other issues. I expect Mudadi to have amended the Party constitution, which we have been neglecting."

"Runo, seriously, you have to do something for your people. This war, declining employment and stagnating economic growth. Do something. I implore you."

"They are not my people. Each man for himself and God for us all."

"Where else do you belong if you reject this nation?"

"My parents were in servitude when they got here."

"But you have a local name, Runobvepi. How is it possible?"

"That was my mother's boyfriend."

"Isn't it good enough that the man was good to you? Didn't he take care of you?"

"He was, and his in-laws became so close to us that we became their nephews and nieces. The eldest son-in-law was so fond of us."

"If that man showed so much love to you, why are you thinking of retribution."

"How do you know if he was not the very reason my father ran away?"

"That cannot be his fault, but your mother's problem."

"I couldn't care less. Someone must pay for it."

"Any idea where they came from?"

"I do. That's the reason I am supporting them in their fight against the fundamentalist dictatorship."

"For now, can you help the cause of your fellow countrymen?"

"I cannot find the will, either in my ribs or in my bones, to do so," Runo was unmoved and showed no sympathy.

"Everyone put his trust and faith in you. You cannot betray that."

"Seriously, I never asked them to. They wanted independence, and I gave it to them. What else do they want?"

"Do you presume your family history will remain a secret forever?"

"It's buried. All evidence has been destroyed, and no one dares talk about it, just like I have covered up your local roots."

"Why this anger, apprehension, resentment and frustration?"

"You won't understand."

"Is it your childhood? They are not your father. They love you. Why prefer some foreign nation over your own?"

"Don't worry, my lady, you know I always will visit home despite my numerous trips abroad."

"What did they give you that you forget your own?"

"The see-eye-all has been good to me. They gave me a job when I was just a hopeless teacher. Imagine me masquerading as a journalist to gain access to the newly anointed leaders of independent Africa. I had all privileges, and I am now Chief Executive cum governor of this nation. When my task abroad was complete, I was reassigned to come home and destroy some novel and amateurish movements that were disturbing the peace of my principals. Their vetting system was weak, and they trusted an enemy whom they brought into their fold. They have lost their struggle but do not even recognise it. My allegiance will always be with my principals since I took an oath, not to this rat-infested nation. Besides, I have several affiliations to keep me afloat and not get challenged for the top post in this nation, the church, the secret club and many business interests benefiting from this country's resources. I am invincible, my lady."

"How could you betray your brethren, and why cling on to power if you have a low opinion of this nation with no allegiance to its people?"

"I have been taught to spy even among my own family, my brethren, to believe no man and to trust no man. As for this nation, it's just a source of resources, income and power. When I do my trips, they will be so happy to have such a privileged leader."

"Your evilness is unparalleled. Have you ever realised how

it pains me to know that my roots are in this nation?"

"Thank you for the compliment, my lady, and you don't have to remind me of things I already know.

The congress endorsed Lady Amai Marunjeya's appointment, and Runobvepi declared no vacancy in the praesidium through Mudadi. Ziva went ballistic as this was against all agreed Party tenets. He bemoaned the hijacking of the Party and nation by a dictatorship unwilling to embrace democracy. Ziva even pointed out all the unfulfilled promises, passing all the blame on Runo and his unwillingness to help his people, preferring to dine with the enemy. His speech was from the heart, undiplomatic, truthful and confrontational. He commenced by calling Ino, who had brought along his nephew, Heartbeat, to the podium (the nephew was the driving force and major cause for Ino to leave the Bellyman and his Party, together with Ziva, who mooted the idea of forming a splinter group. For this reason, the nephew was the heartbeat of the Party).

He lifted Heartbeat's left hand and asked him to wave to the crowd with the right. Ziva thanked Heartbeat and the crowd. "This young man's life, though in his early twenties, is intertwined with the life of the great revolutionary party. He is one of the major causes of the birth of our party. His birthday coincides with that of our great revolutionary Party, and we must appreciate his very existence despite his father being our arch-enemy. Those who know already know." Ziva then paused with a song composed by Cde Paul Chigango, a song that always reminded the rebels to maintain discipline, leaving no window of opportunity for questions:

Kune nzira dzemasoja dzekuzvibata nadzo
Teverai mitemo yose nenzira dzakanaka

Tisave tinotora zvinhu zvemass yedu
Dzorerai zvinhu zvose zvatogwa kumuvengi

Taurai zvinetsika kuruzhinji rwevanhu,
Kuti mass inzwisise zvakananga musangano

Bhadharai zvamunotenga nenzira dzakanaka
Mudzorere zvinhu zvese zvamunenge matora

Tisave tinotora zvinhu zvemass yedu
Dzorerai zvinhu zvose zvatogwa kumuvengi
Taurai zvinetsika kuruzhinji rwevanhu,
Kuti mass inzwisise zvakananga musangano

Tisaita choupombwe muhondo yechimurenga
Tisanetsa vasungwa vatinenge tabata

Tisave tinotora zvinhu zvemass yedu
Dzorerai zvinhu zvose zvatogwa kumuvengi
Taurai zvinetsika kuruzhinji rwevanhu,
Kuti mass inzwisise zvakananga musangano

Awa ndiwo mashoko akataurwa kare
naivo VaMao vachitidzidzisa

Tisave tinotora zvinhu zvemass yedu
Dzorerai zvinhu zvose zvatogwa kumuvengi
Taurai zvinetsika kuruzhinji rwevanhu,
Kuti mass inzwisise zvakananga musangano

The mood was jovial, and everyone was ready to listen to Ziva and Heartbeat's story, but instead, he dived into the congress proceedings.

"Ladies and gentlemen, I stand before you not only as Secretary General of our Great Revolutionary Party but also in my capacity as a founding member and father of our Revolutionary Party.

"We made a giant leap forward by achieving independence

through democracy despite a history of combat activism. It's irrefutable that the battle had been won in the trenches, but we lost the war at the negotiating table on whether to sign for the continuation and perpetuation of colonial rights or not. The world at least looked at us in a different light and had a lot to learn from us. It was an unprecedented move that would go down in history as a test case. In short, greatness was thrust upon us by our very own achievements. While the country has embraced democracy, our Party still yearns for guerrilla warfare. I would have imagined that Party democracy engenders national democracy. It is now my considered view that had it not been for the negotiations we held to end the insurrection, this nation would be under a brutal military command. A life term in office would not have been inconceivable. This nation would also have been under a family monarchy. It is most likely that we will take the same direction, albeit under the guise of guided and legitimised rule.

"Even leading up to this Party congress today, we have destroyed any hopes for democracy in our Party. If we are all prepared to accept the decisions made thus far, then we are not only doomed as a Party but as a nation. If we continue on this path, we may as well forget about the future of our children and their children's children. The goodwill of this nation is being destroyed right before our own eyes. The negative results of politicians usurping a patriotic and nationalist cause are becoming clear. I am baffled by your quiescence and willingness to be cowed into submission by Runobvepi, our leader.

Today, we are doing exactly the opposite by trading our freedoms for beneficence. When will we learn to separate Runobvepi as a person, his role in the Party and his role in government? There is a life beside and after him. Why should we tie the fortunes of the nation to one man? The path Runobvepi has chosen will have far-reaching consequences for this nation. It is a dangerous precedent. You should never allow someone to impose his will on the entire Party. If he can do as he wishes to the Party, then the next stage is to apply the same template to the nation. Each one of us attending this congress is culpable. First was the endorsement without due process of his wife, Lady Amai Marunjeya, as she wants to be referred to now. She was never part of the Party structures six months ago, and today she is not only in those structures but at the apex of the women's arm. No one has lifted a finger. He went ahead and declared a no vacancy for all top leadership posts. Again, this is against Party principles, and now these have to be amended to suit his wishes. Not one of you has lifted a finger again, and it makes me wonder if all of you are the same people who revolted against Douglas.

"It was my responsibility when I, Stick Man and Ino established this Party that we bequeath a democratic institution to the nation. We took time to incorporate every democratic principle in our constitution. Today, you have trampled and turned your backs on what I had hoped were great values and principles. I cannot reconcile the docility gripping some once fearless rebels who now so easily acquiesce to being bullied by one who never held a gun. Being chosen as a leader is not equivalent to being a deity. It is a position of trust. Runo is the same mortal person that we must call to order and not only show a democratic path but demonstrate the essence of democracy. A one-man rule for life is not part of it but the opposite. Leaders must have defined and limited terms in office irrespective of how good or bad they are; democracy has one constant. That constant is change, yet we fail to understand that simple concept. If we cannot do it today, then we have failed as the guardians of democracy. We would have failed as leaders entrusted with the future of this nation. The sacrifices by us and our other rebels, people's hopes, dreams and expectations have all gone up in smoke before our own eyes. We achieved and attained freedom only to give it away because some of us are not racially confident and trust only those who communicate well in a foreign language, our colonial master's language. Colonialism, therefore, never ended.

"A one-man state was never one of the founding principles of our Party. Experience on our continent has shown that it brings the evils of nepotism, corruption and inefficiency. It's not my intention to get personal and, therefore, I will not make any direct attacks on his person, but on his office. For the past four years, how many farms were taken from white farmers for the benefit of our people? How many factories were given to our people? Today, you still have white-only shops and suburbs. How many companies are being run by our people? The simple answer to all the questions is none. I wonder if this was the objective of the war, yet every one of you here chose to keep quiet and are feeling alright or ambivalent. Please explain to me why you are ready to betray your own so early into our rule. Is this the death of our democracy? Why is Runobvepi afraid of the ballot box, yet he talks passionately about democracy?"

Mudadi started singing and booing Ziva. Other Party members followed suit. Mudadi took to the stage and announced, "Let us agree here and now that we shall never allow our anointed leader to be challenged at any congress. In addition, no one shall disagree with our dear leader for the good of the nation. His level of education is worthy of respect, and we cannot brush aside such hard work to please a few power-hungry individuals."

Ziva was utterly disgusted and responded, "I would not have any qualms if Mudadi stuck to the rule book or the law. Instead, he is dishonest even to himself. I cannot say he is just wrong on our constitutional provisions, as that would suggest an excusable ignorance. Neither is he amoral, as this would point to an incapacity to distinguish right from wrong. His preferred choice of mob psychology is bent on transgressing and violating our constitution. This is not only dishonest deception but extremely immoral, which makes him a very doubtful, if not a dubious lawyer. This nation is not a one-man state, and we should not let it slide into one. Mudadi is a pathetic excuse of a lawyer for pretending not to understand simple principles of democracy. We should not be fooled into worshipping education that does not deliver results. Progress is more important than displaying papers in your offices." Mudadi challenged Ziva on his lack of education, and Ziva was quick to pick him up, but before he could crash him to the floor, security swiftly intervened. The confrontation ended. Lady Amai Marunjeya was ecstatic that her dream had come true. She could afford to relax, knowing very well that life as the first lady was guaranteed.

Mudadi worked overtime to tarnish Ziva's image, painting him as an unstable, rambunctious maniac, an unmitigated disaster, an accident in the making, a man who could not be trusted by any peace-loving and law-abiding citizen. He referred everyone to the peace accord and the principle of forgiveness adopted when they came to power. Mudadi even insinuated that all whites would be expelled from the nation or be killed should Ziva come to power. Ziva reminded people that this was just hyperbole, stuck to his guns, and a rift between him and Runo grew wider every day. In a bold move towards a one-party state, Runo formed a Party politburo and Central Committee. These two organs did not only serve the Party, but their decisions were binding for the nation. Mudadi and Runo went on to abolish the post of Secretary General, merging the position with that of the leader of the Party. Runo, therefore, became both the Party leader and Secretary, creating a single centre of power for the Party. Ziva was left in the cold. The superior role of the Chairman was reduced to being of lesser importance and lower than the Party president. The only stumbling block to his becoming a supreme leader was the Bellyman, as the former oppressors had become an insignificant minority.

*

Election season came, but Runo's government was unprepared for the exercise. There was no voter roll, and it was discovered that there was a need for a delimitation commission to demarcate constituencies. The election was delayed by four months. Breaching the constitution was very likely due to a perceived lack of foresight. Maybe it wasn't, but just for convenience. When all preparations were complete, there were nineteen days left for parties to campaign before elections could be held. Runo never spent much energy on excessive campaigns. The youthful arm of the Party had done enough groundwork for him. Every night in the suburbs, they would gather and move around in groups attacking any known non-Runo supporters, singing and chanting slogans. Each household had to avail a member or its sons for the cause. If not, the family would be labelled as traitors.

Even those without any Party affiliation or interest in politics had to pretend. In other instances, the youths would inspect Party cards at each household in an operation dubbed door-to-door campaigning. The intimidation by Runo's youth brigade brought terror to his opponents. The forced immortalisation of Runo was sufficient to guarantee a victory. Runo's challenge was mainly from the Bellyman. He was back in the country from exile. The Bellyman never stopped talking about progress and reform. For instance, he criticised the lack of preparedness to hold the elections. He further suggested that this could have been by design. Runo was not willing to reform the electoral process, much to the disadvantage of his foes. He was probably hoping they would stop their political movements or Parties. Despite the atmosphere, Bellyman continued with his campaign. However, given the insurrection, not many wanted to be associated with him. His hands were tied to the back and his feet in leg irons, yet he was expected to perform in the ring. Gaining new ground proved difficult. A further hurdle was from Runo's youths brigades, who would not allow the Bellyman's campaign team into most constituencies.

The national media, which was all government-owned, never gave the Bellyman and opposition Parties coverage. It only covered them in the negative. Some tried hard to mention this fact, but Runo labelled them as cry babies. He always referred them to the elections that ushered independence as a test case where the Collar Man and Douglas lost. They lost despite having monopolised the media to themselves. Runo, however, forgot to mention that there wasn't any intimidation. Those who assumed the nation was free for everybody paid the ultimate prize. The Bellyman lost eighteen candidates during the election period. Bellyman, however, never subscribed to the issue of tribes, stating that this was simply a political game by Runo and that no tribe should hate each other as they would fall into a political minefield. Runo never accepted responsibility for the deaths. In his campaign, Runo never stopped accusing the Bellyman of intending to subvert authority.

His message was very clear, "Lets vote for peace and shun war. A vote for the Bellyman is a vote for war." In short, a vote for him ensured peace, and a vote for the Bellyman meant war. Without shame, Runo praised his one-party state mantra in public. Runo repeatedly used the slogan, showing his disregard for the Bellyman and other political leaders. He, however, came short of imposing a one-man state slogan. One journalist almost derailed Runo's campaign. He introduced the issue of land and resettlement. This matter was supposed to be a closed chapter with all its injustices. Runo tried to be diplomatic but was not convincing. It was clear there was something to hide. If only the journalist had probed further, then the truth would have come out. He feared for his life, but at least he had introduced the subject to whoever wanted to investigate further.

Runo won resoundingly, further weakening the Bellyman's position. The Bellyman lost ground from his previous position at independence. It became apparent that the Bellyman's political career was limping. Even his power base had become more tribal, further destroying his national credibility and appeal. The insurrection, however, did not stop. It was clear the election was never a democratic exercise but a choice of the same menu.

Chapter 7

The *pidigori* man released more songs critical of Runo and his government. He blasted the cronyism, corruption, selfishness and love of other developed countries over theirs. He made popular hits such as *Vanotongera mundege, Chimurenga ndakarwa nani, Corruption, Kwapera makore mangani takangomirira.* The corruption buzzword on the streets was that not a single relative of Runo was unemployed; therefore, you had to take care of your own. In no time, the phrase *Chana chavatete* (aunt's child) was coined to mean a favoured one and *mwana wanhingi* (someone else's child), for someone not to be considered for any favours. Runo was thoroughly displeased by an individual bent on causing public despondency and fomenting dissent. He could not publicly attack him but made sure he got fewer and fewer government platforms to perform. Runo was particularly passionate about discrediting the man's hair-locks as heavily infested by lice. It did not work, and the singer's popularity shot through the roof. The singer had once been incarcerated for supporting Runo's rebel movement and, therefore, the people felt they had a hero in him. Runo could not keep him down.

Another, the Dancing singer, did *Inhlanzi yeSiziba* denigrating Runo for abusing the prison system by incarcerating any opponent irrespective of whether there is a case to answer or not. Runo did not quite understand the language; therefore, the dancing singer did not get a significant backlash.

Fearing worse reprisals, the dancing singer went underground. *Zuva rekufa kwangu* was released by another singer, a Revlon Hairman, mocking the unproductive state of Runo's loins. It inferred a constant and persistent wearying, wearing Runo down daily over the matter. The song was a mega hit whose repeated airplay rivalled it only to the anthem. Runo could tell this singer wanted to pick a fight with him; therefore, he ignored it, pretending that no harm was done and freedom of speech was widely accepted.

After a while, and without any headline scandal, Runo and his leadership decided to compensate themselves for injuries sustained during the war. Money for this fund had been donated to the nation by well-wishers. Instead, Runo kept it a secret and information was availed only to the privileged top leadership. For some reason, former rebels who were part of the national army managed to sniff information about the fund. Sloppy Man was quick to silence them as they prepared to make their claims. He asked them a few questions: Are you in a wheelchair? Do you use crutches? Are you bedridden? Are you blind? Did you lose any limbs? If the answer to the above questions is no, then you have no business claiming money from the compensation fund. All soldiers were, therefore, shut out of the compensation fund.

Runo went on to appoint a certain man whose Nom de Guerre during the war was Clever Militia Man, a veteran of the struggle and a doctor, as the specialist responsible for the assessment of war victims. No other views or opinions were permissible. This gave Clever Militia Man an important role in the matter. Runo allowed him to claim a 120% disability so that he could be lenient to everybody making claims. Sloppy Man had his share. Heli claimed 93% disability, but she had no injuries. Runo claimed 98% disability even though he never held a gun, nor was he present at any battlefront. Besides, he was still the head of the nation and the Revolutionary Party. Lady Amai Marunjeya was dismayed by his level of avarice.

His clout was helping the Party retain many supporters and voters. This worked well for any ambitions she was harbouring, and she didn't want anything to come in the way. She, therefore, confronted Runo and asked him:

"Did you have to claim such a high level of disability when you are still the leader? Are you going to return the money?"

"I thought you, of all people, know very well that I am no longer a man," he showed little interest in the subject and never looked her in the eye.

"You are my husband, Runo, and you are of the male gender. Are you losing it?" She was concerned.

"Gender, yes, but where are the results?"

"What results, Runo? Are you hallucinating?"

"Everyone is mocking me, and you even have this singer talking about my barren state. Imagine, *Zuva rekufa kwangu* is being played like a national anthem now. This man lacks discipline and respect."

"You can ban the song Runo. Stop crying." She smiled.

"Then everyone will know it was for me, and the anthem chorus will grow."

"What are you thinking?"

"I will shame him quietly and diplomatically."

"How?"

"Mudadi will think of something, but for now, I have to think about ending this war with the Bellyman."

"If the compensation issue becomes public knowledge, will you return the money, or you may want to do it now and save yourself the public embarrassment?"

"You don't know me as yet, my lady."

"Loyal to yourself, selfish and narcissistic."

"Thank you for the compliment."

A vehicle manufacturer approached Runo's government with a proposal to set up a car assembly in Runo's nation. The talks went smoothly with Runo, and hopes were high that the deal would sail through. Runo later sent his emissaries to negotiate a commission. The representatives reported these perceived rogue elements, and he promised to take action, but nothing happened. Runo's Ministers continued to lobby for a commission before a deal could be signed. After a month of the pesky Ministers applying pressure, the vehicle representatives packed their bags and left. Another vehicle manufacturer, whose brand was already being assembled on a small scale, approached Runo to promise him a much better and bigger deal. They even donated a lot of goods and money to assist the government.

In a surprise move, negotiations for a commission by a Minister were tabled. It was unexpected and unprecedented to have a parallel negotiation, and they exposed the indecent approach to Runo. These representatives also attended one of Simo's public addresses in one town that they had sponsored. They had hoped that on such a platform, their company banners would be displayed and their impending deal publicised. To their surprise, they were never referred to, or their company mentioned, and even the deal was not discussed at any point. The writing was on the wall that they needed to agree to the commission or else the deal was off. The vehicle company moved to a neighbouring country, was allocated space, and became benefactors of a small town. During the same period, a broadcasting company based on a new technology approached Runo's government, hoping to set up a continental base in Runo's nation. As usual, the talks were positive. However, after a while, the commission issue became a sticking point. Nate, Runo's Information Minister, who was supposed to ensure that a licence was granted, publicly bashed their new investors. The broadcasters tried, again and again, to knock sense into Runo and his Information Minister, but nothing worked. In the end, they were forced to set up shop in a politically volatile neighbouring country.

Kumbi was at it again. This time, he requested construction funds so that a gravel road leading to one of the nation's landmark bridges would be turned into a tarred highway. It was also in honour of the landmark as it had been recognised by the government with its image permanently engraved on a twenty-cent coin. Everyone agreed to his proposal. The road stretch was about a hundred and twenty kilometres. Kumbi ensured that only half a kilometre was tarred from both ends, after which all the funds were diverted for personal use. Anyone passing through assumed that the construction of the road was complete. Kumbi went on to violently influence all cartographers to mark the road as a dual highway. This was often a source of confusion in defining a dual highway for school children from the district affected by this new highway. After amassing the funds, Kumbi went on to fence off his homestead from intruders. A local community dam close to his homestead was also incorporated into the fencing project. It became part of his property for the rural home. No one could access the dam, and the community livestock and wild animals that depended on it were plunged into a crisis. People had to travel long distances to get water. He was proud that the locals could finally see him in the same light and class as commercial white farmers. These had their farms fenced, and no one was allowed access or to carry out any activity therein. They were considered the bourgeoise of society, and Kumbi wanted his community to feel the change in his social standing despite it mainly being derived from ill-gotten gains and depriving the people of their rights.

*

Runo thought and thought about finishing off Bellyman but could not find an answer. The battlefront was not yielding positive results, and he was growing desperate. His token head of state, the obscure Professor Reverend Banner, was not helping matters either. He was truly obscure that he only featured prominently at football matches, scouting for suitable candidates. His contribution to the nation was ceremonially negligible to non-existent. On the extreme side, he increasingly humiliated the nation each time he was on an international visit. His background of having hailed from Sodom was becoming too much of a burden and threatening the moral fibre of the nation. The public was wondering why Runo had created his role in the first instance. Even his contribution to the struggle against Douglas was of little significance and limited to a few skirmishes with the police in the company of his church congregation.

On the other hand, Runo also realised that this man was becoming a stumbling block to the sweeping changes he needed to make to achieve total control of both the Party and the nation. He needed to reduce him to a general civilian. Runo was desperate for a solution on a dignified and fitting exit. Given his dilemma, he decided to deal with Ino, his defence point man, first. He called him for a meeting at his Palace under cover of darkness.

"Since the insurrection started, we have not made any progress, Ino. You started this Party. How can you fail us?" Runo was in no mood for socialising or negotiating.

"Your Excellency, we have to be careful not to wipe out our own. The Bellyman is unreasonable. He is not even ashamed of his involvement in this conflict and blames us for everything while being used and abused by international players."

"I assumed that what he did to your sister would provoke much anger and ignite that spark of vengeance to want to finish him off. You raised his son as your own."

"This is beyond personal emotions. Starting this Party ensured that the Bellyman would never rule this country. Let's wear him out and save lives."

"You must know where your allegiance lies. The longer this drags on, the more my reputation will be tarnished."

"I advised you on the best method to win this battle, but you would not listen."

"Ino, my man, you have to decide if you are with us or them. Otherwise you will lose your post."

"Why are you turning your back on me when I have never been disloyal to the Party, to you and this nation?"

"I am in charge now, Ino, and you have to do as I say."

"Come on, Runo. I never expected you, of all people, to be a dictator. I propelled you up the ladder together with my friend Ziva, hoping for sensible leadership over the Stick Man. It has taken me such a long time to realise you are egoistic and selfish."

"You must know that you are being disrespectful of your one true leader who can appoint and disappoint. Before you chose your responses, you must have realised that you never won any electoral constituency and, therefore, you are serving at my pleasure."

"Are you threatening me, Runo?"

"Do your job, Ino. I don't need excuses. There is everything you need at your disposal. What lives do you want to save when you know there is collateral damage in war?"

"I am speechless, Runo, at what you are in private, yet you wear a different character in public. As you wish, Your Highness, I shall deliver."

Runo stormed out of the meeting room in a rage. Being challenged or reminded of the wrong decisions he may have made in the past was a very unwelcome move to Runo. For that, Ino was going to pay dearly. It was only a matter of time and opportunity. Runo, in his mind and his world, was always right. Anyone who dared not respect his view faced retribution at some future point, whether the relations were good or bad. He wanted no one to cross his path, although he kept it a guarded secret. Ino was put on strict surveillance because Runo wanted to know every step he made.

Runo went straight to the Great Crocodile's office the following day, frustrated that he did not have any other choice. In his lifetime, begging was the worst position he wanted to be in. He had no option but to do it. Failing to conceal his frustrations, he simply plunged into the issue before he could extend any greetings. The Great Crocodile had to rush and close his office door; then he asked Runo to be comfortable.

"What can I do for you, Runo? I thought this would be the last office you may want to be associated with."

"My Great Crocodile, you have proved to be valuable before, during and after the war with your intelligent intelligence. Your precocious mind and pernickety are unparalleled," he was unsettled and appeared very serious.

"I know. What's new?" Great Crocodile was dismissive.

"Believe me when I say Mudadi put me on this path against the Bellyman, and Ino cannot finish it."

"How can I help you?" Great Crocodile was puzzled by Runo's state of mind.

"I need you to clean up this mess."

"Once I am done, then you look for ways and means to get rid of me or sideline me as usual. Do you want to use me as a doormat? Talk to him and end the conflict. Words have more power than bullets."

"It's for the good of the nation. For the glory of the Republic, Great Crocodile. Anything you want, all you have to do is ask."

"*Totenda maruva tadla Chakata!*"

"Don't doubt me, Great Crocodile. I am very sincere and swear by that very sacred passage that gave me life."

"You know I can finish this off in a few months, but you must shoulder the blame for the unintended consequences of war. Don't mention my name in this mess."

"Where were you, Great Crocodile, when I could not find a solution to this mess?"

"You hate me with a passion, Runo. It's only desperation that pushed you to me."

"Don't say that, Great Crocodile. Hate is too strong a word," Runo hugged him.

"At times, we must be candid with each other rather than pretend we are friends."

"I never said any hate word to or about the Great Crocodile. Don't harbour any ill-conceived feelings about me."

"You don't have to say anything, Runo. Remember, I have a whole file on all your activities before you demoted me to a less important ministry."

"That was treasonous, Great Crocodile. You should never do that to your leader."

"How was I going to help you if I didn't know your thoughts, habits and generally everything about you? Now, look at the security and defence system I put in place. Impenetrable and strong, but do I get a thank you? No. I instead get the boot."

"Don't worry, Great Crocodile, I was very emotional at that time."

"Then and up to now because you never wanted any close association with me. I know you have even set a trap for me with this conflict, but I hope one day you may come to your senses."

"Trust me, Great Crocodile. I am not at all close to those evil things you say about me."

"Even serial killers say the same."

"I implore you not to be harsh with me."

"I get you, Runo. Before I can do anything, it's time to give Ken his marching orders."

"Why, Great Crocodile?"

"He is double dipping and fuelling the conflict. How do you suppose everyone around the world is ahead of us in terms of intelligence on the conflict? Ken is an undesirable element. He is busy feeding information to Maggie and our very neighbourly enemies. This is the reason we cannot keep tabs on their contribution to the conflict. While we blame Bellyman, of course, he is culpable, but sometimes he is not even aware of what's happening around him."

"I will do it, Great Crocodile, but I don't like your exonerating of the Bellyman when you know he is an enemy."

"We are done here, Runo. You can go. I will relay the results."

"I always knew there is always that good man in you. Thank you, old friend."

Runo left but still held on to the deep resentment of the Great Crocodile. He could never forgive him, but he knew he needed him. Several attempts had been made on his life, but only the Great Crocodile had come to his rescue. It was just his infinite insecurity, selfishness and cowardice that ignited the passionate hate for the Great Crocodile, but he knew he needed him always. In his timidity, he could not handle anything successful except rule by intimidation. Any tactic he had employed to try and eliminate the Great Crocodile had failed. He was unashamed of his lunacy, though.

Ziva, in need of Party reforms, failed to garner enough support within the Party to change Runo's dictatorial tendencies. He had been dropped out of the executive by Runo, and his financial well-being had been reduced drastically. Mudadi was a hopeless character to try and convince. The Great Crocodile was too immersed in the conflict to spare time for Ziva. Besides, the Great Crocodile also seemed to be getting close to the Bellyman. Ziva tried the legal route and failed. Ino was too busy thinking that he could convince Runo to keep him in the executive and did not need more trouble in his life. He had discussed endlessly with Ino but to no avail. Their last conversation left Ziva with no option but to undertake his project alone, although there was a window of hope that he would eventually join the proposed new front.

"My lifetime buddy, Ino, we have proved that we can achieve great things together. Please walk with me again."

"I appreciate your assessment, and the results are there for everyone to see. Our baby is now in charge of this nation."

"We have thrust that baby into the foster care of a marauding dinosaur, a demented monster and an unmitigated disaster."

"That I concur with, but probably there is hope to save him from his madness."

"I have tried several times, Ino, for the past seven years, but the man is hopeless. He is dark-minded, selfish, and vengeful, and, with time, all his former allies will be eliminated from the Party, if not from the face of the earth. He wants to be a supreme ruler, supreme commander and leader."

"I am in a bind, Ziva."

"That's the reason we should join hands."

"I have created enemies and do not want to continue doing it."

"What enemies, Ino?"

"I am not on talking terms with the Bellyman, being viewed as a betrayer, then when we formed this Party and now in this conflict."

"That I understand, but leaving to do our project will pacify him as we will send a message that we need the Bellyman more than Runo. Who knows, our two parties can merge, and we will be assured of beating Runo in the next elections."

"It sounds interesting, but Runo is on my neck and wants me to prove my allegiance."

"Leave him so that once we are set up, we quickly contact the Bellyman for a grand coalition."

"It sounds a great plan, but why don't you do it and then I can join you later."

"Don't hesitate. Let's hit Runo at once then we know he is finished. The project has already started, but I want you to be part of it. Imagine you calling the Bellyman for a meeting. That day would change the future of this nation."

"Give me time to think, Ziva. I just want to make sure I have tied up all the loose ends, but I am sold on the idea now. When we talk next time, I may have already had a chat with the Bellyman. There is, however, a small problem with the Bellyman because, of late, he has been frequenting and being hosted at the Great Crocodile's house. I do not know if he wants to recruit him."

"That will work in our favour if Great Crocodile leaves the Party."

Public opinion never gave Ziva much to work with. It was inconceivable to conjure up the necessity of another political Party. Runo wasted no time when he got an update that Ino was too close to Ziva. He quickly summoned Ino and interrogated him on his conversation with Ziva. Ino's life was threatened, and he had no choice but to stab Ziva in the back. After that event, Runo quickly realised he was going to be the biggest loser and put a plan in motion. This did not stop Ziva because eventually he formed a splinter group and took on a few disgruntled members with him as he received support from well-wishers. Lady Amai Marunjeya felt sorry for him, knowing how ruthless Runo had been on his case. She had to be selfish and put her interests first. His threat made her uncomfortable, and she wanted Runo's assurance that all would be well.

"Runo, I am not ready to be a commoner, yet Ziva threatens us with that idea. How can the situation be salvaged?"

"My lady, if I want to be life president, then you have nothing to worry about."

"But Runo, look at the progress he is making while you are watching, and the insurrection, on the other hand, is tearing the nation apart."

"Relax, my lady. He conceived his idea too early after our independence, and that's a negative. People are not ready to move on."

"Is that supposed to give me comfort?" She responded, staring into his face and ready to poke him.

"Ziva is stubborn, headstrong and too much of a maverick to survive politics," he calmly responded, trying to cool down her temper.

"Will you have him eliminated?"

"Everything does not have to end in bloodshed unless we have completely failed. As suggested by Mudadi, we shall wear him out financially and tarnish his public image. Once close to the elections, we will give the public the idea that he is our project to have a phantom opposition."

"Really?"

"If you are done, I have coffee with Professor Reverend Banner and will see you later. We have more important business than to discuss your worries."

"I have never heard you consulting him before and neither has he made any contribution to this government."

"Relax, my lady. There is a first time for everything."

Runo left to join Professor Reverend Banner at his residence a distance away from the Palace. Runo had picked up the vibes that Bellyman and Great Crocodile were busy mending relations even though the conflict had not ended. Prime Minister Runobvepi felt betrayed and sought to steal the thunder, and hand it over to Professor Reverend Banner in the process. Banner was surprised to see Runo gracing his home, and he asked:

"What an honour to be visited by Your Excellency. What did I do to deserve such an honour."

"I will be quick and direct, Reverend, in the interest of time. I know you have another appointment later this afternoon," he said in a hurry and not ready to entertain any jokes.

"Go ahead. I am listening." The Professor looked withdrawn.

"Reverend, you know I gave you this post, but you never deserved it. Now you are busy engrossed in your Sodom roots. It will be such a public embarrassment if the press sniffs out your secrets," he said, pointing a finger at him.

"What do you suggest, fire me over a sexual preference or just an alternative lifestyle?"

"Your exit has to be more dignified than that, Reverend. Your distasteful habits have to be concealed, and we should protect the public from your excesses."

"You have stolen millions, murdered and have done the unthinkable, yet you want to sacrifice me. How dare you, Runo?"

"Imagine one headline about your Sodom roots. Will there

be time to defend yourself, or will you immediately become a villain? If you have to stand trial for all your cases on this matter, how will friends and family feel about you?"

Professor Reverend Banner thought about it, sunk in his chair, holding his chin and said, "Anything is better, Runo. The nation is not ready and sophisticated enough to understand. Let's have a compromise."

"That's what I thought."

"No press, Runo, and not any form of publicity. The international complaints must be covered by my immunity. Name whatever I should do."

"As you are aware, the Great Crocodile is close to annihilating the Bellyman and his insurgency. Talk to the Bellyman."

"*Kumisa pfambi hunge une mari.* What do I have to offer?"

"You could offer him a carrot to join us and forget about all the public scorn. Even these divisions in the country along regional lines are not necessary. Besides, there seems to be a development between Great Crocodile and Bellyman. Finish off the discussions and you will be able to clean up your exit."

"If that happens, what will be the next step?"

"You would have sacrificed your post for the sake of unity. Imagine what a great honour it will be."

"What will I do for sustenance, Runo?"

"You will still be entitled to your full benefits, Reverend."

"Great. Give me a few months to fix it."

"Time is of the essence because if you wait for the Great Crocodile to clean them out, then we have no deal. Months is not acceptable. You have to fast-track the negotiations."

Runo was delighted with how he was using everyone around him to his advantage. He was content with how he was going to destroy Ziva's plans as well as the Great Crocodile with a single stone. Ino was in the bag, waiting to be disposed of, and obviously, the Bellyman would consider talks with Runo and not Ziva, given that his relations with Great Crocodile had thawed. It was a more practical option, and the Great

Crocodile was efficiently delivering on his promise, save for a few pockets of resistance still operational in some bushes.

Mercenaries from the unneighbourly neighbour and their friendly countries around the world were squeezed hard, and many facing imminent termination had to quickly exit the scene. Otherwise, everyone was cornered and destroyed. All the units that respected Bellyman's call had long since given up arms. This was in line with the Bellyman and Great Crocodile's friendship and gentleman's agreement. Great Crocodile knew very well that Bellyman was a good man but not the best politician. For that, he loved him; hence their talks were successful. Bellyman feared Great Crocodile and knew that being on the same side as him was the solution. One of the last rebels standing was Gwese and his team. He terrorised villagers, buses and passengers, motorists and anyone unfortunate enough to cross his path. Many started fleeing their villages and farms as his terror campaign grew. His activities were widely publicised, and a bounty for his capture was offered. The infamous terrorist was eventually captured while raiding a bus and died in a shootout. When his body was sent for post-mortem, the police were overpowered by the public. His body was instead taken by the public and stoned. For a few days, the police could not access Gwese's body due to public anger. The press enjoyed splashing pictures of Gwese's dead body being stoned at a city central station.

Runo did not want Great Crocodile to take the credit; hence, he started parallel negotiations to undermine his efforts. The Bellyman responded positively, assuming this was an extension of the negotiations with Great Crocodile. Bellyman and his team were ready to sign an agreement to end the hostilities. Banner only got involved in the drafting of the agreement and set up of the future government. The agreement also included the drafting of a new constitution and absorbing the Bellyman's team. The Bellyman's Party was to be dismantled and forgotten completely. This was not what the

Great Crocodile had envisaged. His negotiations with the Bellyman guaranteed the continued existence of both Parties. Bellyman, however, felt a sigh of relief with an end to all hostilities. People could, at last, have some semblance of freedom and not live in fear. The Bellyman made a huge sacrifice. He knew there was no other solution because his opponent was divinely bestowed with infinite and unconscionable ruthlessness. Runo was a sadistic and depraved individual. Any deal that could make Runo win and end hostilities was better. The luxury of negotiating for concessions had to be forgotten for the good of the Republic. In honour of the Bellyman's stance, it was not inappropriate to award him a medal, but no one did, and that was a tragedy. Professor Reverend Banner was relieved of his position. Runo was on his way to becoming the supreme leader.

Chapter 8

Runo was now at the top of his game. He played from the left to the right without many noticing his tricks except a few like the Great Crocodile, Bellyman, Ziva and Ino. He approached Mudadi and said to him, "It is done as you planned, Mudadi. The Bellyman will work with us without a Party."

"Congratulations, Your Excellency."

"It's thanks to you, Mudadi."

"If you say so, but credit also goes to you for being so patient."

"Now the Reverend has to leave because of his perverted state, and you have to craft a new constitution, Mudadi."

"Me, a new constitution?"

"Of course, Mudadi."

"That I can arrange and deliver a beauty."

"It must serve us and us only."

"I know that after you, I shall be the leader and have to safeguard our interests. Supreme and Executive leadership is the objective."

"Wonderful. People are still celebrating. Make your mark and impress me."

"I will show you what I am made of, Your Excellency."

"If intelligence fails, bark and bite to make sure it sails through."

"I can cite any constitutional case around the world more

than anyone in this country and could never fail on this one."

"The number of degrees between us outnumbers our fingers, and our command of the Queen's language should confound them. Do it, Mudadi."

"The Bellyman and his team are in no mood to reject anything. We have cornered them."

"I have waited for this moment for a long time."

The two had fun while Mudadi was partaking in a bottle of whiskey. They talked until late at night. When Runo eventually left, Mudadi could not even say his name. He was led home to bed by his bodyguards. Even the ladies that had been called in to entertain them had to be dismissed. While Mudadi was having occasional flings, Runo almost had permanent concubines.

When Runo got home, Lady Amai Marunjeya was waiting for him, and she demanded an explanation on the pact with the Bellyman.

"Are you excited, my lady, that I can play this game better than any politician in the world?"

"Far from it, Runo. You got yourself in trouble this time."

"Not at all. Look at the big picture."

"Don't you imagine Bellyman will give you trouble once he settles comfortably?"

"You are slow to learn, my lady. The Great Crocodile sealed this pact secretly, and I had to usurp the credit. Instead of keeping it, I had to pass it on to the disgraceful Banner to give him an undeserved dignified exit for my political gain. Besides, Bellyman loves wealth."

"Yes, he does, and he is wealthy already."

"Do you know how much wealth he needs?"

"I don't know."

"Good, neither does he. That is the way to keep my jaws and paws around him."

"How?"

"Keep all the attractions around him to lure him. Once in

the pit, I will never bother to arrest him."

"Do you intend to continue keeping a dirty crowd around you?"

"I see them as dutiful and faithful servants rather than corrupt officials. They never refuse any orders, and each time they loot, the bigger portion belongs to me."

"You will lose credibility."

"Not at all. The more you have them, the more you will be viewed as the only shining pebble on the beach."

"Your eastern backers in the struggle have not benefitted anything, neither have you done a single deal with them since the end of the war. Give them something. Even a token deal."

"The world's best always have the last laugh. We are not at war anymore."

"Where will you turn to if something goes wrong?"

"I have many options, my lady."

"Your friends have a bad reputation for dumping their own when a bad situation arises."

"Let's cross that bridge when we come to it."

"It's contingency planning, Runo."

"Options are not exhaustive for me."

"What other options do you have?"

"We talked about the church, the business community, the secret club. Besides, any negative development will bring out the great diplomat in me. Imagine how I dined with independent Africa when I was just a teacher cum undercover journalist. People are gullible, my lady. I can find many friends in the face of adversity. If all else fails, then cash and resources will deliver the obedience I need."

"Is that the reason you always had access to everything? I always wondered what kind of a special teacher you were. I now wonder if you did graduate those several times."

"You are too slow to discern, my lady. The kind of friends around you determine your options in life."

"What a devious character you are!" She had loosened up

and was hooked by Runo's fast thinking while smiling from ear to ear.

"Thank you for the compliment, my lady." His job was done.

A new constitution giving Runo sweeping executive powers and stripping minority groups of their parliamentary rights was adopted without any opposition. The nation became a de facto one-party State and a one-man State. Professor Reverend Banner was retired on full perks credited with uniting warring factions in the country. Runo, in his usual grandstanding, made the coalition day an international event. He never wanted to miss international praise. The newly created pool of academics from primary level to tertiary institutions never for a moment listened to the content of Runo's speech. They were busy debating and admiring his command of the Queen's language. The complex sentences were joined by commas; therefore, however, hyphens and many more linguistic gymnastics were their source of inspiration rather than what Runo could do for them. His profile as a man of peace was elevated to dizzy heights. Even in song, he got a timeless praise song from some unknown musician who found himself topping the charts every week for his poor efforts. Nobody could be heard singing along or reciting the song, yet it was topping the charts. Teenagers who loved their weekly radio top chart songs would be glued to their stereos or some portable wireless receivers but then end up with expensive repair bills. After an hour or two of counting down good music and suddenly being subjected to some Runo damp squib rendition was unbearable torture. The immediate reaction was to toss the stereo as far away as possible or crush it to the ground. This musician, however, would be invited by Runo on every occasion to belt out his tune.

*

People would trickle out of any music gala once they heard those words. Unfortunately, the broadcasters had no choice but to schedule the song every day.

Runo approached the Sloppy Man and invited him for a secret conversation at his Presidential Palace. His idea was to sow seeds of disunity and mistrust among all Party cadres in the new dispensation. He wanted everyone to at least have more trust in his leadership compared to any other potential candidate. Since Sloppy Man was head of the army, it was his idea to neutralise his power by misdirecting any anger he could have to another phantom adversary.

"Welcome, Sloppy Man, my Commander-in-Chief and General. Please make yourself comfortable."

"Thank you, Mr President, but why do you seem to exalt my name and title above the sky?" Sloppy Man was flattered, and he put on a smile.

"I am one of the very few that regard your title and position highly in this society."

"If you do respect my title, then it should be automatic that everyone must follow."

"It's not that simple, Sloppy Man, because others are bent on undermining the authority of others. They disregard protocol and take matters into their own hands, stepping on the toes of others."

"I didn't realise that was happening."

"Take, for example, the events in the fight against the Bellyman's rebels. At no point did Fly Half and the Great Crocodile refer to you. They executed their plans without even my knowledge. He has too many friends in the army and sympathisers in the Party. The Great Crocodile even negotiated with the Bellyman to end the war, and I was only appraised of the development when I questioned why our bullets had ceased penetrating and ripping the bodies of Bellyman, his crew and his supporters."

"I am beginning to make sense of the conversation," he

said, almost getting upset.

"Relax, Sloppy Man. He shall pay dearly. I am telling you all this so that you can begin to see the power dynamics in the Party and government. The Great Crocodile wants to position himself to take over the Party and government. He is slowly creating a strong following around himself. As your fellow tribesman, I cannot let you lose the opportunity."

"Do you want the army to take him out?"

"This is politics and you have to be smart. The days of Joe are over. Start mobilising to counter the Great Crocodile's moves. Your position gives you an obvious advantage, and when the time comes, you must be ready. Don't be intimidated."

"I am a man familiar with commandeering. There is no way I can fail. I will deal with him."

"It pleases me that we are both reading from the same page."

"How about Mudadi, who seems to be closer to power than anyone else?"

"Leave that to me; besides, the new dispensation takes him away from the centre of power. Barking dogs seldom bite, and therefore you should not worry about them. The only other potential threat is most likely to come from Dumi."

"What shall I do with him?"

"Get closer to him, befriend him and avoid any possibility of a partnership between him and the Great Crocodile. However, you must keep an arms-length relationship."

"I will certainly do that, but these political chess games can get complex to read in advance. In such instances, how will I save myself from the Great Crocodile?"

"Don't forget that I am the patron of your faction. I shall handhold that which I have created. Good luck."

"Thank you for the insight, Mr President."

The conversation marked an emergence of toxic and arrogant political cliques. When factional fights set in, Runo was overjoyed that his plan had magically come together. Instead of mediating, he would, in a soliloquy, say, "*Mudzimu waro bonga kuwana huku dzichigwa.*"

Runo called on Nate and Diesel next. Diesel was one of his trusted Tribal men. He had never been involved in the war against Douglas. He only joined the Party and war at the time of the talks to end the war. Runo was making the whole nation believe Diesel had full war credentials. It was just his attempt to surround himself with his tribesmen. Diesel had a dry smile that never corresponded with his body language. He would smile at just about anything, whether funny, serious, sad or downright stupid. Diesel knew he did not deserve all that Runo was bestowing on him and, therefore, he had to play to that tune. For survival, as a leader, he needed these two on one end. It was time to put together what he had been taught, to plant seeds of jealousy and hatred between communities and people that were at peace and incite them to do deeds of blood and war with each other.

"Good evening, Your Excellency."

"Welcome, my friends."

"It is an honour to be invited to your Palace."

"Of course, you deserve the honour. Nate, I will start with you first."

"Should I step out then?" Diesel asked with a smile.

"No, Diesel, stay. It concerns both of you men."

"Alright then, Your Excellency, we are all ears."

"Gentlemen, we are in danger that this new dispensation is most likely going to result in the leadership of this nation landing in the hands of another tribe. I do not believe it will be a welcome development under your watch. The Great Crocodile has threatened our grip on power by bringing in another Party."

"You must stay for longer, Your Excellency, to assist in coming up with our succession plan. We need a foolproof plan that will be innocently accepted by many. We must build a reputation for certain individuals from our camp to make it automatic for them to take over," Nate suggested.

"We must also soil the reputation of any potential candidate from the wrong tribe so that the leadership remains in our favour. Already those from the Bellyman's camp have no national appeal anymore," Diesel added.

"Good suggestions, which brings me to your standing, Nate. Our tribal Party you represented did not appeal to the people, and your future cannot have any leadership ambition. All we can do is reward you in your current position or any other position. You are an asset to our discussion because of your experience in tribal politics."

"Diesel can still do it, and the time is now to start campaigning for him," Nate responded.

"Very good, Nate. However, we cannot make the outcome of this meeting public. We have to operate secretly. Diesel should be our man but should not have any following or grouping around him. He, however, must help stop our enemies from ascending to power."

"Who are these enemies that we should focus on now?"

"I had hoped you all knew by now, but since you are not aware, I will let you in on the secret. The Great Crocodile is the man to watch. He is threatening to get too close for comfort and too powerful to contain."

"It shall be done, Your Excellency. Time to get to work," Nate responded.

"Good luck, gentlemen."

✳

Ziva's grand coalition dream vanished overnight, although he soldiered on with a solo project. Mudadi was overjoyed that one day he would rule with executive powers. A sole centre of power for the Party and nation. He did not, however, realise that the problem that he thought had gone was back. The Bellyman and most of his men were senior to him. His ascending the ladder was now only dependent on Runo's benevolence. Ino lost his job in the new executive line-up. Frustrated, he gave a press briefing denigrating Runo and his war of attrition against the Bellyman. It did not work, and Runo was left unscathed. If the press briefing had any impact, it affected mostly Ino himself and the Great Crocodile and his role in the conflict. The Bellyman was content that he was finally closer to power than having to operate in a political wilderness, always being vilified by Runo. He had access to all the deals he wanted and hoped to build further on his wealth. His appearance had matured, all his hair had turned grey, and so was his trusted beard too. Only custom-made pants could fit his oversized belly. A dress, a priestly robe or a traditional robe could have been the perfect solution for his wardrobe.

Runo had a few planned casualties in his new executive. The Great Crocodile was allocated a less influential ministry yet again as punishment. Bellyman could not save him, knowing that Runo might start another fight. Nate, Diesel and the Sloppy Man were seemingly instrumental in advocating for the demotion of the Great Crocodile. The trio was heavily tribal-minded and were agents of Runo in promoting a super tribe. Dzinga faced chastisement for his educational policy. Runo was very unhappy with this man, not only because of his educational policy but because he hailed from the same roots as the Great Crocodile. Besides, Runo wanted to take credit for Dzinga's success and become the only diamond in the rough. Tribal cleansing was therefore on his mind. When Runo invited him to his office, Dzinga assumed he would get praise for the success story on educational policy.

"Dzinga, my colleague, make yourself comfortable."

"How are you, Mr President? Congratulations on the unity accord." Dzinga was in high spirits.

"You are welcome, Dzinga," he said with very little interest and looking aside.

"Mr President, you don't seem happy. What could be the problem?"

"You are my biggest problem, Dzinga."

"How is that possible?"

"You and your educational policy, it is haunting me, and I wish I had insisted on not having it implemented."

"Mr President, you are now the continent's number one on literacy. You are on top of the world now. How can you ever doubt the policy?"

"You still don't understand, Dzinga." He showed a stern face

"Mr President, I know it's costly, but we can slowly change it and introduce a token tuition fee to reduce the government spending on education."

"Put yourself in my shoes, Dzinga. Look at the big picture."

"We are only left with consolidating the gains by adding a few universities, and our country will be a jewel of education. Our neighbours will send their children to our nation, and we shall be earning much-needed foreign currency."

"Stop, Dzinga. Your ranting and raving are irritating me." He banged the table.

"That is too harsh, Mr President. What is the matter?" he asked, showing concern that the President was losing it.

"Your policy has produced too many high school graduates who have adversely affected the unemployment rate. Where do you want me to put them? It's reflecting badly on my leadership."

"Our colleagues in the other ministries are not pulling at the same rate. If they did, our conversation would be different."

"I despise your self-proclaimed sainthood. You are the problem."

"Would you give me a chance to articulate my vision for the nation, Mr President?"

"Never. The vision is mine, and you should follow instructions."

"Seriously, Mr President? This is as clear as mud, yet you think otherwise. Do you dislike me that much? I cannot comprehend why you should be dissatisfied with a good policy."

"Unemployment makes me look incompetent. I will not have any of your lectures. Leave my office with your rhetoric."

"I am speechless. *Inga varikuno vanoshura, kuviga nherera mhenyu vachisiya muzvari afa.* It may be best for me to seek alternative employment or go into private business."

"Suit yourself and be gone, devil. By the way, you must stop associating with the Great Crocodile."

As Dzinga was preparing his exit, the nation kept featuring as a test case in education on many international forums. Runo received several praises for the success story. It became difficult for him to just let Dzinga leave and take all the credit when his executives knew who the brainchild for the policy was. To avoid negative reviews and Dzinga revealing his position, he decided to offer him another post, although their relations had hit rock bottom. He created a Higher and Tertiary Education Ministry but with less responsibility because someone had already been appointed to the Education Ministry. Dzinga decided to take it but was very demoralised and disheartened by Runo.

It was not only Dzinga who was frustrated by Runo; the Great Crocodile was also extremely disappointed by Runo's consistently devious character. He went straight to Runo's office one day before they closed for the day. Without observing any protocol, he barged into the office.

"What a pleasant surprise, Great Crocodile!"

"Lying is a virtue for you. I wonder how she puts up with such a child," the Great Crocodile was not shouting despite the stinging attack.

"Leave my mother out of this and state your business before I eject you out of my office," Runo was unapologetic and defiant.

"You have been avoiding me, and you can run, as usual. It's your choice."

"I am the Executive President of this nation, and I don't have to run."

"Good. Now that you have rewarded yourself and enjoy every privilege in this nation, when you look back, was it worth the betrayal?"

"What has to be done has to be done, Great Crocodile."

"I clean up, and you place your chair and those of your new friends around. Is that how it works?"

"Hold on, Great Crocodile, that is not true."

"You have the Bellyman on your side and have offered him the best, pushing me to the back of the queue."

"Your methods, Great Crocodile, and usurping my powers."

"What about my methods? Were you not praising each step towards victory? Besides, did my negotiations not usher in the new era that you have dissociated from me?"

"You were too harsh and terrifying everyone around the country. I can't afford to have you scaring my people, and you have to wait until the emotions have gone."

"Which people are scared, Runo?"

"Everyone in this country is afraid of you."

"Everybody, you say, or it's just you?"

"You have to reform and stop this militancy."

"You pardoned scums like Peter, Douglas and Ken for their heinous crimes and atrocities, yet you brand a saint like me a villain. Grow up, Runo. Besides, you are the leader, and all the blame must lie squarely on you and less on your new friend, the better man, but soon to be culpable Bellyman."

"That's my decision, Great Crocodile. I cannot change it without serious consequences. At least you must know I have trust in you. You must also stop creating a mob of followers around you when you know I am the leader of the Party and nation."

"You stabbed me before and have done it again, you worthless prick."

"We don't have to go that far, Great Crocodile. At least you are lucky because I had to dispense with your colleague Ino."

"That is not an acceptable form of betrayal, Runo. What

you always do is inexcusable, unacceptable and beyond pardon. Maybe what you need is a military takeover."

"That will not stand under all conventions. Everything has to be legal and above board."

"What legal issues did you consider in crafting that illegal constitution? Everyone around the world must be mocking us for ever having adopted such a shameful document."

"It was adopted by the majority; therefore, I had no choice but to take it."

"You, of all people, never take anything that does not benefit you. You knew it, and those were your specific instructions. I am surprised by your allegiance to the Queen as you maintained all the provisions for the promises made seven years ago. It was the perfect time to start afresh, but you think you owe her more than the people of this nation; therefore, you chose to please her over your own."

"Let's not argue over things we cannot change."

"Don't you cross my path, Runo; otherwise it could be you in the grave? Anything I want, you shall approve."

"Tone down your voice, Great Crocodile. People will hear us."

"I know you don't want anyone to know the truth. Everything must be kept secret with you."

"What truth, Great Crocodile?"

"*Poshi haagwigwi*, Runo. Do you know what Bellyman did to my people during and after the war? Can you picture all those people suddenly changing their language, names and surnames just to survive his terror? Imagine people being forced to meet their maker for not being able to answer to the Bellyman's language or not carrying a name related to it. Kids had to be moved from some regions in baskets, bags and drums to safe zones. Visitors without any knowledge of this brutality had to walk to safety under cover of darkness to avoid death. Now you sit with him side by side and sing praises of each other. Have you considered how my people feel?"

"It's water under the bridge. There is collateral damage in every situation. Let's move on and bury it."

"Bury it, my foot."

"You will always be my trusted point man. Please work with me on this and let's not open another can of worms."

"Your stupid church has already done a report claiming thousands, ten times over the actual number to be precise, were killed compared to the war with Douglas. You have said nothing because they vindicated you, and now that this is on me, you let it fly in my face. You have set a sword for our people, and the future doesn't look bright. Get rid of this evil church and reject its report to avoid the enemy taking advantage to brew conflicts in the future based on these lies."

"I certainly have no control over them."

"Yet you have done nothing to correct their nonsense. Tell me, how many people were murdered at those refugee camps by Douglas and his cronies."

"All put together, probably over fifty-thousand."

"In 1976 alone, the Selous Scouts murdered 1257 civilians, and 400 of our fighters had been captured and killed the previous year. At Chimoio, over five thousand helpless refugees were murdered by Douglas and his kind. I can get to a hundred thousand off the top of my head. The war record only has less than one and a half thousand total casualties, which are fewer than the soldiers we killed. Can you imagine that? I can go on and on with the numbers, yet your religious friends covered it up. If I add those who were murdered at Nyadzonia, Freedom Camp and many other places, what numbers do you come up with? Over fifty-thousand lost their lives."

"These things happen, Great Crocodile, and we have nothing to gain by opening up old wounds."

"Did you keep the records of all the skulls and bones collected and buried after the war? Do you have the statistics?"

"No. We just needed to clear the land so that people could live freely without being reminded of the war every day."

"I know you and your deliberate convenient actions. It was no coincidence that such an important exercise could take place without any statistics being collated."

"Just let it go, Great Crocodile. I am in no mood for a lecture," Runo responded angrily.

"Don't tell me you were involved in all the refugee and rebel massacres by the way you buried all those cases. You were clearing and cleaning your path to power while I was blindly assisting you. I can now tell that you even set up Stick Man. You were going to be a winner whether the war had been won or not. Hail great betrayer, hail great traitor."

"Stop accusing me, Great Crocodile. I am your president."

"Don't you believe that you have become a cruel, heartless, murderous leader, Runo? For how long do you think you can protect yourself from such shame? I am not here to fight you and have no intention of doing so. I am not accusing you of anything. All I care about is the glory of this nation."

The Great Crocodile knew he had to make seriously calculated political manoeuvres to avoid losing out to Runo. Everything was being twisted to suit Runo's agenda. Runo could not care less. His interests and those of the Bellyman were well served, and they were relishing in the new dispensation. Runo had every reason to bask in glory, knowing very well that he had crushed the strongest dissenting voice in the nation. He went on to establish his secret service department, which was independent of the national intelligence service. These men and women were on the civil service payroll but reporting directly to Runo. None of the senior government officials was aware of this development. A directive was, therefore, issued that no payroll audits were to be carried out without Runo's approval. Runo's recruits received specialised training and complemented his terror activities. These men and women would kill with no trace, be it through the use of biological weapons or guns. Fear was instilled into the population because of this department's activities. Runo was so pleased that he became comfortable that his position could not be challenged.

All executive meetings under the new coalition went smoothly, beyond everyone's expectations. In situations where members felt dejected and tired in the executive meetings, the Bellyman was their inspiration. He had a favourite song by the Bundu Boys, *Faka Pressure*, that he would always recite to uplift everyone's spirits. His favourite part was;

Pasi apa, pane minzwa pane minzwa,
Pasi apa, pane minzwa pane minzwa,

Kana uchinge wabaiwa, rega kuponja faka pressure
Faka pressure, rega kuponja faka pressure

Faka pressure, rega kuponja faka pressure
Faka pressure, rega kuponja faka pressure

Kana uchinge wabaiwa, rega kuponja, faka pressure
Faka pressure, rega kuponja, faka pressure

Each time, he would stand up and sing with his traditional walking stick in hand as a choirmaster. The big-bellied old man gave a fresh new look at conducting government business. He and Runo had transformed from *makara asivonani* to a successful marriage of convenience. Age might have been the factor behind Bellyman's transformation. He neither had the stamina nor the acumen to continue fighting a career-winner and non-forgiving foe like Runo. It was very apparent he would lose both the public sympathy and any political goodwill left in him. But old habits die hard. Maybe he could pull off another trick, but Runo was well prepared.

Runo had not forgotten about the *Zuva Rekufa Kwangu* singer, and he still planned to act on it. He also wanted to celebrate with Mudadi and pacify him as he was beginning to make demands on concrete plans for succession. At that moment, he knew that he needed Mudadi less because of the great accomplishments he had made. At least maintaining a calm arms-length relationship was better than pushing him away completely. The worst he would have wanted was to have him join Ziva. He, therefore, handled him with caution. At least he knew he was safe with the Bellyman, considering the serious mistakes he had committed that cost him his possible ascendance to power. Runo, therefore, invited Mudadi late at night to the executive bar next to the Presidential Office. They could talk freely without any interference. In a very calm mood, he asked Mudadi.

"How do you know if your children are yours?"

"Only the mother has full knowledge is the answer you are looking for," he responded, looking at Runo's desponded face.

"Does that bother you?"

"It depends on what you want to achieve in life, Your Excellency."

"You mean a father figure can be just a social construct?"

"Exactly. Let me tell you a hypothetical story, Your Excellency."

"Go ahead, Mudadi."

"A story is told about a barren senior Police officer. He knew about his condition, but the wife was not sure. She feared for her marriage and tried every scientific solution to no avail. In the end, she got pregnant by some Prophet. Things worked well because the Police officer was not under any more pressure socially. She, however, got pregnant again by the same Prophet, and the Police officer killed him."

"So he knew what was happening?"

"Of course, Your Excellency."

"Thank you, Mudadi. I will sleep on it, but for today, let's celebrate."

"What are we celebrating?"

"The Bellyman is now under our belt and has no hope of

getting to power. Imagine, they chanted slogans and songs of his ineptitude and foolishness."

"It's expected of him, Your Excellency. He has always been a self-betrayer or is always trapped in a series of wrong turns."

"What do you mean?"

"Remember that he could have been the leader long back had he just signed on that dotted line, and the war would have been avoided."

"Silly him. What he thought were his people are now ours."

"We have killed two birds with one stone. Even Ziva cannot dream of winning anymore."

"You are a genius, Mudadi. Truly *uri mhumhi yangu isingadli chakafa choga. Bonga Chihwa, the revered wild dog*," Runo appealed to Mudadi's emotions by reciting his totem praise poetry.

"I wish I could reciprocate, but those privates are unpalatable and not easy to deal with in public. I hope you understand, *Muchero waNegondo (Negondo's fruit), Sango dema Jiri remuchero (a fruit buried in pubic hair), Kugara pasi kusimuka zvobgwire vhu (a fruit which collects dust when a woman sits), Mbwerambwetete (the formless fruit), Mutinji wahwera (dangling labia), Gunuuswa (a passage under the grass/where pubic hairs meet), Zhengeni (a vibrating fruit), Mutupo uri mumakumbo (a totem which is in between the legs), Mutupo ugere mai (a totem carried by mothers), Kuchipata kusingabve ruoko (the passage that gives pleasure), Usavi hwevarume (a favourite dish for men), Chitsime chisingapwi kana nemuchirimo (always wet and lubricated/ eternal spring), Mupata...,* that sacred passage which gives pleasure to men. Except, of course, Professor Reverend Banner, who didn't know what he was missing. It's a pity we had to retire him early."

Runo was quiet. He was angry but looked down, contemplating an appropriate punishment. He wished he was strong enough to batter Mudadi with the back of his hand. How dare could Mudadi recite such a private totem?

Later, he said, "Of course, what would men do without it? It's very vital and makes the world go round. Even you cannot keep your pants on for a single day. That's why I have arranged the best in town for you. Sip on your whiskey, and don't rush."

"I know our friendship is blossoming."

"Of course, Mudadi, it's between me and you. Have you ever imagined how it would end?"

"Just a smooth transition and nothing horrific."

"It's a wonderful thought. Enjoy for the rest of the night, Mudadi."

The ladies invited were among the pioneers to be infected with a new chronic pandemic. Mudadi was not worried about the looks, and Runo knew any female would do the trick. Mudadi's favourite line when it came to women was, *dhadha haridliwi musoro*. When being philosophical, he would say, *Zhou mutupo pane vanhu, paseri machikichori!* And for the ladies of the night, he would say, *Nzenza mumvuri asvika anovanda zuva*. He never really believed in love since arranged marriages tended to last a lifetime compared to those based on fleeting emotions and some very unreliable neuro-chemical reactions within the body. To him, friendship, companionship, aligned values or being duty-bound were more compelling reasons for marriage. Gossip among some of his close female companions was that he was the king of drama on intimacy to the extent of belting out the song *Chimbambaira chiri mupoto* during the act.

These women were believed to be part of the team that had gone through routine medical checks in the army, a routine that Ziva was opposed to. Runo had one of his concubines, a married woman. He was sixty-three then, while she was only twenty-one at the commencement of their affair. It was the year the nation's most prolific singer, Gwaindepi, released *Gunzvezve*, a timeless masterpiece of a love song that topped the music charts and won many accolades. Rumour had it that Runo would always refer to this concubine as My Gracious *Gunzvenzve*. He was head over heels and truly, madly, deeply infatuated with this young lady, most probably of his grandchild's age. Runo also assumed that a double effort of assassinating Mudadi's character, isolating him and dealing with a terminal disease was the ideal situation. He knew that he was done with him, especially from this night. It was just a matter of time before Mudadi noticed that he had lost the game.

Chapter 9

A war in a neighbouring country was likely to result in the toppling of its leader, a friend of Runo. The same leader, Marshal, had given Runo and his rebels refuge for the tenure of the war against Douglas. It was Douglas and Ken, the Secret Service leader, with the support of the world's leading nation, who had formed this rebel group to destabilise Marshal's country and derail Runo and his movement. After Douglas had lost power, a hostile neighbour took over as the conduit for directing the operations and funding of the group with assistance from the leading world nation. The continued support served to sabotage Runo's government in getting fuel supplies as the nation's pipeline ran through this neighbouring country.

At first, Marshal had opposed the rebel's idea of bringing Runo on board, knowing an intellectual would usurp their agenda and topple it. After Runo ascended to power, his friendship with Marshal grew from strength to strength. Runo decided to save his ally. It was not only a payback, but Runo knew Douglas had created the rebel group to derail Runo's rebel movement by destabilising their base. He, therefore, sent army regiment reinforcements. Marshal's army was facing defeat, and reinforcements worked around the clock just to try and maintain their positions. Many young recruits from the conflict against the Bellyman were reassigned to this war.

Several of them lost their lives in the initial stages of aiding Marshal's army.

The terrain was unfamiliar, and tactics were different. One-man-standing and only survivor situations were a common phrase for many who deserted the battlefront. A significant number of deserters were recorded. It seemed hopeless, and Marshal was likely to lose his leadership. Runo called up army reservists and unemployed youths to enlist in the army. Many went not because of the opportunity but due to economic push factors. There was no choice because employment standards had been raised. For most jobs, one needed to have passed a minimum of five subjects at the ordinary level, including the Queen's language. The bar was later raised to include mathematics and a science subject. Local languages were later dropped from core subjects for consideration for employment or progressing with academic studies. This standard reflected Runo's value system. His inclination was towards destroying the local languages and values to promote those espoused by the Queen's oppressive lot, Douglas and his crew included. Many students wondered why the Queen's language had to be compulsory when they never dreamt of visiting the Queen's country. All they wanted was to perfect their local language and pass on the legacy and pride to future generations.

One clever captain realised that they were not going to be successful. The rebels were well-equipped and well-funded. Some of their equipment was so complicated that they could not even use it. Their bush operations in the impenetrable forests gave the captain an idea. He flew in several fuel containers and air-dropped them in the forests. These were then blown up before touching the ground. Several acres of land went up in smoke, trapping some and killing many of the rebels. In other instances, they used noise pollution to disorient the rebels, giving ground troops the easy task of swooping in on the enemy and eliminating them. This was the breakthrough they needed. Progress had finally been achieved, and body bags from the war front became fewer and fewer. The army could afford to relax, strategise and execute their plans successfully.

After a year of operations, several senior officials in Runo's executives saw many opportunities. For a start, it was the Sloppy Man. Soldiers on the battlefront had spent a long time without returning home. They were not even aware of any pay rise due to them. He decided that for those on the battlefront, it was easier to pay them in cash. Sloppy Man arranged with all his employees' bankers. Some did not have bank accounts and were paid directly in cash. He, therefore, collected cash from the bank and delivered the cash directly to his men. In the process, he retained the increased portion of their salary. Nobody questioned such a move by the Sloppy Man since the soldiers did not need cash at the battlefront. The Sloppy Man amassed a lot of cash from the exercise. His interest became less in winning the war and rather in prolonging it for the benefit of his bank balance.

A certain gentleman with rugged good looks by the name of Turtle Man (he was just a common man but was associated with the top leadership that even some less influential politicians avoided getting in his path. Due to the presumed protection he had, the public thought he had the protection of a turtle shell hence the nickname Turtle Man) made friends with Sloppy Man and decided to sell him a life insurance policy. They were at some exclusive bar, and Turtle Man was using all his resources to entertain Sloppy Man.

Sloppy Man then asked, "How do you benefit from selling me this policy, Turtle Man?"

"That's easy, Sloppy Man. I get a commission."

"How many more of my men do you intend to sell such policies to?"

"As many as I can get. I need to make money, Sloppy Man."

"If you sell to five thousand of my men, how much money will you make, assuming the same value as the one you want to sell to me?"

"Let me take out my calculator because large figures are involved."

"Go ahead, Turtle Man. We have all the time in the world," he spoke in his unimpressive slow voice, occasionally taking a seemingly forced sip as he never seemed to be enjoying the taste of the beer.

"That will be $2.8 million, Sloppy Man. Why do you want to know?"

"I will give a directive, most of my men will sign up for the policy, and half of that commission will be mine."

"There is no harm, Sloppy Man. This is a deal of a lifetime."

"Let's do it then."

Turtle Man became a rich and famous businessman after the transaction. He invested in many businesses and became influential among many politicians. Due to his influence, one of Runo's concubines is alleged to have become his girlfriend as well.

Bellyman and some other senior officials decided to deal in wildlife poaching. The war was going to be a perfect cover for their activities. They used the army to carry out their activities, and Sloppy Man had to be part of the clique. Runo knew he had won when the Bellyman accepted to be part of this robbery scheme. The business venture took centre stage as the counter-insurgency was becoming less prominent. Not all soldiers approved of the commercial activities. Some were up in arms with their seniors condemning the activities. Many were silenced. The activities did not end because some army officers who were not involved reported the matter.

Captain Ed was at the forefront. He approached senior army officials at the head office back home. The reception he got was very cold. Captain Ed received no recognition or praise for his whistleblowing role. To his surprise, he got a lot of home time, away from the battlefront and was eventually moved out of the war zone completely. His treatment at work had changed, and he received several threats. He decided it was time to approach a monthly publication with his story, and it went public. Captain Ed also approached the police and other army officials. The harassment did not stop, and men with dark glasses were put on surveillance around the clock to monitor his moves. Even on a train or bus, he would be followed. For every development, however, he made sure he updated the paper, his wife, friends and the police until the whole nation knew what was happening. It did not help his case either, and this scared him to death. The security minister, a doctor with the nom de guerre Diesel, opposed to the Great Crocodile, a leader of his faction created by Runo with no followers, never issued a public statement or denied the allegation. Runo approached Diesel to put an end to the public spectacle.

"Diesel, what do you think you are doing with Captain Ed's story?"

"I want to scare him so that he can stop his public antics."

"Has he stopped?"

"No, he is getting worse with each tactic we employ."

"Is that good for my leadership?"

"I guess not, and I wonder why he just doesn't get the message."

"What are you going to do about it?"

"We can hope and pray that eventually, he will come to his senses."

"How about the stories in the press?"

"They will fade, Your Excellency."

"Foolish, Diesel. I want this matter closed without any further delay."

"Will the publicity end if we eliminate him?"

"It's your problem. I cannot have this defenceless boy exposing us every day."

"It shall be accomplished, Your Excellency."

Captain Ed was moved to his hometown base away from the paper he was feeding with his stories. It did not stop his attempts and updates. He also reported that some men had tried to abduct him from the barracks. Still, no one came to his rescue. A few months later Captain Ed disappeared from the army barracks without a trace. Those who had witnessed something were threatened and changed their story. Officially, he was charged with desertion in absentia. Two months later his dead body was found decomposing in the woods near the barracks. It was ruled a suicide because he had been diagnosed with suicidal tendencies. Everyone was shocked, but in a few months, the case was forgotten.

Fear of the government apparatus grew among the people. Captain Ed's wife pursued the matter legally until a commission of enquiry was established. It was just a diversion. Due to a lack of evidence, the enquiry had to close its case. Captain Ed's wife did not stop her grieving anger and was later put into the ground as well. The case died a natural death. Although there was sympathy from the public, it did not matter until and unless someone marched in the streets or took up arms. Sympathy only was of no consequence or effect.

Marshal never publicly made comments on the commercial activities in the war zone. Whether there had been talks and apologies behind the scenes remained a big secret. The only information that could be ascertained was that he was displeased by the wildlife slaughter and made it known to Runo. His visits to Runo, however, continued. One day, while returning from an international visit, his plane crashed, and he died.

A bank colloquially known as the bank of crooks and criminals by the public decided to invest in the nation, giving a financial boost to Runo and the Bellyman. Rumour had it that the bank owners were Runo's close friends and used to offer him some regular payments. Other banks protested when the bank's licence was issued, arguing that the economy was over-banked, but Runo turned a deaf ear. These were the same banks that had held Runo at ransom when he wanted to implement economic reforms. At the point of setting up their operations in the nation, Runo and the Bellyman got huge payments. After that transaction, however, Runo continued to receive regular payments and, in certain instances, got invitations to all special occasions held by the bank.

This bank disrupted the activities and profits of its rivals, and rumour started circulating that it was involved in illicit transactions around the world, and coincidentally it became subject to several investigations. Transactions that took place between the bank and the two top men in the nation were news-shy, although there was a feeble attempt by the media to disclose it. After Captain Ed's death, it was understandable that the media grew cold feet. The deal marked a dearth of principles, morals and ethics in the person of Runo and his leadership. The man was after enriching himself at any cost without any regard for the welfare of the national economy and the general public.

Besides, this was Runo's chance to get back at the colonial banking institutions, and re-channel government business from them to another preferred partner to weaken them. He had never forgiven them for holding him to ransom when he had intended to implement economic reforms. A few more licences were further issued to newly formed local banks. From this time on, he watched the colonial banks daily as they lost business slowly and surely to the new banks that served the local population better. The colonial banks had been long reviled by the locals for being pedantic, favouring and serving the white population only. For that, the people were moving in droves to the newly formed banks. With the rapidly declining white population, it meant that it was only a matter of time before the colonial banks had their backs against the wall.

A shortage of vehicles crippled the nation. Senior officials were given the privilege of first preference at one of the nation's vehicle assembly plants. Most of them started buying and reselling the vehicles at exorbitant prices. The anomaly was reported but ignored. Runo never cautioned anyone. Some officials stopped, and others continued with the racket. Other well-placed individual vehicle dealers were also well-connected in the scheme of things in the scandal and benefitted immensely. The commission was due to some of these buyers for their repeat business, and in one mistaken transaction, a commission cheque was posted to a consultant of the company and not the dealer. The consultant was puzzled because the initial on the cheque was different. This consultant was Obi. He knew very well that he was not entitled to a commission.

He tracked down the owner of the cheque, resulting in the press knowing about the scandal. One newspaper editor, Dream Boy (the man lived, imagined and dreamt of a perfect world and got disappointed by any anomalies he encountered), was irked by the greed and did an extensive investigative piece. Therein, he named and shamed everyone involved. This was the same scribe who had reported on the Bellyman's insurrection. This time around he had assumed a senior position. Runo was in a bind. If he ignored the report, his arrogance was going to be a public secret. People were also going to question his integrity. It was obvious that somehow he was involved in the scandal. He had no choice but to respect the law. Besides, he made a strategic decision. This scandal had come in handy for Runo's selfish dreams.

In his heart, Runo thanked the scribe. He had never assumed there could be an opportunity to dispense of his war colleagues in large numbers without shedding blood. For a moment, Runo had never thought that letting his friends financially help themselves illegally was such a good thing. It turned out that there was a silver lining in crime. He went home satisfied that his dream of a life presidency was shaping up in unexpected ways. Only one problem remained. His lady's direct involvement. Lady Amai Marunjeya was worried when the case had to go before a commission. Her image was going to be shredded to pieces. The commission was set up on a fact-finding mission without any mandate for stipulating or imposing sentences for the offenders. It was just an enquiry.

The potential expose rattled her that she spoke at length with Runo on the matter.

"Runo, my husband, did you have to succumb to this editor?"

"I thought I had buried the matter, but this man kept harping on and on about the scandal."

"Does he comprehend how power works and what could happen to him?"

"You must take pride in press freedom, my lady."

"I thought it was not on your agenda."

"Of course, it's not, my lady."

"Are you going to terminate his life then?"

"He has done me a huge favour, and credit must be given to this overzealous judge too. Initially, I had chosen to ignore the case, but this publicity gave me a chance to reflect yet again. On second thoughts, it is for the best, and I will go along with it."

"You will be weakened by the judgments."

"Look on the bright side, my lady. Everyone involved has impeccable war credentials and spirit, which I cannot afford to have if I want a life presidential tenure. They could potentially upset my plans."

"They are your friends, Runo. You need to be there for them. Besides, you enjoyed part of the spoils."

"There are no permanent friends in politics, only permanent interests. This is my only chance to have absolute power over my Party elders. The list is impressive. If they don't fall by the wayside voluntarily, then I will simply drop them, but I will be wielding excessive power over them should I need their services in future."

"How about the scribe?"

"His fate is sealed. Mudadi has suggested that we reassign him and not renew his contract once it ends."

"Do you realise the sacrifice could cost me owing to my involvement too? You have to suspend this commission."

"I know, but you were not directly involved, were you?"

"You know I used one of your officials."

"It's simple, you see. He can be the fall guy, and we will save him later."

"If he refuses, what shall we do?"

"Let's take each day as it comes, my lady. We will think of something. He can be the last in line for all the cases. By that time the judge may have left his job, or the case would have died a natural death. No one is going to jail if that is the satisfaction you need."

"Will your self-loyalty and selfishness ever end? My name, my reputation is at stake."

"Time will tell, but at this rate, it's not conceivable."

"Hail great betrayer. Hail great deceiver."

"Thank you for the compliment, my lady."

After Runo's conversation with Mudadi, the President decided it was time to uplift his image and shame his detractors. For a few years, he had been involved with a young, beautiful and intelligent lady from the Intelligence Service and a good-looking assistant from his office, his first concubine, the married woman. The intelligent young lady, his second concubine, was Rachel, and the good-looking assistant was Marujata. Runo often said that she had the beauty to sacrifice or die for. Even breaking up his marriage was not off limits because he was dazzled by this vivacious, unfaithful charmer. From the day he forcibly kissed her before professing his undying love, he often swore by that sacred passage that gave him his life that she was going to be his for the rest of his life.

Runo discovered that Rachel was very ambitious and held too much information on all his activities, but it was too late to withdraw from the relationship. She was assigned a security detail who was on guard all the time. She wanted to replace or be Runo's second wife at any cost. Runo, for his part, wanted a Western image and to portray an international image free of African tradition. For Runo, a one man, one wife principle had to be upheld in public despite the duplicity of a secret life. Thunderbird was the leader of the security detail for Rachel. Marujata, on the other hand, was married with a child but had two other boyfriends besides Runo and Turtle Man. This did not deter Runo's advances towards Marujata. This affair had been carried out even in the office and on all trips where Lady Amai Marunjeya did not accompany him. Even in the same house, the Presidential Palace, when Lady Amai Marunjeya was asleep, Runo and Marujata would hit it off. Marujata was also very ambitious, hoping to leave her husband one day to become the premier lady. It was suspected among security detail that she wanted to poison Lady Amai Marunjeya so that she could take over. Runo was determined to have a normal family with children. He had to implement the notes he gathered from his conversation with Mudadi. It was only a matter of time before he became a father figure.

It was not only Runo who needed total satisfaction by engaging other women to assist their official wives in core matrimonial duties. The Bellyman had one sweet lady he used to provide for with everything, and the relationship was going smoothly. However, it did not work well for one of his drivers. The driver paid dearly for keeping the secret. At the height of the colour television craze in the nation, she asked the Bellyman to buy her one. He gladly complied and brought one when he returned from one of his trips abroad. This set was not sent directly to the lady as he forgot and took it home with him. His wife noticed but did not say anything as she suspected him of having several other families. The Bellyman later instructed his driver to deliver the television set. He complied, but the wife stopped him and searched the car. She accused him of theft in front of the Bellyman to ensure she got the confession she had always wanted. The Bellyman pleaded with the driver not to say anything using signs. It worked. She insisted, but the Bellyman stuck to his guns. The driver was arrested and jailed, but no one spoke up. He was released after some time, and the Bellyman rewarded him with a fully paid house in one of the capital's leafy suburbs.

Simo, Runo's deputy, had his share of relationships. He did not hesitate to buy an activity house for each of his ladies. However, he never put the houses in their names. It was working for him as the public never suspected he could have been Mr Loverman in private. The problem was that he sometimes went for some young schoolgirls. In one incident, his guards mistakenly brought him his daughter from another concubine. He was extremely embarrassed and had an altercation with his security personnel.

Another Minister, Herbie, a doctor and friend of Mudadi, had over forty official children, and everybody wondered how any amount of wealth could support them. The Sloppy Man was especially notorious. At one point, he even left a man wounded and paralysed over a fight for a girlfriend. He had also married two more wives. They, however, remained officially unrecognised as Runo wanted to maintain a certain image acceptable to the Queen. Runo took advantage to get insights into the Great Crocodile's life and plans by pushing one of his secret agents to befriend him. It did not take much time before the Great Crocodile associated with this young lady as his part-time sidekick. Runo was assured that the threat from Great Crocodile had been neutralised. Such were the goings on in Runo's executive team.

Elections were drawing close, and Ziva had made significant gains. His movement reached all corners of the nation. Runo paid many youth gangs to chase away the campaign teams for Ziva in many situations. He eventually spread a rumour that Ziva was his project and, therefore, a vote for Ziva was the same as voting for Runo. The two were lifetime friends, and there was no way they could fight on opposite sides. His objective was to limit the number of constituencies that Ziva could win. If this went according to plan, then Ziva's movement was doomed. For his Party congress, Runo made sure everyone endorsed the top team formed after the Unity Accord with the Bellyman. This team comprised Runo, Simo and the Bellyman. The tradition of endorsing the praesidium without any democratic process was almost becoming the norm for the Party.

During the election campaign, Runo made populist promises as he went around the country canvassing for support. It was necessary to do so as he had met most communities at the last round of elections. For some, he had never visited them since the nation achieved independence. All those involved in the vehicles scandal were relieved of their duties, with some looking for alternative employment outside the nation. Dzinga also left as he had been on the wrong side of the law. Towards election day, Runo paid off most of Ziva's trusted lieutenants, who gladly accepted and deserted him. These were publicised as having been unhappy with a demented Ziva and decided to rejoin the only true Party for the nation. Some who were confident of winning in their constituencies refused. Five lost their lives in the violence that followed.

One of those who refused posed a serious challenge and was going to embarrass Runo's Party in one constituency. They decided to eliminate him too. He nearly died after sustaining serious gunshot wounds. His shooters were arrested and charged, but it did not take much time before they were pardoned. This sent shivers to aspiring politicians. The *Pidigori* man sang to warn the man against adopting a political career in the song *Jojo chejera*. All former supporters of the Bellyman were, by default, now part of Runo's establishment. Ziva was handed a comprehensive defeat, although he had a strong showing. Runo secured his third term in office.

All other obscure political parties that were participating in the electoral process were only validating the democratic process rather than carrying any hopes of ever making a difference. The process was just one-sided. The independent press had seriously been depleted. Our dear ambitious editor of the vehicle scandal, Dream Boy, was eventually transferred to head office. His contract expired and was not renewed. Some of the political opposition leaders were very old and never capable of offering an alternative. Anyone who ever thought of starting a new movement had serious hurdles. More than the backlash faced by Ziva.

Runo summoned one of Marujata's boyfriends. The man was scared to death and even soiled his pants to the extent that he needed brown trousers to conceal his state. He assumed that he would involuntarily donate his severed head to Runo for getting involved with his girlfriend. This man was aware he was sharing Marujata with the President. Some of the gifts she got from Runo, she, in turn, passed to him. It was, therefore, logical for him to assume that he was going to meet his maker.

"You look worried, my good friend. What is the problem?"

The man could not speak. He was in extreme shock.

"Relax. I have good tidings for you."

He was paralysed by fear that he only managed to look up at Runo, and then he mumbled.

"Speak up and be open. I have a proposal for you."

"What proposal, Mr President, for a commoner like me?"

He hesitated before speaking. "Our paths have crossed, and that means you, my friend need a better connection. You need a new intimate life with Marujata."

"Mr President, she is yours..."

"Hush, my friend. It is done and agreed upon. My relationship with her has nothing to do with you. You work as instructed."

"Hmmm, but Mr President..."

"No buts. You shall have your reward. Ensure she produces

good offspring, but I will determine at what intervals."

"What if the security detail betrays your trust? It will be a big embarrassment. Let's not have this deal."

"They call me the Nob, my new friend. I treat traitors ruthlessly."

"If you say so."

"Marujata shall never know of this conversation."

"How about her husband?"

"If she had you, me, and others, does she still care about him?"

"Probably not."

"Good. We shall assist her to accomplish her wish. Leave it to me. I expect you to attend my wedding and all ceremonies as I demand of you."

"I understand, Mr President."

Meanwhile, Rachel was keeping track of all developments and had her arrangement with Thunderbird without Runo's knowledge. Runo, however, had one too many weak moments in the office with Marujata, and things did not go well. Lady Amai Marujeya was so embarrassed that she called him to order.

"Runo, why did you demean your stature and my societal standing? Why the embarrassment when you are just some eunuch, Runo?"

Runo did not respond and just stared at Lady Amai Marunjeya.

"Are you deaf, Runo? Did you have to tarnish my public image after supporting you for so long?"

"You started it."

"No, Runo. I never did such a thing. I have always been faithful to you and your family."

"If you are as you say, would I have murdered my brother?"

"At least I would have given you a product of the same bloodline. I am such a decent and understanding human being who values family."

"For how long will you shout if you don't have to offer a

solution," Runo knew he had lost the argument.

"Runo, I am past childbearing age, yet you decide to stab me in the back. How cruel and heartless of you?"

"What other choice do I have?"

"You are so insecure and sensitive for a man. It was just a song, and everyone has forgotten about it. Do you have to hold grudges for a lifetime?"

"I had to do something and prove myself."

"You are foolish, Runo. I hear she is pregnant. Do you want to give your mother a heart attack? I hear Rachel is pregnant as well, if you did not already know?"

Runo fell to the back of his chair, shell-shocked.

"What do you have to say for yourself?"

Runo thought for a moment and then said, "It can't be. That man crushed me, and I have always vowed to kill him since the incident. He took away the most valuable thing in my life. It can't be, but at least my mother doesn't know."

"You are very stupid, Runo. How do you think it was possible for me if she didn't know?"

"No, no, no (looking defeated and hopeless). She went along with the introductions and was happy for her future granddaughter."

"I feel sorry for you, Runo. Your mother could not hurt your feelings. Have you admitted to being a failure both as a leader in capturing and killing him?"

"He deserted his post after our talks for independence. No one knows where he is. He has not set foot in his rural home for over a decade. I suppose he is keeping a very low profile, and I can't get my revenge."

"Even if I knew where he was, I could not tell you owing to what you have done."

"My lady, I beg you. I have to kill him. Please help me."

"You have a mess to clean up. Fix it and forget about shedding blood. Get to your senses and think about what you should do," she pushed him hard to try and command him going forward.

"Give me time and let me think. I am in too deep."

"In too deep, Mr President? You shall pay dearly."

"Are you working against me now, my lady?"

"It's not necessary. I am sick and have to think of protecting my reputation rather than relying on some selfish pathological deceiver. You need to tell me how you are going to clean up your image."

"I faked a moment of stress and mental disturbance. There is a brain scan due in a few days."

"Will the results be made public?"

"Of course not. It's just a diversion from the lusting story."

"Good gracious, how did I end up with a bad choice like you?"

"I am the best that you could ever have, and I gave you the best too. You were in a dead-end marriage. I rescued you and brought you home."

Lady Amai Marunjeya smiled and went on to attend to other business. She knew he was right.

The official used by Lady Amai Marunjeya did not cooperate and continued to make demands long after the commission was supposed to have concluded its findings. His case remained pending as he failed to attend hearings and dodged giving evidence. He continued to profess his innocence publicly. When Dzinga became a casualty of the vehicle scandal, he gave Runo a sigh of relief. Many other individuals resigned from their jobs after negative findings by the commission.

Young Rachel made demands from Runo. Runo's intention to prepare for Marujata to take over if Lady Amai Marunjeya could not successfully win the battle with her sickness was unwelcome to Rachel. She was prepared to go public on the affair, the pregnancy and Marujata's situation. The news, unfortunately, reached Runo's mother owing to Rachel's anger. She gave her too much information than she could handle. Runo's mother suffered a massive heart attack. It was fatal for her age that she remained in a critical condition. Runo realised that she could not stomach his lies and even went ahead with another man's family. He was personally devastated because they were very close. It was suspected by the public, and rumour had it, that all her witchcraft secrets had been passed from mother to son instead of mother to daughter. Now the son had contributed to his mother's ill health. It meant a stroke of bad luck for Runo would soon follow. She remained in her vegetative state. All his attention was directed towards providing care for his wife and mother.

Meanwhile, Lady Amai Marunjeya's security personnel worked very closely with her fall guy in the vehicle scandal. Numerous appeals were made to cut a deal with the man, but he refused. The silence was not guaranteed because he was too jumpy. When everything had failed, they persuaded him to make peace with the world. The official committed suicide by allegedly taking a suspected poison. Lady Amai Marunjeya was finally free of the scandal. The case was going to tarnish her image, but that ghost had been exorcised. The man's family was, however, very unhappy with the development, given the way things had been handled towards his death.

Runo attended the official's requiem mass and press address at his house, after which he went home livid. He started ear-bashing Lady Marunjeya until she showed him that she had her earphones on. He had to start all over again.

"My lady, I was embarrassed today because of your indiscriminate actions."

"You kill and maim every day, and I never say a word."

"How you execute yours leaves too much doubt and suspicion leading to me."

"If you cannot cooperate or help me, what am I supposed to do?"

"I am the President, for goodness sake, and some silly low lives wanted to stop me from attending my junior's funeral. How dare they do that to me?"

"You have to learn to work with others to avoid paying a

heavy price. This self-loyalty has to end."

"The people are still talking about that boy who started the child charity organisation, and they think I had a hand in it. When will you stop, my lady?"

"You have bigger fish to fry, Runo."

"Don't divert attention when you know you have become a burden to my ambition. I should have listened to myself because great men work alone. They do exceedingly well without the urge and need for some gratifying greatness of a sacred passage."

"Suit yourself, Runo. I cannot attend any functions because of my failing health, and very soon I am likely to be deficient in the power of locomotion or gone. Listen to a word of advice for once, my husband."

"I shall not have it."

"What are you planning, vengeance again on some grieving family? No, Runo, it's immoral."

"Watch me. They shall beg for assistance. I am the Nob."

"You are such a pathetic excuse of a President."

"I am out. My judgement is final."

He slammed the door as he left.

Rachel disappeared during the same period. Her whereabouts were unknown. No one at her workplace cooperated. Her friends had no idea, and her usual accomplice, Thunderbird, professed ignorance of her situation. He refused to talk most of the time. The family was not satisfied and pushed the matter further. They filed a missing person's report with the police, but it did not yield any results. To progress the matter, they engaged a private investigator. After a few weeks, he was found dead. The family's anger worsened, and they suspected foul play. Rachel's case exploded as the family talked to whoever cared to listen; family, friends and the press.

Chapter 10

Marujata had a child secretly tucked away. Runo was very pleased that he could present a family to the world, but not yet because Lady Amai Marunjeya would not approve of him taking another wife. Besides, Runo wanted to keep up appearances. Runo had to deal with his presumed international image as well as a religious one; therefore, the new family had to remain secret. He named the daughter after his mother and hoped that the next child would be a boy. Marujata had stopped working at Runo's office to become a full-time mother. The donor was allowed visitation rights only at family functions when there was a crowd around. He had received life-changing donations and was undertaking many business ventures. This was to avoid questions from the child later on in life. His mother never said a word but simply went along as if everything was normal in her failing health. She was devastated that her son was such a great pretender willing to lie to his mother. Since Runo assumed leadership, she had always been on his side. He supported her and cared for her. Every little knowledge she had about strengthening his grip on power, she had passed on to him. Knowledge on prolonging one's life, she passed on to him. He, in turn, treated her like a god. She felt proud, but Marujata and Rachel's incidents made her doubt her son's sincerity. It drove a thick nail into her heart.

Rachel's disappearance could not be buried. It exploded

into a daily headline. The reports started as little stories but grew each day and everyone looked forward to getting new updates. Each newspaper realised that they could capitalise and make money if they devoted time and space to the story. It was deserving of the publicity and, therefore, allocated front page status. The family wanted justice and would not relent in achieving their goal. Eventually, the authorities had to acquiesce to an inquest as the best option to resolve Rachel's disappearance.

Lady Amai Marunjeya was completely bedridden, and her ailments were worsening. She tried again to have a conversation with Runo, her husband, before she died to help him have peace in his life. Her frail state frightened him. The doctors' prognosis, though diplomatic, was not encouraging. There was no hope of saving her. Instead of being compassionate, he instead was hostile and angry. Runo had no clue how to handle her sickness.

"I know you are itching to have a word with me, but it never crossed my mind that it might be important."

"You are indeed selfish that I need to make an appointment with you."

"Your family is always around, and that should give you comfort. I don't need any distractions at this moment."

"Runo, listen carefully. My health is failing. What you have done with Rachel has destroyed any will I had to survive. Her disappearance worsened my plight for a normal life after your retirement."

"Who is going to retire? Me? That's a foolish statement."

"We have to stop. You have gone too far."

"We are both culpable. If you are weak-kneed, that is your problem. You have to understand that power, royalty and money are sustained by murder and oppression. Without shedding blood, no man can be saved. If you can't support the idea, then we don't belong together."

"Runo, we have done our part. Let's leave it to others."

"Never, not in my lifetime."

"How are you different from Douglas?"

"Douglas never sacrificed for this nation. I spent ten years in detention and then lost the essence of my manhood for this nation. Everyone must feel and share my pain."

"I have thought about that manhood issue and realised that you have been lying to me."

"You must be getting very sick. I never lied to you."

"Think about it, Runo. All the women after your divorce and before me, but no results. Before the incident, we couldn't get one either. You must have had an untreated disease that destroyed your functionality. That is the reason you never bothered to look for the man you accuse of destroying you."

"You know very well that I could not find him. If I had, you would have heard stories. But how did you know about my first wife and children?"

"Liar. With your vengeance and all security apparatus at your disposal, there is no way you would not have nabbed him. You knew he was just flogging a dead horse, and you used it to your advantage. How come I managed to track him down, even your first wife and her children? That is the reason that boy does your birthday interviews every year. Even the teenage schoolgirl you raped when you were a teacher, I found her together with her child. I now know you were relieved of your duties after the incident. For this reason, Douglas had an axe hanging over your head, and you opted to betray your own to avoid doing time. The other side of you is way too dark to contemplate. You can't keep any secrets from me. I had to dig up all your dirty laundry after the Marujata affair."

"Enough of your madness. Why mention it now when you were quiet all along? Do you want a confession? Please spare me the Holy Grail patronage!"

"Yes, confession is good for your soul. Was it gonorrhoea or syphilis?"

"I don't have the luxury of giving someone power over

me. Confession is the worst covert, publicly planned and accepted voluntary method of gaining secrets at no cost. You should never do it to save your soul but only to help someone in need."

"I am in need because I ended up adopting a child to deal with the loneliness."

"Well done for the calculation, my lady. You deserve a compliment and a medal. The adopted daughter has done well. Are you happy now?"

"I feel sad that I never at any point realised that you were such a pathological liar and a sadistic dictator. Your brain may have been affected by the same disease. That is the reason you behave abnormally. You may be brain-dead."

"Thank you. Now that you know, walk with me and be my partner once again."

"I cannot travel that journey with you. I would rather die in peace."

"What peace when you have always been a part of this? You cannot absolve yourself of the guilt just because you are on your deathbed."

"Save me if you can, but I am going. You will face the people alone."

"The token economic recovery programme has given the nation a new impetus, and the people will think that I love them and I have this nation at heart. It will be a pity if I don't get over 90% of the vote next time."

"Winning a vote is not the point. People choose for different reasons. It may be to avoid war, retribution, to pretend to go along with the system to get privileges, or simply because of the absence of an alternative. We don't have any alternative in this country, yet you think you are the best thing since bubblegum."

"Say all you want, my Lady, and say it loud, but I don't care."

"You will be the most reviled leader by the time you die. If it's your childhood upbringing you cannot make peace with, then you will have a sad future. If you cannot go past that anger, then you have been a failure in life. I am happy I don't have any children with you, and I feel sorry for that one you are expending your energy on. It's not too late to let go."

"Never," Runo was not amenable to unsolicited advice.

"The sympathy you will get as a widower and even when you announce a retirement for the good of the nation will be great. Think about it, Runo."

"That fortune teller at the Industrial Showcase I officiated last year told me that I could get to 100 years. Have you ever imagined how it feels to stay for so long under someone's rule?"

"You will still have all the privileges and peace of mind."

"I shall die in power. If the economy crumbles, who cares? I will still have my piece of cake."

"You forget that Rachel's case will seriously dent your credibility."

"On the contrary, my dear. They shall fear me after this one."

"It's nothing positive but an anger-raising process and vengeance trigger."

"I shall build a bigger and better machinery to oppress them in that case," he showed no emotion or regrets, feeling like he had conquered the nation and the entire population.

"You can only become a nefarious, deceitful and cold-blooded dictator." She had realised that power corrupts and wanted to make peace for the good of the nation. Her last pleas and appeal to Runo were delivered in tears.

"Thank you, my lady," he said, not paying attention.

After this conversation, Runo assembled a small team to destroy all records of his parents, first wife and children, the girl he had raped, his criminal records and anything that could potentially spoil his career.

The court enquiry had many twists and turns. These had not been anticipated. The courage displayed by Rachel's family was unprecedented. Thunderbird, who was expected to take the fall and then receive a pardon later, was scared to death and reneged on his promise. He thought he could be sacrificed and threatened to take down everyone involved in the case.

His infamous statement was, "I will not go down alone. The one responsible has to pay." He was immediately removed from the witness list even though he was the key witness. It became clear who was responsible and whose interests were being served when he was taken off the witness list. The enquiry had to be suspended due to a lack of evidence, even though Thunderbird was around. Even press interviews for Thunderbird were denied. He was put under heavy guard to prevent anyone from getting access even to his house.

Rachel's family gave press interviews and continued to ask one key question, "Why are they preventing Thunderbird from making a sworn statement if he is not a suspect and the leadership is not involved?"

That question went unanswered or never got the answer it deserved. People talked, and rumours filtered through the public sphere. It was suggested that Rachel had been stripped of her organs to restore Lady Amai Marunjeya's health. Others said that her body had been dumped in an acid container and, therefore, nothing could be recovered. Some suggestions pointed to a cremation. These were all theories, but it was clear she was gone. Anyone with information and willing to talk disappeared quickly from the face of the earth. These actions forced the public into their shells. Runo's machinery was once again displaying its capabilities.

While the nation was still engulfed with the Rachel story, Lady Amai Marunjeya died. She had been on life support at a city hospital. Theories were never short from the public opinion pool, given Rachel's case. Some were of the view that Runo no longer cared for her since she was never referred to a foreign hospital, as was the norm with other senior officials. It was also suggested that Runo himself had pulled the plug to free himself from the burden of looking after a terminally ailing wife. Others suggested that she had instructed her carers to end her life because she could not take Runo's neglect anymore. A few who had information on Marujata suggested that she had breached security and poisoned Lady Amai Marunjeya. Due to Lady Amai Marunjeya's death, Marujata was said to be simply waiting for all traditional protocols to be observed before officially tying the knot with Runo.

Lady Amai Marunjeya's funeral, however, was conducted like a celebration. Runo declared a week of mourning. Those who were hungry from the nation's economic malaise had an opportunity to feast and take some home for future consumption. Everything was extravagantly provided. Buses from the nation's parastatal ceased their normal operations. They were directed to ferry people from around the nation at no cost. Runo allowed anyone who wanted to pay their last respects to the mother of the nation as a way to manage his grief. Reports were commonplace of people fighting to get a place on the buses and enjoying being hosted by the President. An opportunity for corruption had once again arisen for Runo's Party touts as they selected suitable candidates for the event. Lady Amai Marunjeya received the highest honour as a hero of the nation for her role in caring for the leader of the rebels. The expenditure for the event was astronomical, but no one dared report on the matter.

Runo's mother died soon afterwards. Very little attention was given to her death by both the press and the public. There was too much fatigue from the activities at the funeral of Lady Amai Marunjeya. Her funeral was less colourful. People felt sorry and assumed that Runo would leave his role as well to get time for himself and to recover from his loss as he had been left alone. They were wrong and underestimated his resolve. Power was his to safeguard at any cost.

Immediately after the tragic events in his life, Runo quickly got back to work and consolidated his grip on power. It was surprising to many. Public opinion had no option but to downgrade the events from tragic to just a loss and not even a great loss. It seemed that the events did not mean anything to him. A former judge had launched his Party and had won a few vacant constituencies while Runo was dealing with personal issues. Ziva was still bubbling with confidence that with additional resources he would wrestle power from Runo in the next elections. Runo swiftly changed the rules for political Party funding. He raised the bar high with Mudadi's assistance to ensure that any funds due to Ziva ceased promptly. Ziva's pleas went unanswered, and nobody dared to fight in his corner. The judge was also affected by the same law. Runo still was not finished. He wanted absolutely no competition in the next election. He had to solicit some ideas from Mudadi. This time around, the discussions were more mature, and the venue had changed. He invited him to his Presidential Palace, where he was reflecting and refocusing everything. It would seem that he wanted to strike the keynote once again before pursuing the tune. He wanted all his political ducks in a row.

"How do you do, Mudadi?"

"Your Excellency, I am surprised that you have been nationalised and naturalised by the Queen."

"How so?"

"You seem to have adopted one of their worthless and irrational greeting modes."

"Why do you think that way?"

"Do what, Your Excellency? In Africa, we personalise our greeting and connect emotionally with the person we are greeting. Even our handshake is different. We are completely sentient human beings." This was the last straw for Runo, but Mudadi continued pretending to be oblivious to his insults. "The British have no sense of shame either. They have no dogs of any value to the world but some ugly creatures that they have to put up with. Instead of naming them the British Hideous Dogs, they instead are selling them to the world packaged as the tenacious British Bull Dogs. I wonder if the females should be the Cow Dogs?"

Mudadi needed to be eliminated. He calmed himself before responding, knowing this was a direct attack following the publicised newly imported dogs for the first family.

"I get the point."

"Thank you for taking my advice, but what do you have on your mind, Your Excellency?"

"This judge and Ziva are getting on my nerves."

"They don't have much clout, and your recent amendment to the constitution will financially starve them. It has already done a devastating job on their finances."

"I mean, how do we finish them off?"

"They are not a threat anymore. It's just a matter of time before the limping animal will fall to the circling vultures. We may not need to expend our energies flogging a dead horse."

"No, Mudadi. I have to think clearly without any distractions."

"Forget about them, Your Excellency. I promise you that nothing significant will come from these two."

"Crush your enemies completely and ruthlessly. I have to make an example of them," Runo was resolute.

"I see. That will not be a problem."

"We must be on the same page. Go on and proclaim their deaths."

"We need some inside men or an inside man to do a smart job for us."

"What will that man or men accomplish for us?"

"Vote the leaders out. A no-confidence vote or motion will do the trick."

"Very smart, Mudadi. A house coup is the least anyone can expect. Well done."

"Thank you, but there is one thing you keep overlooking."

"What is that?"

"You have already done two terms, now serving your third

and working on your fourth. Where do I fit in the big scheme of things now?"

"As you know, I have been overwhelmed by personal issues lately, and I may not be able to put a plan for you at present. It is not my intention to rule for life. Certainly, we should put a plan in place by the time we go for the elections."

"I will hold you to that, Your Excellency."

"I don't have a problem with that."

*

The Sloppy Man arrogantly perfected his money-spinning rackets. The army was tasked to aid in a longstanding war in one of the countries in the neighbourhood. This nation had vast oil reserves and gem-quality diamonds. Countries in the international community were using rebels as a conduit to access and milk the resources. Runo's army had a reputation for delivering results, and rebels were going to be on the back foot once the army had landed. A lucrative deal for the soldiers was packaged to ensure they took out the rebels in record time. Each soldier was going to receive a net monthly salary of three thousand eight hundred dollars, with all expenses catered for. This payment was in addition to their normal monthly salary from Runo's government. The Sloppy Man only made a tenth of the deal on the salary available to the soldiers each month. When the soldiers complained, he was very blunt about it.

"Is our national government not meeting its monthly salary obligation to you?"

"It is, Commander Sloppy Man."

"Are you not getting an additional monthly allowance for your tour of duty?"

"We are, but..."

"If you answered all my questions positively, why do you want to complain?"

"It's lower than what we signed for."

"Firstly, you belong to this nation and the army. Secondly, this deal was made available to you by our national government. Thirdly, the government needs to recover its costs from your adventure, and finally, in each situation, you must remember that livestock feed on the fodder while the grain goes to the farmer. You must never forget that."

Runo was so pleased with the payoff that he even buttressed Sloppy Man's position by saying that only a Contractor gets a compliment for a job well done and not his employees. He, however, could not have imagined that someone else had a higher tolerance for avarice than him. All he could say was 'ukaravidza chembere muto wegwaya, mangwana inofira mudziva ichitsvaka hove'. He began to have misgivings about Sloppy Man. The pay cut was too excessive. Although he had no regrets about making money, he doubted how much more he could have been losing to this man. However, his influence in the Party, as head of the military and with financial backing, continued to grow. His group could rival the Great Crocodile at any moment, and Runobvepi Runobvepi offered assistance as this grouping was a direct result of his influence to keep the Party divided but allegiant to him. Two individuals, Mudadi and Diesel, were expecting to take over Runo's position; they were waiting to be handed the stick. Two warring groups were at each other's throats all the time, Great Crocodile and The Sloppy Man's group, assuming one of them was likely to get to power. Runo knew this power balance would help him in his quest to rule for life.

The deception of the defence forces did not end there. A world leader or world bully toppled a government of another African country and installed its preferred candidate. The gesture was not welcomed by the locals, and an endless war erupted. Even the bully was unable to bomb the people into submission, although they continued to exert their influence daily. Key influences for the bully to interfere were oil, a strategic passage of sea cargo and a free ocean dump site. Fishermen of this country were pushed out of business as the bully used their ocean to dump toxic industrial waste. Locals fought back and were labelled pirates on each international news station. To prop up its image, the bully promoted a movie where the locals were portrayed as savages disrupting organised international assistance, in *Black Hawk Down*.

Even when the bully was overwhelmed by the war, it would not relent but unleash more terror. An African head of the United Nations at that time pushed for peacekeeping efforts and a cessation of hostilities. The bully was enraged. The leader had done it in a few troubled spots in Africa where the bully was promoting terror. He was, therefore, put on notice. Luckily, the African leader, Khali, was not harmed for defending and protecting Africans like one of his predecessors, Dag. Under the peace deal, Runo's army was given a contract to help maintain peace efforts. Again, the army men and women were fleeced of their financial windfall.

Manu, an ambitious young man, and a few colleagues joined Ziva's Party. He proposed to stand as a candidate in the capital. His friends wanted to help the Party campaign's strategy and public relations. Ziva accepted his recruits after three months of negotiation and vetting. Themba and some others joined the judge. The judge did not scrutinise his new members and assumed his Party was growing. Within six months, Manu started having disagreements with Ziva. Ziva exercised patience and did not expel his recruit. He tried to educate him on the Party ethos, and Manu seemed to understand. When Ziva did not expect it, Manu and his friends moved a motion to replace Ziva as the Party leader. Some Party members sitting on the fence received handsome amounts from Manu and his crew. These did not hesitate to vote with Manu when the motion was moved, and suddenly Ziva was on the back foot. He tried to fight but the credibility of the Party was already questionable. It did not take long for the Party to fold after Manu and his hired guns had left. Ziva realised that it was time to cut his losses. Themba and his colleagues gathered together one day and expelled the judge at a press conference. They assumed control, and the judge had to take them to court. By the time he won his Party back, he had lost ground and support. He, however, continued participating in all elections, although it was just an academic exercise for him. Runo had an election victory before the election.

Runo received advice from the world's leading financiers to adopt an economic reform programme. Under the programme, he had to liberalise trade instead of protecting his home industries. He had to float his currency as opposed to managing and commanding it. Government expenditure had to be downsized, and this meant cutting down ministries, reducing expenditure on education (removing policy on free education), cutting down the size of the army and reducing health expenditure (removing policy on free access to health) as well as the removal of government subsidies and introduction of tax reforms. The currency had to be constantly devalued to stimulate exports. Parastatals had to be commercialised or privatised. Some of the objectives were self-defeating as a child had to grow up in poor health, defenceless and uneducated. The currency was normally recommended for devaluation after every annual budget exercise or when exports were low or seemed expensive. This meant the budget became obsolete before implementation. Import demands for trinkets shot up, putting pressure on the free exchange rate. Within a few years, the value of the currency had halved, companies could not compete with international giants and, therefore, export growth was never achieved.

Some companies even exported their products clandestinely to their newly created foreign subsidiaries and resold them back into the nation to earn money in a stable currency. Taxes were reduced drastically, and unintended consequences resulted in more than halving government income which was now based on lower numbers. Still, Runo did not abandon the project. On the contrary, a local Blue Book had been developed which had identified key industries that needed support for retooling and or development, all import substitution products, key success factors for parastatals and operational targets, separating business and politics, separating Party business and government, appointing leaders based on merit and not patronage and several key issues which would have guaranteed a prosperous, sovereign and debt-free nation. Runo had decided against this option because, under the international programme, loans had been promised. He then wanted to lay his hand on that money. Unbeknown to him and his appetite for money, it was the nation's focus on economic growth and freedom that was written all over the Blue Book that leading nations wanted to destroy. Through their independent proxies, the international financiers, they achieved their goal of stifling this growth and independence to limit competition and keep the nation as a source of resources and a consumer for their finished products. Besides, they wanted to limit Runo's financial capacity to assist his peers as he had become a regional centre of relief. This, they could not allow.

The Queen granted Runo his lifetime wish. Runo was allowed to host the Queen and all members of her common club of chihuahuas. Hosting of the event took centre stage in every activity. Even Simo would not leave out mentioning the event at every gathering. The press was awash with the event publicity and positive stories about the impending visit by the Queen. Preparations for the event were given precedence over any economic issues. Opportunities for corruption were opened up by the event. Friends and relatives of Runo got contracts to supply vehicles and other materials. Even that man he had made a deal with on Marujata got a piece of the cake. By this time he had become a flamboyant businessman. Some of his financing had been channelled through a newly created Local Business Association. A staged terrorist bombing took place to aid in securing funds for security and other logistics for the event. It worked, and the leadership feasted on the funds. The event itself was less glamorous than the publicity it had received. The economic benefits expected from hosting the event were not tangible. It was the opposite, as the country received no benefit after overspending.

To boost government revenues, Runo tried, as he had done a few times before, to push for an agenda for trade in endangered species. His previous attempts had failed. The illegal killing of animals and the sale of their valuable ivory were cited as the reasons for banning the trade. For his nation, the population of the endangered species was huge and reached unmanageable levels. It was, therefore, best to utilise these for the benefit of the nation. Maggie, who was still the leader of the former colonial master of the nation, was very unhappy with such a development if successful. She, with her friends, wanted to prove that Runo could not contain or manage the illegal activities by promoting poaching through Runo's neighbour as she had done previously. The only difference was that this time around, the poaching activities were too rampant and intense. Runo lost once again. He was furious because he never accepted defeat kindly and, therefore, sent in his army to hunt down all the poachers.

To his surprise, almost all heads of poaching units were top army officials from a neighbouring nation. Runo engaged his colleague, Kenny, over the matter, but nothing changed. This man, Kenny, although publicly touted as a supporter of the liberation movement, was a spy for Maggie's government. Kenny had made several attempts to derail the movement. Runo realised that this was his chance to fight back at this counter-revolutionary element. He, therefore, promoted civil unrest in Kenny's country. Kenny had been in power for forty years without a single election. The people marched on the street calling for his ouster, and went on strike for several weeks. Kenny realised that his nation was slowly becoming ungovernable; therefore, there was a need to restore order. Runo was the first person he consulted to help end the impasse. President Runo advised his colleague to conduct an election to legitimise his rule and end the civil unrest. After a few sessions, Kenny agreed and informed his nation that a new constitution would be put in place to allow for elections. When the constitution was ready, it was put to a vote as a delaying tactic. People voted overwhelmingly for the constitution, and Kenny was left with no choice but to conduct the election. He didn't realise the vote was a protest against him. Elections were conducted a year later and Kenny lost dismally. He learnt the hard way that *Werengenya haachiriki moto*. Runo was too sadistic to pick a fight with, especially when your own house is not in order. At least Runo had made a good call to eliminate a sell-out from among his kind.

That bank, which had been paying Runo handsomely, went into liquidation after its shadowy activities had been exposed internationally. A run on the bank was imminent and, therefore, the only option was to liquidate and avoid further probes. To hide his shame, Runo quickly arranged for the government to take over the institution's local network. The bank was quickly rebranded, and it retained most of its customers after guaranteeing their deposits.

After the Queen's event, Runo went for his next step in eliminating everyone opposed to him. Two top army officials, the Sloppy Man and Tunga, felt that there was no succession planning and democratic principles were not being upheld. Sloppy Man was even planning to topple Runo, but Runo was saved by the Great Crocodile before the plan was executed. Sloppy Man's estranged wife, Heli, then exposed the whole plot. Runo had a talk with the Great Crocodile on the matter at his office.

"How are you, my good friend indeed? *Miviri iri sei?*"

"*Haiwa, ndiri njanji! Ndakasimba somutanda wehambautare.*"

The two men laughed their lungs out.

"Thank you, Great Crocodile, for foiling these soldiers' plans."

"I thought you would thank me for saving your neck."

"That's a given, Great Crocodile. I never thought it was necessary to talk about it."

"You have something on your mind. What do you want?"

"They say, *kukwira gomo hupoterera*, my good friend. That is the reason foreplay is a necessity," he said passionately.

"Since when did you become romantic, Runo?"

"Things change. If I don't, how do you expect me to remarry?"

"Just let it go. Age is not on your side."

"Never, *musha mukadzi*, besides, I have needs, you know. *Ndodawo kugara ndichiridza ngoma nenyama* like any normal man."

"*Baba angu shumba iwee. Zvatichaitigwa mashura. Inga gumbo retatu rinoparira, mushenjere uyu, muhwezva uyu!* (he laughed and Runo joined in). I hope you are not looking for anyone new and going along with some familiar concubine."

"Leave that to me, Great Crocodile. You know that she is a thread of grace, *dzvetera matadza nzungu yomunanzvigwa*, a thing of beauty, *gona mashavi nyoka isina ruzhowa* (smiling from ear to ear and shaking his head from side to side with total satisfaction), *kunonga bvupa muderere, bungu muridzo, ruva reChitekete* (This he said following Gwaindepi's release of yet another scorching love song, *Chitekete*, which gained the singer worldwide fame)."

"*Zvokwadi watopera pfungwa.* You seem deeply enamoured with this one. Are you completely sure there is no love potion involved for a strange man like you overly praising just a common lady, heeee, *chimurerekedzwa chindiro chine buri?*"

"They say, *mupfuhwira rudo*, therefore, I will be alright, and you don't have to worry. Remember, the best form of sedative or antidepressant for a mature man is a woman and a beer afterwards. The two are complementary. If you take one in isolation you either become a hopeless drunk or a sex addict."

"It must be *mupfuhwira uroyi* but remind me, Runo. How come you have never been attracted to purity, the chaste, something of your own, rather than what others have used, abused and discarded or laid a claim on already and are also fighting to keep?"

"Our wise elders say, '*Mvana ndodzinochengeta*'; besides, the totem my father adopted forbids me from taking up on your proposal. In addition, pursuing a marked woman adds to the fun, especially with power and money on your side. It makes you feel like you are the best thing since bubblegum (beating his chest). They say, *ubuhle bendoda yinkomo zayo*."

Surprisingly, Marujata, on her part, would justify being in a relationship with a grandfather figure by saying, "*Harahwa ndodzinochengeta*". In turn, her friends would mock her saying, "*Harahwa ndodzinochengera*".

"You have already gone ahead of protocol. As an elder, how do you intend to make good that aberration?"

"They say, '*Tsenzi igara wadla!*' *Hee, kwahi vuxhwa bgweNyati ndobguri mudumbu! Vafana vanoti gara wadla magetsi anoenda!*"

The two men laughed for a moment. Runo was proud of his reputation, while the Great Crocodile was trying to make sense of Runo's justification for his irrational acts. He couldn't, so he decided to move on.

"Anyway, we are digressing. What can I do for you, Runo?"

"They say *chirungurira chigwere, ukanyara unofa nacho*."

"I am listening."

"Your arch-enemy might strike again. How do I deal with him?"

"His term is coming to an end, Runo. It's simple. You just recall him from office."

"How do I ensure he is completely fooled? They say, *Ukangosekerera mhashu mangwana dzinokudlira murivo*."

"Once he is out, you can ask him to stand in the forthcoming elections to raise his profile."

"If he does, won't he become too powerful?"

"Sloppy Man cannot even speak properly. He mumbles. How do you expect him to make an impact?"

"That's reassuring. How about Tunga?"

"He is a wonderful gentleman, a rare breed. Leave him in office for the good of our nation."

"Thank you, Great Crocodile, you have been of great service."

Runo instead invited the two military men to his Presidential Palace. He wanted them gone. No strongman was supposed to stand in his way. Runo didn't like the connection between Tunga and the Great Crocodile. It made him insecure. His talk with the two men seemed frank and open.

"Gentlemen, you are my two top soldiers in this nation. No one has fought for this country and protected it as much as you have done. As is traditional in any system that's appreciative of its true sons, you must grow," he used well-calculated gestures to appeal to their emotions.

"How else can we grow when we are already at the top of our respective careers?" Tunga asked.

"Tunga, you are not following my line of thought. If I retire today, someone has to take over from the rank and file. That is progress and growth. As gunmen, you have no hope of participating in running the affairs of this nation."

"I don't speak so well and have no hope of taking over the leadership," responded Sloppy Man, seeming uneasy.

"You always talk of succession. Even a ministerial post is progress. Think about it, gentlemen."

"What is your proposal?" Tunga asked while looking composed.

"You can retire and then participate in the forthcoming election. Once you become members of parliament, then appointment as Ministers becomes easy?"

"It sounds good," responded Sloppy Man, looking convinced and nodding in agreement. He assumed his grouping was now being positioned to take over power, and the chances were that he was going to be the next leader.

"How about you, Tunga?"

"Why us when no one else has relinquished their positions, including you?" He was not convinced and was staring

Runo in the eyes to measure any shred of truth in his proposal.

"There is always a starting point, Tunga."

"Good. Why can't this process start with you?" he calmly asked.

"I have a term to finish, whereas in your case, I need to justify any reappointment I have to make because your terms are expiring according to statute," he was startled by the response he got.

"Do you promise to retire after this term has expired?"

"Tunga, I cross my heart."

"If you don't hold your end of the bargain, what is the recourse?"

"Tunga, we have been together since the war years. Have I ever let you down? We have been in this together for a long time. You have no reason to worry about it. Do I have to swear by that sacred passage that gave me life?" The soldiers laughed, and Runo joined in. Swearing made the difference in Runo's favour.

"If you say so, I may be inclined to believe," he was still not convinced.

"Don't worry, Tunga. You will easily win an election in your home area. There shall be no obstacles, I bet you. Please support me in this quest to renew the leadership of this nation."

"Who else is up for retirement?" again it was Tunga who asked.

"As you know, the police appointment is still relatively new and is, therefore, not up for debate. Intelligence has had many changes since the days of Ken. Therefore, it's just you gentlemen, me and some Ministers."

"Very well then, we shall do it."

The revenge did not end with the two being retired. Several plans were in store for them. To begin with, Runo celebrated with them on their retirement after having brought them the ladies infected with a chronic pandemic he had used on Mudadi and others. Runo was relieved but was thoroughly disappointed by Tunga. He needed to deal with him and ensure this man never got anywhere close to power. He had to keep him out of any government institution. Besides, he knew Tunga was sympathetic to the Great Crocodile's cause. It was a no-brainer that this man could combine forces with the Great Crocodile and topple him. Just as well he had agreed to retire and sign his isolation warrant. Indeed, the two retired and other equally fearful men were appointed. Fox took over from Sloppy Man and Fly Half from Tunga.

There were problems in the administration of football affairs at the mother body in the nation despite a huge following of this religion. From one administrator to another and from one leader to the next, pilferages were rampant and financial statements could never be produced. No audits were conducted either. Runo never bothered to have matters resolved. Instead, he wanted total control of the institution. He, therefore, financed his nephew, Cub, to make a subtle hostile takeover. He was successful but very unpopular with the fans and other football administrators. A conflict between Cub and another administrator grew. This administrator was also head of the nation's Foreign Trade department. He held and operated a franchise of a vehicle assembly. This administrator was head of Runo's favourite football team as well as the association in charge of all matches. The feud did not bother Runo at this stage because the administrator made sure that Runo's team won the championship each year. When the championship was closely contested, he would change the game times and days for the final matches. Runo's team always played last under such circumstances to ensure it could win the remaining matches and also match scoreline requirements. It is for this reason that the team won most local championships, keeping Runo satisfied, although it did not have any credible accomplishments regionally.

Diesel, the Security Minister, was instructed to deal with a perceived rogue member of Parliament, Sid. Sid was critical of government complacency and corruption. He wanted results and accountability, which Runo could not give. Not only were ministers in the firing line from his criticism, but Runo was not spared either. This is the reason Runo wanted him out of the way. He was the last man standing publicly in opposition to Runo. Like-minded colleagues had perished along the way. Runo and Diesel were in the Presidential Office.

"Diesel, my boy, I have an election due next year."

"I know, Your Excellency. How can I be of service? (Almost smiling.)"

"Having any critics and opposition to my will is the last thing I can afford."

"You enjoy absolute control. There is no chance anyone could dislodge you."

"I want total control, Diesel, and I must make sure no one stands in my way."

"Who could pose a threat to a great leader like you?"

"Look at Sid and his rumblings every day in parliament about our failure to meet the needs of the people or grow the economy."

"It's just his personal opinion and of no effect to your person, the Party and the government. Isn't it part of the democratic process?"

"I don't like his disrespect. Silence him and send him to the morgue."

"Is it really necessary, Your Excellency?"

"Let my will be done, Diesel."

"People talk, and it is not good for your reputation."

"What have they done since they started talking?"

"Nothing."

"See. They are spineless jellyfish. I will march through while they are busy wetting their pants."

"Sid has been one of a kind. He is a voice for the voiceless and a hope for the hopeless and oppressed. Let him live."

"Are you suggesting that I oppress my people?"

"Not at all, Your Excellency."

"Follow instructions, Diesel."

"Your wish is my command."

Sid met his fate late at night when he supposedly had an encounter with a black dog while returning from a community visit. While trying to avoid the black dog, he crashed and died on the spot. The story set tongues wagging. Given his history with the government, there was little left to guess or to the imagination on what could have happened to him. His death did not bode well for democracy, as those contemplating joining the political arena were silenced. Runo gave Sid the highest honour of the hero of the nation. He praised Sid for being a voice of the voiceless, a hero of heroes and a unique character, *amadhodha sibili*. Runo took the opportunity to chide any opponent and talked of all government plans at the funeral. This was his usual style. He never at any point had to address the nation. National events like Freedom Day and Veterans Day were used to outline his agenda. Funerals, mainly, were his major platform. Any economic plans for the nation remained a secret. Even an update on the implemented economic reform programme remained a secret, if at all he had one. Sid's elder son fled the country later due to his fierce opposition to Runo. He realised that he was going to be next in line. However, he continued to write negatively about Runo and his cruelty. At some point, Runo harassed Sid's widow after failing to locate the son.

Another high flier in Runo's Party was getting too popular and overshadowing even Runo. He was from the same province as Runo. The public assumed that Runo would embrace him and use him in the next election. He was an asset to the nation, and his name was Informant. Strangely, Informant never got a chance to show the whole nation what he was capable of achieving. He met the same fate as Sid. His death was again through an accident. Runo was happy to preside at his funeral and honour him in his usual style. No questions were ever asked, nor was an investigation opened on the accident.

That year-end, the Party had an elective congress where the post of chairman and other key posts were put to the vote. The Great Crocodile saw an opportunity to ascend to the top of the ladder. Runo could not allow it to happen. He hated the Great Crocodile with a passion. It had been a while since he had his usual secretive chats with Mudadi. Occasionally, Mudadi was tasked to be the Party and government spokesperson and representative. He debated on many academic and legal matters, dutifully representing his government. Mudadi, however, was so pompous and undiplomatic that many people started to view him as a recluse and unfit for public office. This was good news for Runo. Only on one occasion, he had approached Runo to firm up the succession plans, but Runo remained non-committal. Runo, however, knew that in leadership, they would have a common interest with Mudadi and, therefore, it would be an easy one.

"Mudadi, my partner, why are we always meeting secretly so often scheming and plotting?"

"It's for the glory of the Republic, Your Excellency, Runobvepi."

"We have come a long way, my partner."

"Of course, we have, save for the fact that we do not seem to agree on when it should happen."

"That should be the least of your problems, Mudadi, because there is an urgent matter at hand."

"What is it, Your Excellency?"

"The Great Crocodile is campaigning for the congress. He wants to be the Party supremo."

"I have noted."

"Are you going to sit around and do nothing?"

"It doesn't concern me, Your Excellency."

"Assume we win next year's elections and I retire. Do you expect him to let you take over without a fight?"

"I know he is a formidable opponent, but what you have

directed, he cannot dispute."

"Dream on, my partner, but I think your inheritance is slipping away while we engage in an academic debate. I felt compelled to let you know as my only trusted friend."

"In that case, let me fight him. I will present my candidature."

"Your intention and mine will be out in the public as they have always speculated. We cannot be an open book. Hide your intentions until you are ready to strike."

"In that case, shall I find someone to play a front and will always be indebted to me?"

"You are on point, Mudadi. Who do you have in mind?"

"I can work with the Son of the Great Lord."

"Excellent choice. He is a Party senior already, and no one can question his standing."

Mudadi knew that *atengesegwa neisipo*. It was nothing but a test of stupidity, just like the game he used to play during his youth back in his rural village. In the game, one is promised that a healthy fat chick will pop out if an arm is rubbed vigorously several times until the skin bursts open. This leaves a very painful big scar, which takes several weeks to heal. A person with a mental challenge had to endure the pain but for no reward. The game was *Chikuku vata vata* , and the scar left behind was referred to as *Chikuku*. Parents would quickly know, with shame, what a loser of a child they had if they spotted a *Chikuku* on their child. He never asked how he would fit in when all posts are taken up. Despite the full knowledge of the test of stupidity, Mudadi went on to secretly canvass for the Son of the Great Lord. Mudadi was highly educated but certainly not civilised and not wise. In reality, he would have fallen for the fat chick option if he had not already done so as a child. There were several such games under the natives' culture and tradition falling under the critical thinking banner.

As a child grew in society, its position would have already been cut out based on aptitude. It was this aptitude that determined whether one became a farmer, hunter, artisan, miner, teacher, arbitrator, healer, midwife and so forth. Other testing mechanisms did not necessarily involve games but storytelling and problem-solving. A tale such as *Mutongi Gava (Fox the Great Arbiter)* was an excellent example for those in the arbitration role. It sharpened their wisdom in passing judgement rather than being populist or favouring the rich and famous. On colonisation, the white men easily found their way by abusing such characters as Mudadi, who would have otherwise failed in the traditional aptitude testing. Those individuals were the first to embrace religion to abdicate responsibility. They were also the first to go for the white man's education because it was based on regurgitating an established position without critical analysis. It is for this reason that folk tales, crafted after slavery and colonisation, involving deception always had a great deceiver employing prayer as a smoke screen to hide his true craft. This was meant to warn children of the folly of religion and its wickedness.

Mudadi probably felt he was duty-bound to assist Runo since he had no one in his corner to back him. He had based his plans to ascend to the throne on Runo's benevolence. His allegiance to Runo and the Party with no support around him was accelerating his political irrelevance. Mudadi didn't realise that his actions were only benefiting Runo. Son of the Great Lord's candidature was kept secret until close to the date of the congress to avoid a counterattack from the Great Crocodile. Mudadi secretly met the Sloppy Man to agree on a pact to help them fight the Great Crocodile as one front. The Sloppy Man, being of a slow and retarded mind, agreed even if there was no tangible benefit that was going to accrue to him. A band of unperceptive minds, hypnotised by Runo, worked together to fight for Runo's cause. The Great Crocodile was handed a shock defeat. Until that day, he had taken it for granted that Mudadi lacked foresight. It also became as clear as mud that Runo would feed him to the lions at any given moment. Runo's plot against him had now taken its full form.

He had never appreciated being saved countless times before. The Great Crocodile needed to tread carefully in front of the vengeful Runo.

Chapter 11

Runo was cruel, callous and capricious. His inappropriate use of power had taken root, and fear had spread throughout the nation. No potential winners were willing to stand against him in the impending elections. Everyone had been cowed into their shells and were fearing for their lives. They had become well aware that it was treasonous to challenge him not only in public but even in an election. This treason extended to challenging Runo's Party in Parliamentary elections and local government elections. Opposing candidates were often harassed, beaten up, had their properties broken into, or trumped-up charges were levelled against them if they were lucky not to be eliminated from the face of the earth. Strange late-night physical calls or telephone calls were the order of the day to anyone suspected of harbouring political ambitions. A few insignificant ones, however, were still brave enough and willing to face humiliation.

In a primary election, Tunga had an easy victory. Tunga, however, never got a chance to run in the general election. Runo persuaded his deputy, Simo, to stand for the election and be in touch with the grassroots. Simo was from the same constituency as Tunga. The two could not square off in a primary election because Simo, as deputy to Runo, had a right to represent any constituency he chose. This was according to new Party rules announced by Runo. The two men nearly traded blows while Runo was watching. Tunga tried hard to convince Simo to abandon his campaign because he was already occupying a high office. It was, therefore, not necessary for him to crowd out others. Runo kept pushing Simo, and the fighting went on. Simo finally pushed Tunga out in a violent abuse of power and hierarchy. It was an election struggle within an election dubbed the Carpenter versus the Gentleman. In cartoons, a little Carpenter had put up signs saying "No Contest" while the Gentleman was steadfast with a gun on the hip. The primary election results where Tunga had won were declared null and void. Tunga was dealt a big blow, and he realised he had been technically knocked out into the cold. Runo could not be reached for a discussion as his schedule was fully booked. It was said that his election campaign schedule was too tight in addition to his normal presidential duties. Tunga knew he had been cheated. He had to take it like a man and face his supporters. Tunga delivered the sad news that he had to stand down and pave way for Simo to avoid dragging the Party into disrepute and keep his image intact.

Two old timers participated in the election against Runo, the Stick Man and the Collar Man. The judge still had hope for better fortunes considering the stagnating economy. He, therefore, joined the election bandwagon. Runo knew very well that he had no economic agenda to sell to the people. His campaign was, therefore, based on his feigned exploits in the war against Douglas. It was about how he and his colleagues sacrificed for the nation. He, therefore, was insinuating that he had a right to rule and preside over the nation. Simo was his main campaign partner, although Mudadi assisted a lot. Runo just made sure Mudadi's campaign was not televised. He wanted to downplay his role in the election and neutralise his influence.

The Collar Man's campaign was based on Runo's failure and his election rigging machinery. In addition, he complained about the uneven political landscape, which needed reforms.

Collar Man was part of the establishment with Douglas; therefore, he claimed to know all the tricks. He was, however, evasive when confronted about his role in aiding Douglas in the bombing of refugee camps during the war, where tens of thousands perished. He instead was more interested in bragging about his stay in the new world. In his own words, he termed it a nation flowing with milk and honey. His idea was to convince the people that he was privileged and, therefore, the people had to vote for him. During his interviews and campaigns, he never took off his religious collar. The Collar Man also mounted a court challenge to have electoral reforms implemented to level the playing field. In his challenge, he wanted the elections postponed if the reforms could not be effected before the election day.

Stick Man's campaign was mainly about the political system, economics and Runo's failure. In one televised interview, he outlined why people should not vote for Runo. He introduced himself with credentials as the father of the armed struggle for the nation. The famous seven killed to signal the start of the war was his project. He was bitter at Runo's treacherous behaviour in hijacking his Party. The speech was famously dubbed the "Do Not" campaign, whose speech in part was as follows;

"...Do not vote for Runo because he rigs elections. Do not vote for Runo because he betrayed his leadership during the war. Do not vote for Runo because he uses his secret service agents against the people, not for the people. Don't vote for Runo because he has destroyed the economy. Do not vote for Runo because he has no agenda for the economy. Do not vote for Runo because he has made friends with the enemy. Do not vote for Runo because he has killed too many sons and daughters of this nation. Do not vote for Runo because he is the enemy of the people. Do not vote for Runo because his economic reform programme has done more harm than good. Do not vote for Runo because he is corrupt and selfish. Do not vote for Runo because he has destroyed the goodwill of the nation. In my next instalment, I will outline why you should vote for me..."

The voters were wooed by his speech and were ready to listen to his final blow. It was a victory for the Stick Man, but unfortunately, *chiri pamuchena chiri pamutenure*. Little did he know that *nhanga rekuzhira ndimaparira ngozi* despite his mathematical chances of winning. Immediately after the "Do Not" campaign speech, allegations of attempting to subvert Runo's government were levelled against him. He was charged with treason. It was alleged that at some point in the not-so-distant past, Stick Man was seen holding a hand grenade at a bridge, waiting for the presidential motorcade to arrive. Stick Man was infuriated. Only a few people could ask the right questions, while the rest were less interested in following the elections. They felt it was a futile exercise and nothing was going to change. The charges against Stick Man were not only extremely flimsy but absurd. It would have been reasonable if he had been arrested at that point, on that bridge. If he had done it but was unsuccessful and was not charged, what was motivating the charges towards an election? To worsen his plight, the Stick Man was put under house arrest and could not hold campaign rallies. To counter the other insinuations in the Stick Man's speech, Runo had the government newspapers publish positively on the economic reform programme. Some statistics on jobs created due to the programme were published but did not correspond to anything tangible in the economy. They were simply lies.

Both the Collar Man and the Stick Man, however, had agreed that there should be no term limits and that a leader could rule for life. This came as a relief to Runo, who wanted to be life President. It justified his continued stay in power. The judge was clear on his agenda in reducing expenditure by trimming ministries, the civil service and some idle embassies. For a change, he wanted presidential term limits. His financial base was limited and could not field many candidates, therefore, he was viewed by the public as a time waster and a spoiler. The Stick Man and the Collar Man pulled out of the election race a week before voting began. It was in protest as the Collar Man had lost his court challenge for electoral reforms. The Supreme Court had turned down his challenge. The Stick Man was protesting against treason charges and house arrest. His campaign had been compromised and undermined after becoming a victim of Runo's whimsical persecution. Runo, however, forced the election to go ahead, and he won. The Stick Man came a distant second with just a few constituencies. The Collar Man and the judge were an embarrassment. They had nothing to their credit. Despite his win, Runo never withdrew the charges against Stick Man. The judgment seemed predetermined because he was convicted for the flimsy and whimsical case. Stick Man was furious at how, as the former rebel leader, he was now being persecuted in a country he helped liberate. He claimed that the country had achieved independence without freedom. No one came to his aide. What the people did not realise was the risk and consequences of the capture and destruction of the courts by Runo. Several other institutions were already subject to his will, and this was a danger already leading to Runo turning the nation into a Runo State and monarchy while the helpless population watched with disbelief. Mudadi was injured in a car crash while campaigning for Runo. He was hospitalised on the Queen's island.

While the Sloppy Man had won in his constituency, he was never appointed to a higher office. To keep the Sloppy Man happy, Runo told him that Simo had chosen to stand in Sloppy Man's constituency, and he persuaded him to choose his home town constituency. The Sloppy Man was grateful for the assistance. The Great Crocodile kept fighting to remain relevant with quiet diplomacy. Many business people in the Sloppy Man's constituency were happy to have him as a representative. Due to the lack of development in the area, they decided to use him as a conduit to spearhead that development. They contributed millions of dollars for road construction, school development and many other infrastructure projects. Sloppy Man invested the money in his family trust and abandoned the business community that had enriched him. No one was brave enough to confront this former army chief. They held their peace, and Sloppy Man got away with theft by conversion.

Runo never retired, and Mudadi was left out of the executive. He was also dropped out of the Party's supreme decision-making committee. Runo had consolidated power around himself. Bellyman was old and getting too frail to pick any fights. In most meetings, he would doze off and only wake up when proceedings were almost complete, if not right at the end. The public called for his retirement, but Runo never listened.

A noble initiative, a housing scheme, was established by the government to ease housing problems. Civil servants were to contribute towards the construction of their houses, and therefore, a large majority of the civil servants joined the scheme. Private individuals also joined the scheme until staggering amounts were accumulated. Not a single house was constructed, but the leadership kept promising. It then turned out that all the funds collected were being shared among top officials. Everyone pulled out of the scheme, forcing its closure. Unfortunately, there was no recourse to recovering the looted funds. Runo was calm and never made a comment, giving the idea that he had never heard of the housing scheme. No one was arrested, or an enquiry established. The people who lost out never mobilised for mass action. Runo had become a feared name that he could impose his will without any opposition. He became extremely arrogant that he even started appointing some of his friends who had been involved in the vehicle scandal. This further cemented a culture of corruption among Runo's peers in the Party and government. Runo also appointed some of Collar Man's advisors to the executive to utterly destroy his Party.

After Mudadi was released from the hospital, he confronted Runo at his Presidential Palace.

"You have always told me that it was me and you only. Now you have left me out in the cold, out of the executive as well as the Party supreme body. What's next, put me into the ground?"

"You should be the last person to ask. To begin with, you were always threatening to take over my office when there were several Party seniors ahead of you. How do you expect an appointment outside of formal channels?"

"I did not expect such a direct, upfront, and deceitful answer. For that, I thank you."

"You don't have to sound despondent because you can still redeem yourself," Runo never showed compassion or remorse.

"Really? What magic do I have to perform?"

"Your childish behaviour has to change, and your conduct towards me must be respectful. Seriously, you may not be able to cope with some of the duties required of you. I note from your medical report that you have contracted some terminal conditions; hence you took a long time to recover. It may be in your best interest to help the Party the best you can and bury your other ambitions."

"Very profound, Runo, but I don't think I need your counsel," Mudadi frowned.

"Suit yourself, but remember that I am the ultimate authority thanks to your constitution for both the nation and the Party. You can't touch me, Mudadi. You lost out."

"Have you ever imagined what I would have called you in the game of Strangers and Mothers?" This is a game where if a mother danced around her children and shouted "*Chidhange chidhange*," they responded positively and said "*Mai vedu* (our mother)". If a stranger comes and does the same, the children will frown and say "*Mazimbare*" (black spots that develop on

the shin because someone sits around a fire constantly in winter) or other very mean words.

"I cannot say if I have any interest because whatever it is, I
don't care. If you try anything to disturb my rule, I will crush
you," Runo answered pompously.

"*Kuraira kuuya ndokomuromo, kweshamhu kwakapa musimbwa!*"
He tried to strengthen himself.

"You don't dare defy me, pathetic creature!"

"*Heee, ura mapako hunozvara mbavha, mhondi nemuroyi. Kuberekwa
kwako kwaiva kokungobvisa bundu muura,*" Mudadi showed bravery and was ready to take on the invincible Runo.

"I am done with you and will watch that disease tear
you down slowly and painfully. There is no cure if you didn't
already know. *Handichapedzeri hoko padebgwe reshindi,*" he threw
his hands towards Mudadi with disrespect.

"*Ndinozviziva kuti rinogara rivete nemanhede rakateya mapfumo
seSoso. Tichapedzerana.*" Mudadi stormed out of the Presidential
Palace, pretending to hold his head high, but his tail was
between his legs, weeping quietly.

Mudadi was devastated, and he quickly had a caucus with
a few parliamentarians. He assured them that they would topple Runo through a no-confidence motion. What needed to
be done was simple. At least four of them would need to push
a motion that the President must retire because he had overstayed and is a liability to the economy. A few agreed, but others were fearful of Runo's retribution. Mudadi assured them
that he would be behind them all the way. Zoro agreed to start.
Dzika and Nzara were to be next at different intervals depending on the outcome. Others were to support the motion with
Mudadi's backing. Zoro was fearless as he sent the first scalp.

It was not expected, but Runo kept his cool, looking for
an appropriate response before the motion could be officially tabled for debate. He didn't appreciate the call. There
was an election to select the supreme Party leader in Zoro's
province before the motion was tabled in parliament. Mudadi

pushed Zoro to contest. He wanted to humiliate Runo's candidate and friend, Kumbi. Many from Kumbi's camp encouraged him to quit the race. Following Mudadi's advice and support, he participated and won. A few weeks went by and Zoro got an appointment on a foreign mission to take him out of the way. This meant that he was going to relinquish the position that he had just won and his parliamentary seat. Zoro's appointment was, in a surprise move, widely publicised, and Mudadi's team assumed that there were no consequences to their actions. Besides, they assumed Zoro had sold his soul and abandoned them. Before Zoro left for his job, he made one last visit to his home. He was assured by the Security Minister, Diesel, that if there was any problem, he should always be in touch.

Zoro noticed unusual activity around him and many people on his trail throughout his journey. He notified Diesel and was told to relax as there was no threat. A team was going to be dispatched to escort him on his return. He was advised that a vehicle with escort reinforcements would flash to confirm its position, and he should flash back. Zoro did as instructed, and the flashing car went straight for him and crushed him, and he died on the spot. This was the same spot where another high-ranking official had died in an accident.

Runo gave Zoro the highest honour and threatened to change all road rules. At Zoro's funeral, he vowed to have the offending driver incarcerated. Nothing happened. Runo met Diesel after the funeral to shower him with praises for a job well done.

"Diesel, you are in danger of becoming the President's favourite and point man."

"What did I do to deserve such an honour?" He wore a wide smile while nodding.

"First, you belong to the right tribe. Second, you have carried out all my orders diligently," he responded with a fist.

"I thought I was just doing my job."

"It's different, Diesel."

"How, Your Excellency?"

"Without complaining, grovelling and probing, you just do your work. A lack of curiosity is one of your better qualities, and I hope you don't lose that quality."

"I am happy you appreciate what I do. I also didn't know my tribe was special because we have relatives from all over the country."

"We cannot let our people be dominated by anyone. To cut a long story short, you must know my favour has been stolen by you."

"I am excited, Your Excellency (blushing). Just name them, and I will execute, Your Excellency."

"Keep this conversation to yourself, Diesel."

"I know, Your Excellency."

"Have a nice day."

Even Mudadi and his team could not guess what had happened to Zoro as they just assumed he had enemies in the Party. Enemies that were against his appointment and had close relations with Runo. They all presumed Kumbi could have been the culprit but could not find his footprints on the trail. Runo was the last person they suspected, considering his gesture to Zoro. They, therefore, continued with their push for Runo's ouster. Dzika was the next to announce the retirement mantra. He was met with brutal force and suspended from the Party in an instant. Mudadi had no suitable response as his colleagues became casualties one after another. Runo had assumed total control of the political landscape, so he decided to relax the operations of his secret service apparatus. Even the budget was reduced.

Effects of the experiments on army personnel began to show. Several officers became ill and suffered from long-term chronic diseases. One would not die quickly but went on for a prolonged period while slowly losing immunity to diseases. Once these men returned to their homes, conjugal rights became an issue due to the education the women were receiving from civic organisations. Domestic violence became a common phenomenon. The belief was that these soldiers were irrational, oversexed individuals who had no self-control or ever thought of protecting themselves and their partners. It was difficult for anyone to know and understand the intricate details of how most of these people got infected. If the information had become public, Runo was going to face a mutiny. Many enemies of Runo suffered from the disease, including innocent individuals. Projections were pointing to the effect that the nation's population would halve within twenty years as the nation had recorded the highest prevalence of the pandemic on the continent.

A mobile telephone technology craze hit the nation. A gentleman who had been earmarked and trained by the government to spearhead the project decided to implement the project on his own. The government was engulfed in its bureaucratic processes, and this delayed the project's implementation.

Runo had second thoughts on the government's point man. Those in positions of authority were looking for an opportunity to get a fee or commission on the setting up of such a company. When that gentleman applied for an operating licence, the authorities panicked. Some, however, supported him, while others were totally against him, especially Runo. The gentleman had to wait while government departments debated on the issue. This gentleman, Steve, had done some work for Runo and invoiced him for a shoddy job. Runo refused to pay, and legal proceedings were instituted. Previously, Steve had been supported by Runo in a quest to create a tribal business clique and rival those he wanted to keep under his thumb. Runo had used this man through Lady Amai Marunjeya. After her death, Steve got greedy and did not pay a penny to Runo for the business ventures. Runo had been patient, and his time for revenge had finally come. Eventually, the government went on to implement its project first. Steve went to court, but the case was stalled. Heli was tasked to fight Steve to ensure that he gave up his quest. She displayed her total lack of knowledge in the process and ended up fighting everyone.

To deal with the matter decisively, the government floated a tender for a second operator. Steve put his bid against a few other contenders, and he lost. Turtle Man and a few business associates won. Runo had pushed for Turtle Man to keep lucrative projects under his control and among his preferred tribesmen. Turtle Man faced a few problems because his associates did not pay any capital for the project. It was impossible to force them to pay because they were Runo's close relatives. To make the situation worse, the key associate, Cub, was demanding full recognition on behalf of Runo. Turtle Man stood his ground, not realising that Runo had awarded himself the project through him as a proxy. Runo expected Turtle Man to do the maths and come up with a reasonable conclusion. This should have been obvious after a briefing and when team Turtle Man and associates were constituted with a strong hint of Runo's support. However, Turtle Man still didn't get the sense or comprehend Cub's demands. Maybe he was simply playing hard to get.

A few months later, Runo approached him and asked. "Turtle Man, are you unhappy with the opportunities I am creating for the aboriginal people of this nation?" He spoke sternly.

"No, Your Excellency," Turtle Man spoke with a subdued voice.

"If you are not opposed to the policies, how come you don't appreciate them?"

"I don't understand, Your Excellency."

"I gave you that licence, and you were to scratch my back. What's your story?"

"I borrowed, Your Excellency, to put up the capital," Turtle

Man assumed Runo would pardon him.

"What does that have to do with me?"

"How do I assist if no money has been paid?"

"Do you want to play hardball with me?"

"No, Your Excellency. I don't have the resources to pay back if you don't make good your portion."

"Do you feel you are more business-minded than me?"

"I thought we had a deal, Your Excellency."

"Look at your other gentleman. He did a lot of work for me and thought he was smart. He billed me for some poor services after I babysat him for many years and now wants me to licence his operations. He can rant and rave all he wants. Even if the Bellyman supports him, he will not get that piece of paper."

"Your Excellency, I never thought it would come to this. We have never had such a misunderstanding before. I beg you, can you please, at least, meet me halfway?"

"See to it that this deal is sorted. I need positive feedback from Cub. My contribution is that piece of paper you call your licence. Thank you for your time, Turtle Man."

Chapter 12

Magazines and newspapers sniffed the news of Runo's secret family. It was difficult to keep the affair under wraps for a public figure and also because the daughter was of school-going age. The leak was, therefore, inevitable. A magazine that Captain Ed once used broke the story and gave all the details. The public did not believe the contents and assumed it was a money-making stunt. In addition, his eunuch status had become a public secret. After a while, another popular weekly business newspaper carried the story. Runo went berserk and had all the publication's leaders imprisoned and fined. No scribe dared report on the matter again. The truth, however, was out in the open, and Runo never denied it. Information was, however, out in public, and it was clear Runo was being authoritatively dishonest. A few months later, Runo decided to officially formalise his relationship with Marujata. He also pencilled in a wedding date. At that stage, she already had a second child, a boy whom he named after himself. His decision was roundly condemned by everyone in the nation. Civic society organisations and churches had a field day pointing out all the stains on the union. Some speculated that given her level of education compared to Runo, it meant she used a love potion to lure him. Furthermore, it was most likely that he would respond positively to her every wish in the future, irrespective of how unreasonable the wish may be. Runo never paid attention as he went ahead with his plans. He instructed priests to officiate at the ceremony. The Chief Priest refused, and several pleas were made to ensure that the head of state was not embarrassed. He did not waiver. As the days drew closer, Runo realised that only a hostile negotiation would be the ideal solution. Runo visited the Chief Priest at his quarters.

"Good day, Bishop," Runo was very civil in his approach.

"Your Excellency, welcome. What did I do to deserve such an honour?" The bishop suspected something brewing on the horizon.

"We come a long way, Bishop. You probably have a file full of my great association with your confessional chamber since time immemorial."

"That we don't talk about, but is everything alright, Your Excellency?" The Bishop wanted to avoid being sidetracked by technicalities.

"Bishop, you and I know you are of good moral standing," Runo said with sarcasm.

"What's your point, Your Excellency?" He was taken by surprise as this was supposed to be obvious for all men of the cloth.

"You don't want to be embarrassed when your dirty linen starts to dangle in public."

"For the Son of God, I am willing to die for what's right," he thought Runo was bluffing.

"Is that so? Even if you get tainted by his blood?" Runo confused the Bishop, so he continued answering from the previous response.

"Of course, we shall not preside at your wedding, and that's final, Your Excellency. You may have my head on a platter, but so be it. By the way, it's the blood of redemption, not tainting."

"Whoever said I am a shedder of blood? Let's talk morality," Runo sounded reasonable, knowing victory was in sight.

"The morality of this whole issue is that you cannot take someone's wife and do as you please when you should lead by example," the Bishop continued to assume a moral high ground.

"Wonderful, Bishop, just like you took the vows of celibacy."

"Exactly."

"Yet you have trampled on those vows, tainted by that blood like any other proselytes and have become a family man like us, mere mortals," Runo looked away from the Bishop to avoid his expression. The Bishop dropped his rosary in shock but maintained his position.

"I have done no such thing."

"Do you swear, Bishop?" Runo smiled with the fish firmly on the hook.

"I don't swear. My yes is a yes, and a no is a no." It was embarrassing, but the Bishop tried to fight back.

"Very well then. Whose family photo is this?" Runo pulled out a photo from a thick file that he was holding.

"Hmmm, Mr President. That's a confidential matter. You cannot possibly try to blackmail me," the Bishop fell to the back of his chair with his right hand covering his face.

"No, Bishop, I don't do blackmail. I negotiate."

"If I refuse, what will you do?" Defeated, the bishop weighed his options.

"The choice is yours, Bishop. Cast the first stone only if you have not sinned."

"I understand, Mr President. Do you want me to preside over the ceremony or some of my very fine priests to do it?"

"The choice is yours. I cannot interfere with your church schedule."

"I will deal with the issue, Mr President. If you don't mind, you can stay for as long as you like." The Bishop felt embarrassed and could no longer openly comment on morality until cleared by the political leadership.

"It has been a pleasure doing business with you, Bishop, but I have a lot on my plate today."

The Chief Priest personally presided over the wedding. That man, who was involved with Marujata, also attended and the other one. Those who knew the other man's association with Marujata avoided him. They thought they would be caught in the crossfire. Some even deserted their tables just after having been served lunch. It turned out that all the press reports on the union were indeed very correct. Why Runo wanted to persecute people was a mystery. It probably was just in his blood to cause terror and derive joy from other people's misery. Runo's marriage, however, had a lasting effect and influence on the nation. It became a trend for many widowed grandfathers to remarry. They were not only remarrying but looking for young ladies and even teenage girls. This was in line with Runo's example of marrying a thirty-year-old when he was in his late seventies. To manage and massage the anger arising from his union with Marujata, he held a press briefing on the matter at his Presidential Palace. Hand-picked journalists took turns to ask questions but knew they could not dare provoke him.

Another side of his insanity was revealed by the session. One journalist asked, "Do you sometimes feel that you betrayed your former wife, the late Lady Amai Marunjeya, by having children with another woman before her death and now marrying that woman?"

"*As you are aware, one gave me support, was a very close friend and confidante. However, the other blessed me with love and children. I know you can follow the logic.*"

Another asked, "What are your words of advice to all girls aspiring to achieve what the first lady has achieved, marriage?"

"*Be careful, men will abuse you, ruin your reputation and then marry an angel and pretend to be born again.*"

"How about those who are motivated by finances to take advantage of men?"

"*Some girls get physically fit due to hoping from one boy to another,*" the room was filled with laughter.

"Any advice to boys?"

"*If a girl has tattoos or piercings, then she is already used to pain and is fair game, don't hesitate to break her heart.*"

Journalists fielded many more questions, but nothing serious and damaging was thrown at him. The press briefing was repeated a few times on national television to patch up Runo's image.

The father of Marujata's children got overexcited after the wedding. A child donation to the first family was on his mind. Unsanctioned, he quickly rewarded Marujata with one. Runo did not appreciate the unsolicited gift. In his usual vengeful mood, the donor had to bid farewell to mother earth in a freak accident, in a very unlikely situation. He had, however, told his brother about these children. The brother approached Runo to negotiate a deal to handover the children. He wanted the children to grow up among their own. Runo was reasonable according to his standards. He paid off the brother, and the children never got to know their real father.

All close relatives of Marujata were rewarded with good jobs in the government after the marriage. Marujata's estranged father was shocked to learn that her long-lost daughter had landed the first lady trophy. He made all the necessary arrangements to reunite with her.

Marujata was put on a few payrolls, one local authority, the public service payroll and a parastatal. Runo did the same for all his relatives and all farm workers. All executives were allowed to do the same. Strict instructions were given not to make the payrolls public even to anyone leading a parastatal or leading a local authority, especially if not from his camp. Runo wanted this little secret of his to remain hidden from the public eye. This resulted in more than a third of the government payroll being saddled by non-government workers and ghost employees.

The creative postage stamp sector, which was exporting much of its products, collapsed following Runo's wedding. It was time to put the artistic and creative minds out of business and employment while raising Runo's personal and family profile above that of the nation. All new stamps were mandated to bear the wedding picture of Runo and Marujata sharing something referred to as communion bread. Something supposedly sacred or holy being partaken by a husband hopper and a serial girlfriend, and some sadistic gentleman and cold-blooded murderer with no consequences, none whatsoever. After many silent protests by individuals, rumours and insinuations of dictatorship, other postage stamps with an image of Simo as well as the Bellyman were introduced to save face. Faces of other liberation war heroes were also put on a limited number of stamps. These stamps were of no use in other nations, and therefore, no one outside the nation bought them.

Results of mishandling, mismanaging and corrupt activities at parastatals began to emerge. People could, without doubt, see Runo's wanton disregard for economic fundamentals. The bus company was failing to service its routes, timetables had been suspended, and private players were allowed into the sector to ease mounting transport woes. During rainy days, private cars would help the public but charge ten times the cost. Illegal private players would charge double the normal cost. The monopoly situation could not be sustained. Runo's government, therefore, decided to licence private players. The bus company was slowly heading towards closure. Even Runo could not summon the buses to his rallies or other public events. He never felt embarrassed, though, because he never called anyone to order. His close associate was in charge of the bus company as well as one of the biggest insurance portfolios in the country, where the government had a controlling stake. Runo pretended everything was normal.

The national airline also faced its biggest challenge. More and more planes were being grounded due to old age. No spares were available for the ageing fleet, and it was only logical that the fleet be replaced and, if not, grounded. An anticipated replacement process did not take place because there were no funds left, and the government could not afford to assist. The employees were not being rationalised as the number of planes reduced, hoping for government intervention. The situation continued until only five planes remained, with a workforce of more than two thousand employees. It became logical to reduce the number of routes that were being serviced. Salaries were no longer manageable, but Runo insisted that no one would be retrenched. Employee rationalisation was going to reflect badly on his leadership. Service crumbled, and safety became a major concern. The public joked that the airline had decelerated from a tradition of caring to a tradition of scaring.

The national railways' company faced the same problem. Most of the managers, besides drawing huge salaries and benefits, also established competing transport businesses. Besides the issue of incompetence and political patronage, their management style favoured the success of their private businesses. This situation was worsened by the general economic decay in that the revenues declined. Salaries could not be paid on time, and prices for services were increased, which hastened the company to collapse. The control systems were antiquated and cell phones became the new mode of control. Train drivers had to phone each other for positions using mobile phones. Railways signals, both electronic and fixed signs, broke down and were never replaced. Salaries were paid to different groups at different times as Runo would not allow parastatals to run like businesses. Staff reductions were not permitted as these would have reflected badly on Runo's leadership.

The same fate met all parastatals, but the insatiable quest to plunder did not stop; it was instead reignited and reinvigorated with age. Each time a parastatal raised a red flag, a bond issue would be undertaken, and the money made available.

Within a few months, the government grant would have disappeared from the parastatal, and Runo would never question anybody. This became the new model for siphoning money out of the system. These clear scams reflected how Runo entrenched a culture of indolence and an unproductive self-entitlement. Parastatal leaders got all the blame for corruption, but the seniors, especially Runo, were regarded as clean.

Information on the war veterans' compensation fund leaked to the media, and a weekly business paper proffered detailed insights into the levels of looting. Clever Militia Man had been elected to lead the war veterans at that time. The public was overjoyed and celebrated the revelations, hoping that the scandal would culminate in leadership changes. It was rumoured that Heli immediately paid back her loot, and this appeased public anger. After a week, there was no response or comment from the government. Weeks turned into months until the story died down and was forgotten. Runo was never moved, true to his word, nor did he urge his colleagues to follow the rumoured example. The public was disheartened but felt powerless. By default, Runo recorded another victory. His victory was, however, short-lived as the real veterans were irked by the news. They had received nothing, yet the leadership and undeserving individuals took home hundreds of thousands of dollars. The veterans demanded their due rewards and sought an audience with Runo. Runo refused, and they persevered relentlessly. He sent emissaries to silence them, but the veterans could not be taken for granted. Eventually, they demonstrated at the Party Head Office for an entire day until Runo sent some senior Party officials. Again, they refused to meet these officials. All they wanted was Runo since he had self-anointed himself as their patron. He ignored them and sent in the police riot squad. Police used tear gas and baton sticks to fight the veterans.

The veterans employed their war tactics and used wet towels to ward off the gas. These veterans also used unexploded tear gas canisters to attack the police. In the commotion, they managed to grab a few police officers and gave them a thorough bashing lesson. These were badly injured, so the head of police services reported to Runo, and he called for the intervention of the Army. Fox refused to attack unarmed civilians and ignored the call. Besides, he was a veteran like them and could not hurt his friends. It was then rumoured that Clever Militia Man had never finished his military training and never served on the battlefront either. In addition, it was also claimed that Clever Militia Man had not completed his medical training. He was, therefore, not a qualified doctor. This was a rumour spread by Runo to discredit the veteran leader hoping to score some points. It did not work and the battle continued. One of the war veterans, an artist, released a hit song with a hidden message on Runo's devious character and how good he was at lying and not keeping promises. The song was *Sawara*. Runo was unmoved. All he did was make moves towards ending the singer's life. Many women suffering from a chronic pandemic would make themselves available to the singer sent by Runo's emissaries.

It was getting towards Veterans Day, and the veterans kept their cool, pretending that they had given up. On the day of the celebrations, Runo had his usual routine of giving a televised live speech to the nation. When he arrived at the veterans square, he was greeted by a huge angry crowd of veterans singing and chanting liberation war songs. He pretended to be strong and weaved his way in. Runo personally asked Fox to deal with the unwelcome crowd, and Fox told Runo that the army had no business dealing with crowd trouble because it was the domain of the police. People could tell that the two were arguing. Runo could not impose his authority and was devastated that a strongman had stopped him in his tracks. It was an embarrassment, but he tried to soldier on.

The activism was so strong that he had to abandon his speech at the veterans square. In anger, he never addressed them. He was determined more than ever to eliminate them but was not sure how best to deal with them. Runo preferred a slow and painful death to each one of them, especially through an injected disease. How to gather them and spread a pandemic was the problem because he did not have a formal relationship with them, nor were they benefiting from him and his government. A week later, the veterans marched through the streets of the capital, camped outside Runo's office and put mats, blankets and chairs blocking the road. The veterans threatened to block the entrance to Runo's Presidential Palace the next time if he continued to be elusive. Runo instructed the police to shoot. Before the police came to discipline the veterans, Simo was appraised of the situation and quickly stopped Runo's madness. He went out personally to address them and diffused the standoff. After the meeting, he approached Runo for an audience with him. Runo gave Simo the chance to make suggestions but after the meeting he ignored everything. Instead, he was planning to hire some hitmen to eliminate the veterans.

When the development reached Simo, he quickly met Runo to persuade him to change his mind. This he tried several times to no avail. Simo realised that his boss was at it again, and despite the foolishness of his decision, he was going to implement it. He, therefore, asked to see him one day at the Presidential Palace in the early hours of the morning. Simo went with a group of traditional dancers. Once they got into the premises, Simo set them up on the neglected lawn. They sang and danced to one tune three times. The song was *Nyuchi dzinoruma, with Simo in front.* They sang;

> *Nyuchi dzinoruma,*
> *Tora uta hwangu ndoda kuenda,*
> *Dzinoruma,*
> *Nyuchi dzinoruma,*
> *Dzinoruma,*

Vashe vashe woye,
Tora uta hwangu ndoda kuenda,
Dzinoruma,
Nyuchi dzinoruma,
Dzinoruma

The song was used in traditional ceremonies as a coercive last-ditch persuasive measure to summon mediums. The main theme of *Nyuchi Dzinoruma* points to a situation where there obstacles(nyuchi dzinoruma) but one is determined to soldier on. Simo repeated this routine two more times, and Runo was left shaken. At times, Simo served as Runo's spiritual advisor; therefore, Runo assumed that a bad omen was on the horizon. He, therefore, softened his stance out of fear rather than reason. Fear was a key language of instruction for Runo. An agreement was, therefore, cobbled up in a follow-up meeting, and the situation was resolved. It turned out that Simo was very resourceful and a key advisor to Runo. However, Runo still had another ace up his sleeve. He wanted to exclude most of the veterans from the payments and, therefore, ordered a veterans reregistration exercise. Runo's friends and relatives were the first to line up for the payments, which ballooned the known veteran's number to more than double the official number just after the war. To instil a negative public image of the veterans, he ordered some of his friends to do the most foolish things with the payments, like hiring a taxi across the nation, hiring a bus for one person or buying a television set for livestock. Such incidents were then publicised repeatedly in the media.

Runo wanted alternatives and more income streams. He had never been featured in any magazine's rich list, and he felt it was time to go public because he had spent too much time in office. It was not clear why he had this craving to accumulate cash and wealth. Some thought it was a lack of money sense since only a few million were enough to keep him and his family going for over a hundred years. Probably, he intended to show off his capability to accumulate and compete with the leading members of the world, but for what purpose and for whose benefit remained a mystery.

On one end, it was a good thing not to appear in magazines because it made him proud that they could not track or trace his wealth. In addition, it made him feel that he related well with the masses without any extravagant wealth as an ideal public image. Runo identified a few additional channels to capture funds. The first was through local authorities, and the second was through a levy for the chronic pandemic. He also realised he could establish a national pension scheme for all workers. His priority was to assume total control of all local authorities and have access to the funds from these institutions. He decided to create Executive Mayoral posts. The academia, civic society, churches and the general public condemned the proposal. More costs were going to be incurred without any corresponding benefits. Runo would not be deterred by public pressure. He turned a deaf ear to the outcry and continued.

Turtle Man saw an opportunity to make extra money and used his financial muscle to have his nomination endorsed by the Party. Turtle Man had joined Runo's Party and had gone up the ladder to the stage of being part of the decision-making body. Runo was livid at the idea of Turtle Man spoiling his money-making venture in addition to the cellphone deal. He, therefore, stormed the Party supreme committee and forced the cancellation of Turtle Man's candidature. Runo condemned his fellow Party members of corruption for endorsing what he termed a criminal in joining the Party and letting that criminal win nomination for a key post. No one opposed him, and Turtle Man lost his bid to become an Executive Mayor. In another city, Runo's preferred candidate lost, and he had to intervene by making up some trumped-up charges. Those charges were not even true, but instead of backing down, the popular candidate continued. Runo ensured that the popular candidate was relieved of his duties from his government post as well. Finally, Runo won his case, but his image had been battered.

In a third city, Runo's candidate never got a chance, and he had to let go because he was bruised and battered. He tried to buy his allegiance diplomatically and avoid a confrontation that would have completely shattered his reputation. It was obvious Turtle Man, and the other unwanted candidates were going to spoil Runo's plans. The Executive mayoral project was one of the worst ventures that Runo had ever embarked on. His preferred candidate in place of Turtle Man eventually won but had a disastrous tenure in office punctuated by endless problems. The candidate later approached Runo, proposing to leave office because of the low confidence displayed by the people.

"Your Excellency, I think it's time for me to move on."

"Where to, my Mayor?"

"The people are not happy with my leadership, and I think it's best for the city and the Party."

"You don't have any problem, my Mayor, hold on."

"I don't understand. My low rating could affect the Party and you."

"Look at me. The whole nation could not care less if I leave. They hate me with a passion, but will I leave my office? The answer is an absolute no, not in my lifetime. Go back to your office and enjoy."

"How about the reputation of the Party?"

"Let me worry about that because you are my project."

The mayor went on to build the most lavish mayoral mansion, whose price kept rising by the hour. Complaints got worse, but Runo was unmoved.

The national scheme had no hurdles for Runo. It was the best money-making venture he had ever come up with. This scheme was made compulsory and under the total control of the government. It was not subject to regulatory controls by any regulator in the nation. He, however, faced a small problem. It was difficult for him to access funds. The leader had to be relieved of his duties due to an extravagant executive lifestyle. All members of the public bought the story and never sympathised with the leader. The next leader was the former head of an insurance company. He did not last long either due to his professional conduct. Owing to too many demands by the government to access the funds, he resigned. After leaving the national scheme, he encountered too many accidents because he held too much incriminating information. He later realised that things were not normal, and he skipped the country. Runo then started appointing his hand-picked and preferred individuals.

Runo then created a new tax to cater for drugs and treatment for the chronic pandemic. People never protested because of the public sympathy and the sorry state of most patients and the health delivery system in the nation. It was hailed as a brilliant idea and a progressive step towards care as well as research and development. This fund went for three years without being used for its intended purpose. When drugs were finally procured, senior officials suffering from the disease were the first to help themselves.

Runo brought in a new member of the executive. This man was Igi. A homeboy and close relative of Runo. His level of corruption was unprecedented from the time he was appointed. He hit the ground running and was always on every news bulletin. Igi was Runo's favourite minister. He never improved anything but destroyed everything in his path. Education was an exemplary ministry with some of the best standards. After a year in office, everything was in a sorry state. Students from tertiary institutions were scrounging for food after he changed the procurement system, where Runo's farms and companies became the suppliers. Igi's wife also got involved. Produce was being paid for in advance despite supply constraints. Faced with an imminent collapse in standards and service, students went on strike and demonstrated against Igi's incompetence on several occasions. Many were beaten and briefly detained for causing public disorder. Eventually, they got tired and succumbed to the heavy political hand and also because no one seemed to be listening. Above all, the institutions were threatened with closure, and Runo was already taking steps to close them.

A tender to extend and improve the nation's only international airport was floated. Runo wanted the contract, and he assigned his nephew, Cub, to represent his newly registered company. The company came in fifth place according to the published tender rating scores. Before the tender could be formally awarded, Runo intervened, and his company won the tender. It was reported that the company had won based on their proposed designs despite the cost and competence issues. An obvious fact was that Runo's company would subcontract a more experienced contractor and pocket the difference. The story made headline news for a few months until people forgot about it. Runo never responded to any allegations and accusations.

An attempt to oust Cub at the Nation's football mother body was gathering momentum. Runo was irked, so he instructed the man at the centre of the controversy to be purged. That man's office at the Foreign Trade Department had its keys changed overnight, and an article placed in a weekly business paper. It was hurriedly inserted to the effect that changes had taken place. His motor vehicle assembly franchise operations were abruptly terminated, and all his bank accounts were frozen. The palace coup was averted, but the remaining foot soldiers still managed to regroup and force Cub out in a no-confidence vote. A new leader was appointed. Before long, Runo had the new leader charged for various offences committed many years back. Cash Back, Runo's brother, easily got the appointment, especially with the financial muscle to push his agenda.

It was Cub's association with his uncle that presided over

the demise of several companies. Cub had been asked by Runo to change his surname to match that of Runo. On behalf of Runo, Cub would approach many companies as an investor or outright buyer. Within six months after a bargain or token purchase, they would strip the company of all its assets and move on to the next victim. Cub's first experience was in a steel and pipe company where he mercilessly stripped and drove over a thousand employees into destitution. After this successful transaction, Runo's other close-foot soldier, Fine Lips, a more charismatic and maverick character, joined in. He was more focused on destruction and was more unapologetic than Cub. Runo was extremely pleased with Fine Lips, so he allowed the man to even sell the most closely guarded party and government secrets for a fee. The public referred to the two as lacking financial wisdom but awash with opportunities to get rich.

Bellyman died, and an extravagant funeral was held for him. His funeral or death became a festival rivalling that of Lady Amai Marunjeya. They made the public feel it was a great loss, and Runo used it to his full advantage. It was time to take advantage of an unfortunate situation. A lasting impression had to be created. There was song, dance, drama and poetry at the funeral of this hero. Bellyman was posthumously named Father of the Nation. The public, however, preferred to remember him only as a Nyongolo. Even his former post was renamed Nyongolo by the public. Bellyman, however, had a final scalp on Runo before he died. He had published his memoirs detailing all his grievances, blaming Runo and those not of his ethnic group. Unfortunately, Bellyman was not aware that the tribe he thought he belonged to was not even his. Stick Man and Simo were his clansmen and the major family grouping in the nation. The three were family. Runo had no chance to respond or get revenge as it was published posthumously.

Son of the Great Lord was appointed to take over the

Bellyman's position. The Great Crocodile tried again to fill the post left by the Son of the Great Lord and failed. A certain Cowboy, who was a close relative of Runo, won. Cowboy was Runo's brother from a different mother. Mudadi, despite his precarious position in his political career, did not fight for the Great Crocodile again but instead worked in Runo's camp. He was an embittered man with no hope and could not even support his fellow brother in attaining the leadership of the nation. Great Crocodile and Mudadi did not only hail from the same rural home but shared the same bloodline. They belonged to the same clan and family. Nate, having reached his career ceiling, announced his retirement. Simo also indicated his intention to step down at the end of the term of office and not participate in the next elections. A few more old-timers were under pressure to do the same.

Chapter 13

An attempt to form a political group by some worker representatives was made, but all efforts were futile. There was no traction from the public or business community. Its leadership tried to make a further test of power through a demonstration against Runo's government and shut down work. Again, the demonstration and call for a shutdown failed. Finally, they decided to negotiate with the diplomatic representatives of the world's leading nations. The diplomats bought the idea and decided to run with it. They even entered into talks with the representative body of companies to lobby support for the new party. They negotiated with every small Party in the country to join hands. It worked, and a two-day violent demonstration was staged, which was a resounding success. This process was repeated a few times to make sure the new set-up was well received. The political party was, therefore, formed as an ideal. Its name and leadership remained unannounced after realising that Runo would crush them before they could even spell their names. They, therefore, decided to organise under disguise. The disguise came in the form of a Constitution Reform group. The leader of the group was Sabi, a former workers' union activist. Runo was not worried about the development because each time there were elections for the national worker's union, Sabi was his preferred candidate. He would, therefore, direct the result to be in favour of Sabi.

Funds for the political Party were raised under this banner as the leadership made all necessary publicity stunts. Parallel political Party structures were taking shape religiously in the shadows. Others quietly remarked that should this political movement come to life, then it would mark the beginning of more disasters for the country.

Runo decided to put them out of business by starting a constitution review process. An independent constitutional-making body was swiftly put in place. Among the commissioners in the constitution-making process was Tadpole. Tadpole was a war deserter, a sellout, and was actively working in the ranks of the oppressor to scuttle the war efforts. He was also rumoured to be the Stick Man's child. He was the best example of a hired gun and could offer services to the highest bidder. Any prize to change loyalties and prevaricate could not fairly and honestly pass this gentleman by. His spewing of inanities, mindless and pointless arguments made a grotesque mental pollution to any enlightened listener. A happy and progressive community made him sick, made his head spin and gave him constant migraines, which provoked him to mindlessly attack anyone and any subject.

Tadpole was using this political assignment to hide and also seek protection from his past misdemeanours that warranted a jail term. His moral compass had never been normal, and a replacement was difficult to come by. His cob-shaped head was a subject of ridicule and scorn, making cartoonists' tasks extremely easy. This cob-shaped head was bald at the top and he must have received massive discounts on each visit to a barbershop. Many referred to it as a circumcised head. Tadpole's face was marked by a flat nose covering a quarter of it.

Runo thought it was best to have someone to feed him any information he needed. Mudadi and the Great Crocodile were tasked to represent the Party's interests. The two led a team that presented to the commission the views of the

Party. Each civic group came up with the same setup, but the Constitutional Reform group did not participate. It was opposed by the Constitutional Commission. Mudadi and the Great Crocodile shared the same passion for ensuring that Runo was taken out of the system. The two, however, did not discuss the matter between themselves. The Great Crocodile preferred to keep everything close to his chest. Mudadi was so frustrated that he made his wishes about the constitution public. Tadpole quickly relayed the message to Runo, and Mudadi was pulled out of the Party team before it completed its task. The Great Crocodile gladly incorporated everything that Mudadi had suggested without antagonising anyone.

People of an alternative lifestyle – homosexuals, gays or perverts – pushed for recognition in the constitutional-making process. This was a new concept for the nation. The people concerned even gathered at an annual book fair to present their material. Runo had them chased away because the nation was not a Sodom resurrected. He made international headlines for going against these sick people. More of their kind around the world gave support, and the fight grew. For his stance, Runo gained a lot of support from within the nation. Runo aptly described them as beasts, and the majority agreed with him.

Unfortunately, some countries that referred to themselves as the international community vilified him for taking a correct stance during his tenure as president. No financial support was going to be extended to the nation due to Runo's utterances against this hopeless bunch. They were determined to force everyone to accept and adopt their abhorrent behaviour and make it a normal practice. At least Runo had taken the first step in shaping and creating a better future for his kind.

Coincidentally, soon after the furore on homosexuals, a policeman gunned down a soccer fan at a football match. This policeman, Jeff, was a former security man for Professor Reverend Banner. He was immediately arrested and charged with murder. In the court proceedings, he pleaded not guilty to the murder charges, and the nation was shocked because he had committed the crime in broad daylight and at point-blank range. Jeff, in his testimony, told the court that he had been provoked and humiliated by the man he shot. He alleged that the man had labelled him as Professor Reverend Banner's spouse. This dehumanisation drove him to commit the crime. When asked why someone would refer to him as the former president's wife, he advised the court that it was because of the former president's presumed condition or aberration. He was asked to elaborate and the prosecution team vehemently objected, knowing that they were going to lose their case. It took a few sessions to finally have his testimony admitted into evidence. He also told the court that he was prepared to name all the men or girlfriends that the former president had been involved with. The prosecution's case collapsed like a deck of cards, leaving Jeff with a slap on the wrist.

In the public arena, information was being shared on all the sodomy incidents that Professor Revered Banner had had with football players, his security detail and college students. The court was compelled to open an inquest into the matter that the former president was summoned to court. His lawyers made frantic efforts to stop the case, alleging that Jeff was saying anything to secure his freedom. All their attempts failed. Runo was also under pressure to show that he truly despised gays and supported African values. The former president found himself in the dock. It emerged that he forced himself on any man close to him, imposing his political office and power to sodomise his victims. An invitation to some ball-room dance he had learned in another nation was his main pointer or intention to sodomise a victim. It turned out that Jeff had, on several occasions, beaten up Professor Reverend and sometimes thrown him into a pool to stop his advances. Witnesses had to be turned away because there were way too many to accommodate in just one case. Professor Reverend

Banner approached his estranged wife and summoned her back to the nation to stand by his side during the court proceedings. His legal team had hoped that this could sway judgment and attract public sympathy. Details of how he had forced her back into the nation emerged, and the public felt sorry for the wife instead of the Professor. Professor Reverend lost his case and was imprisoned. The title of Professor became a poisoned chalice such that in certain situations, it was used negatively. For instance, a trailing soccer team's supporters, any losing sportsperson's supporters or even those in a mechanical game or computer game, always claimed that their team would come from behind like a Professor to snatch victory. 'You could face a Professor', became a warning that a person likely to be encountered was a homosexual.

The economy took a nosedive on many fronts. The first was from the peasants who wanted recognition from the government and to get land. Public land allocations had been done for a few years after independence. Any allocations after that were for senior officials due to limited farmland. A certain chief and his people moved on to white-owned farmland but were removed forcibly by Runo's policemen. A few months later, the same thing happened, but the police came in handy for Runo. It reached a hopeless stage when the same process was repeated over and over again. It became apparent that the public impatience could no longer be contained. Something had to be done, but Runo had no solution. He tried to have a land conference, but this resulted in many foreign investors pulling out, causing an infamous economic Black Friday meltdown. Runo engaged the former coloniser to fulfil its obligations on land.

The response Runo received was devastating. It had been written by an immigrant turned Minister in the coloniser's country(Clare Short's letter to the Zimbabwe government). It read in part, "*...I should make it clear that we do not accept that our country has a special responsibility to meet the costs of the land purchase* *in your nation. We are a new Government from diverse backgrounds without links to former colonial interests. My origins are Irish, and as you know, we were colonised, not the colonisers...*" The response was an abdication of responsibility and a deliberate intent to throw Runo under the bus. The former coloniser wanted Runo out of power for asking what had been agreed upon many years before when the pact for the continuation of colonial privileges was signed. Runo read the letter in public to share his anger and ease the pain while planning his next move.

The second was the dismal failure of the economic reform programme that Runo had implemented. Many companies had closed and unemployment was skyrocketing. Runo also introduced many taxes that were burdening individuals and companies. All employee benefits were taxable, and people needed to work extra hours to maintain the same lifestyle. Educational fees, vehicle benefits, club benefits, holiday benefits and anything that employees received in the form of benefits became taxable. Companies assembling vehicles and industrial machines had their imported components slapped with duties, and prices spiked.

Runo's finance minister had advised him against the policy and seemed to understand. However, one day, while addressing a funeral, he went on a tirade against his minister, which forced the minister to capitulate. In another incident, the minister had suspended the payment of bonuses for civil servants due to a lack of funds, but Runo reversed the decision at a political rally. It took more than six monthly instalments to pay the bonuses as the minister was battling to raise the finances. For any small problem created by Runo or his corruption scandals, he appointed committees, commissions and subcommittees to investigate. These absurd structures ensured that nothing tangible came out of the enquiries. In addition, these bodies were weighing down on the treasury, and the country was running an unsustainable budget deficit. Individuals started to explore the option of rioting to send a strong message to Runo. Runo, however, never responded positively. He was heavy-handed in dealing with the people. He also wanted to continue borrowing to keep the government afloat. That decision was roundly condemned because borrowing from John to pay Peter or digging one hole to fill another was never a sustainable solution. Runo only looked for short-term gains and was quick to respond to criticism. In his witty style, he referred to the press to all developed nations and their debt levels. He then closed off the argument by saying, "Have you ever heard of a government that collapsed because it is over-borrowed?"

Heli's ministry was given the task of making sure that each rural community had access to clean water within reasonable distances. Due to the frequent droughts being experienced by the nation, boreholes were the only feasible method of achieving the goal. This goal was made public, and all rural communities got promises. This made sure that a vote at the next election was guaranteed. The lady took the liberty to drill boreholes at her farms and her houses around town with the resources. She then did the same to all senior officials, including Runo's properties. At the end of the exercise, only a few rural communities benefitted from the little resources that remained. People complained about the unfulfilled promise, so Runo quickly appointed a commission of enquiry and reallocated Heli to another ministry. The report was completed very quickly and Heli panicked. She approached the head of the commission of enquiry, Dan, who used to belong to the Collar Man's party but had kept this a secret to get favours from Runo. She threatened to expose his political past and to harm him if he made public the results of the enquiry. Dan abandoned the project, and Runo was overexcited by the absence of the report.

Kumbi, a former ally of Powerman, drained all the grain stocks, acting on Runo's instructions. He sold three years' worth of grain reserves. Nothing was left to feed the nation, creating a crisis. Runo turned a blind eye to the scandal. One singer made a song on the scandal, and Kumbi sent some touts to discipline the singer. Other corrupt deals wiped out all fuel stocks, resulting in queues forming around the country's fuel stations. The queues were an average of over a mile. No one was arrested. The public made very sensible comparisons with many countries in conflict or without a government but still capable of managing their fuel situations. Calls were made to liberalise the sector, but Runo was adamant that the situation was under control.

It turned out that the reason the fuel was more expensive than other neighbouring nations was due to the national fuel company procuring the commodity from Runo's company. If the sector was liberalised Runo was going to be the biggest loser. In this instance, Runo's company was under scrutiny from the former coloniser's new leader, Poodle, and his associates, making sure that it received no supplies. In other instances, they would buy out any supplies destined for the nation through Runo's company. The misfortunes of Runo's company became a burden to the nation, but he never cared. In other instances, many companies were registered for the sole purpose of procuring fuel. These companies would be allocated foreign currency but deliver nothing. The process would be repeated several times, creating wealth for a few individuals at the expense of the nation. Runo went on to transfer the only oil pipeline for the nation to his friend's company. He had hoped to change it later into his name, but in the interim, he was receiving a dividend when the country used it to transport fuel.

A housing scheme that was helping many civil servants for a few years shut down. This was after a new Minister responsible, Runo's blue-eyed boy, Igi, and Marujata had shared all houses constructed after her marriage to Runo. Chiko, popularly known as the Rhino Man due to his looks, had been reassigned to another portfolio after he refused to offer Marujata favours on the houses. Runo decided to appoint his trusted man in crime, Igi. Marujata's power over Runo was at work. All construction materials and equipment were looted in an instant, forcing the scheme to shut down. In addition, the scheme operated on a revolving basis. Allocating the remaining houses to themselves destroyed the revolving fund basis to keep the scheme going. One old man was pulled out of his job in the ministry and put in charge of collecting rentals for the two. These two did not want any records of the transactions in case the man sold the story to the press. The money collected would be entrusted to Igi, and Marujata would collect her portion from Igi. There was one month when Igi did not pass on Marujata's portion. He had paid services for his several concubines, and instead of owning up, he accused the old man of theft. Marujata ensured the man was imprisoned. The prison system at that time had collapsed, needing serious attention. He failed to cope under the filthy conditions and died a few months after his release. Runo put Igi in charge of the bus company to oversee its revival. This was the last time the bus company's fleet made an impact in the transport sector. His looting frenzy was unprecedented.

A war broke out in one nation in the neighbourhood. One career rebel and traitor, who had become the head of some tiny nation, was being funded by some leading nations to foment the insurrection. He was promised a hefty reward for assisting in dividing up one of the largest countries in Africa into five small countries to facilitate the looting of resources by the world's bully. This traitor was responsible for genocide in his nation, and his friends had worked hard to clean up his image and repackage him as a saviour. All regional heads agreed to rescue their friend. Runo committed several troops and resources. When boots were on the ground, Runo's colleagues all reneged on their promise except one, Sante, whose nation was directly threatened by the war. The colleagues who chickened out had been paid handsomely to look aside while the insurrection was growing.

This was Runo's second step in making and creating a future conducive to his kind, a correct decision. Due to the poor state of the economy, Runo had to drain resources from government coffers and all quasi-government institutions. His participation in the war was roundly condemned by the Western world, and they pulled their financial support to Runo's government. Nobody mentioned or questioned Sante's participation. Neri, a publicly revered leader of a neighbouring nation to Runo, was happy to take the glory as Runo's international ratings faltered. He had pulled the rug from underneath Runo's feet and had fallen prey to the former colonisers' machinations where they always set a brother to destroy his kind. Instead of sending troops, he had stalled the process, and when diplomatic efforts were mounting, he put the decision to a directed parliamentary vote and debate. Neri was branded as an open and democratic leader by the international media.

On attainment of his nation's independence, Neri had declared a policy of unity and inclusivity without equality and land for his people but maintained colonial privileges and superiority for whites alongside native scorn and poverty. To bolster his position of openness, he ushered a reconciliation commission of enquiry in his nation to expose the rot in the system of governance by the former colonial regime. Over 99% of the interviewees in the public hearings were natives, and a handful were from the colonial regime. The majority of the adjudicators on the Commission were white. No political players that instituted and implemented the oppression were called upon to testify. The judges that administered the oppressive system and companies that benefitted from it were never summoned to testify. Neri had rigged the outcome in advance. It was a circus and a shame. Conclusions from the commission were that most crimes were perpetrated by natives on natives. Blaming his kind was part of upholding the belief that the oppressor was smarter and the native brother was always junior, inferior and cursed.

He was assisted in crafting a new constitution, which was the first in the world to recognise unions of perverts. Coincidentally, his country's new flag was named after the rainbow, and the country was also named a Rainbow Nation. The international community praised him for not finding fault in their kith and kin. They further made statues of Neri and put them in public places honouring his legacy. Disappointed natives started divulging information on how Neri had sold out during the struggle for independence. It turned out that he was out of prison for a long time while being purported to be the longest-serving political prisoner. Others even suggested that he was just a double, as the original had long been murdered. They made him divorce his wife because she was too radical and unfit for the white man's agenda. Neri had promised to defend colonial interests if power was transferred to him. So far he had upheld that end of the bargain by continuing to sponsor rebels created by the colonial regime in the region, defending a horrific Bantustan ideology and maintaining cold relations with his neighbours.

Snubbing Runo and other regional leaders was part of that puppeteering deal. For that reason, no single leader in the neighbourhood had even opened an embassy in Neri's country since his ascendancy to power. Runo was, therefore, branded as the Lord of Misrule. It did not end there. Neri was instructed by his master to howl Runo out of any leadership position in the regional groupings. This would stop his influence. Gladly, Neri caused a stir by fighting for leadership in the region to become the new school headmaster and bully on the block.

What started as a noble Rainbow initiative in honour of the celebrated natural phenomenon led to an expropriation, plunder and destruction of the symbolism by associating it with a minority clique of a confused and perverted mentality. Neri's nation became a guinea pig in exporting and marketing the ideals of homosexuals and those bent on conquering the alphabet by creating long acronyms for their groups.

Progress on the ground was, however, swift and within a few months troops were comfortable to draw safe zones and hot zones. It was obvious that a win was on the horizon. At that point, the international community called for a cessation of hostilities, citing the use of superior weapons not suited for the war. They also called for talks. Runo did not take them seriously and maintained his position. Once the rebels had rearmed, re-strategised and were ready to start again, the talks were terminated, and the fighting resumed. It did not help much because Runo's forces had made significant progress, and commercial activities by both the political and military leaders took centre stage. Runo went into a deal with the leader of that nation, which saw the two controlling one of the key minerals. They withheld supply and the price of one mineral rose eighteen times to their advantage.

Further deals were made that saw Runo's generals making huge amounts of money that helped them in building massive mansions. It was rumoured that Runo was in charge of a safe deposit box, a vault, for all the precious minerals and cash for their deals at the presidential level. The vault, however, needed biometric recognition features for both presidents to open it. Any attempt to break in resulted in the destruction of the contents as a safety precaution. As the war dragged on, other plans were put in place as the two gathered wealth to rule the world. To easily access the wealth and transport it safely to Runo's nation, Runo and his friends funded the construction of a highway through a neighbouring country to their destination. Generally, the road was a dual carriageway but had several lanes between certain towns. Runo had never undertaken a project of such a magnitude in his nation. This was a true reflection of his selfishness. Runo's new friend became a casualty of the war and died. This new development meant that the vault would never be opened. An instruction was, therefore, issued to charter the dead body to Runo's house in order to open the vault. Meanwhile, everyone's attention was diverted by discussions to find a suitable replacement and successor. Reports were also rife that he was still battling for his life at a private hospital. Once the vault was opened and a successor named, the leader was declared dead. The vault idea set Runo's mind running wild. He ended up transferring all the nation's gold reserves into this vault as well.

Runo was faced with a myriad of issues to deal with. Everyone assumed that this was the end of the feared leader's rule. He put more emphasis on the constitution to divert attention, but the Constitutional reform group was discrediting it until everyone lost faith in the Constitutional Commission. He also set up a commission of enquiry on the corruption deals to redeem his lost credibility. These were designed to delay as much as possible and help buy him time. His efforts were in vain, as everyone talked about the outcome more than the process. Runo tried some publicity stunts to denigrate the accused perpetrators of corruption. The troubled president famously said he would not shed a tear when any official was convicted. He stage-managed some arrests of the alleged perpetrators. But some technicalities were used to have them remanded out of custody.

Towards election time, all leaders of the Constitutional Reform group officially took up positions in their political Party. Runo was under immense pressure. His Constitutional Commission was also ready with a new constitution. Tadpole took the document to Runo, and they had a secret chat.

"Your Excellency, the document is brilliant but bad for you," he looked shaken, blinking continuously while changing his posture frequently.

"What have you done, Tadpole?" Runo looked straight into Tadpole's eyes to read through any mischief he could have done.

"Your Party representatives suggested some of the most progressive clauses, but they spell doom for you," Tadpole was blinking continuously and was jumpy, and Runo, for a moment, didn't believe him.

"Did the Great Crocodile not look out for my interests?" Runo gestured with his open hands, almost confronting Tadpole.

"I suppose he was happy as he never opposed the clauses that nailed you. He seems content."

"I see. He wants me out then."

"Most probably, Your Excellency." Tadpole attempted to clear himself from the mess.

"Any specific clauses that refer to me in the document?" He put his hand on his chin.

"No, Your Excellency."

"Why, then, do you say he has a bone to chew?"

"Your tenure in office has been limited to two terms, Your Excellency."

"It gives me time because I have ten more years to go. Once Sabi's threat is out of the way, I can change it."

"You don't have that much time."

"What do you mean, Tadpole?"

"The constitution has no start date to accommodate you. Technically, you will be the outgoing president once the constitution is adopted."

"Is it that bad when it's a brilliant document, as you say?" Runo looked pensive yet confused.

"That's exactly what I have been trying to explain. Good for the nation and democracy, but bad for you!"

"Let's deal with him."

"How, Your Excellency?"

"We cannot just accept the constitution without a revised outreach."

"Are you suggesting that we take back the constitution to the people for further review?"

"Why don't you make it a feedback session?"

"We can always be negative about the feedback and tell them that some of their suggestions were not taken up."

"Exactly. Probably we can get a mass uprising to help us set aside the process."

"If it does not work out that way, what do we do?"

"As a democratic nation, don't you think we should put it to a vote?"

"We have elections pending. Don't you think we will be chasing too many birds in the process and ruin our chances of success ?"

"Not if things are going our way, Tadpole. We have to explore every avenue. Our enemies are many. We have the Great Crocodile in the Party, Mudadi, Dumi and then the opposition that's gaining ground by the hour."

"Let's deal with the constitution first, then we can gauge the mood before working on the next hurdle."

"Agreed, Tadpole. Go ahead."

After the feedback sessions, many were left disgruntled, but there was no uprising. Tadpole had tried to undermine the final document as much as he could. He used several documents in the sessions, referring from one document to the next. This way, he could put doubts into people's minds. For contentious items, he would tell the people that the views were not taken up to score a quick victory. In some instances, he would tell them that the views were taken up but were not yet in the main document. Runo and Tadpole met again to review their strategy after the feedback sessions.

"Tadpole, you should give me some suggestions because you are my man on the ground," Runo seemed disappointed. He wanted to put pressure on his point man.

"I was too involved in this document and could not abandon the process. My peers could ruin it for us, Your Excellency. Our project could collapse, and we will all be out of our jobs," Tadpole was running out of ideas to please Runo.

"No, Tadpole. I have to take revenge on the Great Crocodile for standing by and being willing to let me lose power. We are behind time."

"That's exactly what I have been doing, Your Excellency. Let's put it to a vote then."

"Without a doubt, we should do it."

"Can we make him the spokesperson for the project while I work on a lacklustre campaign?"

"Brilliant, Tadpole," Runo nodded and smiled at the guarantee of securing his position.

"How do we safeguard against losing to the Great Crocodile?"

"The opposition hates everything we do. They will do exactly the opposite of everything we want. Besides, this *Mutekwatekwa* they call Sabi wants power like me. He could never accept a document with term limits."

"Why do you call him that, Your Excellency?"

"It's just like what others call *Murinda*, in their clans. In the Sabi clan, that is the name they use because he doesn't belong."

"That should be a campaign bonanza, but don't you think if he opposes and wins, it will boost his confidence?"

"It doesn't matter, Tadpole. We have to choose our battles carefully. Some you win, and some you lose. Just as long as you win the important ones. All the elections Sabi has ever won were because of us twisting the outcome in his favour, and now he assumes he was very popular," Runo pulled a lecture on Tadpole. Lowering his voice, he gestured with his right hand, the left resting on his thigh and he was firmly relaxed against the back of the chair.

"If his advisers and funders tell him otherwise, what shall we do?"

"Tobby is way ahead of everyone on elections. He never fails to deliver," Runo was tapping the chair with his fingers and tapping his right foot, bubbling with confidence that victory was in sight.

"That's a plan, Your Excellency."

The constitutional referendum was held in many places while under heavy floods due to excessive rains. It worked well for Tobby as he delivered a positive result for Runo. The Great Crocodile was devastated, and he had to adjust quickly and concentrate on campaigning for his constituency. He had lost the big prize. Sabi celebrated Runo's win as his own. He was a pathetic excuse of a political leader; he was just an opposition political figure. The general public and the international community were of the view that Runo had been handed his first defeat. They were wrong.

Chapter 14

"We need a miracle to win the parliamentary elections, Your Excellency," Tadpole was visibly shaking and his hands trembling, reflecting a panic mode.

"No, Tadpole. We have bagged the biggest win of them all. The nation has not only lost the most brilliant constitution that was costly to me but one that would have moved the power carpet from right under my feet and propelled the economy to dizzy heights. I have to rejoice, Tadpole. You, too, must count your blessings because if the Great Crocodile had won, you would have gone back into the hands of those who wanted you behind bars," Runo was unmoved, rolling his swivel chair with ease.

"Thank you, Your Excellency, for saving my life." Tadpole posed to gauge Runo's view.

"Don't mention it, Tadpole. Now, we need to tackle the next hurdle. What's the bad news, Tadpole?"

"Sabi has received a lot of funding following the constitutional defeat. They are on cloud nine. They even want to field candidates in all constituencies and can afford to do anything. We could be history," Tadpole looked hopeless and defeated.

"You sound worried. I have another fight to finish at this opportune moment, and yet you have already run out of ideas."

"Are you not worried, Your Excellency? All your white allies are now supporting Sabi."

"You don't say!" Runo pretended to be ignorant of the development, yet his teeth showed with a cunning smile. "While I am scared to death because of the unexpected turn of events, I am also rejoicing. I believe it's difficult to lose to a character who puts on a pink shirt and a yellow tie. Imagine, Tadpole, *hembe yakakangavira nemudzipanyota weruvara gwenhundugwa here*? When he goes casual, he spots a blouse instead of an informal shirt or a T-shirt. However, I have to take a gamble. Fortune favours the brave! I must take revenge against those ungrateful white flies." He further responded with his face punctuated by a sly grin and eyes full of mischief.

"What do you have in mind, Your Excellency?" Tadpole could not see a silver lining in Runo's hints and slightly scratched his nose, preparing to put on a smile.

"You are going to be the Party campaign spokesman since you are not representing any constituency. Diesel shall be your silent partner. You shall invoke a constitutional clause stating that my election is due in two years. Technically, this should pour cold water over Sabi's early celebrations."

"Anything special that you want me to work on with Diesel?" He breathed a sigh of relief.

"I want the Great Crocodile out, Dumi, Mudadi and a few of the old guard to lose. Call Diesel and leave us for a moment."

Diesel was ushered into the room.

"Diesel, You know my heart chose you, but too many people are senior to you in the Party. You and I want those seniors to you out at this opportune time so that you can easily claim the throne. You are my only senior tribesman in the Party. Tell me, how can we achieve that?" Runo had his hands on his legs, occasionally shuffling his feet, looking deeply at Diesel. Then he moved his hands and held them together, resting them around his tummy, appealing to his emotions.

"I am also fighting for my survival because the opposition is breathing hot in my backyard," Diesel put on a dry smile devoid of any suggestion or hope.

"Diesel, you worry too much. Be man enough. Have balls of iron," Diesel closed his eyes and covered his face. Later he moved them lower and bit his right thumb, looking on the floor digesting Runo's suggestion before responding.

"Your Excellency, if we do not concentrate on the opposition, we could lose everything."

"Listen to me, Diesel. You shall do as I tell you. Get Tobby in here."

Tobby was ushered into the room.

"Tobby, how can you help Diesel win the election?"

"That's easy, Your Excellency. I will give him all the postal votes."

"Now that your problem is solved, how can you help to ensure Mudadi, Dumi and the Great Crocodile are out?" Runo asked Diesel.

"Your Excellency, there are too many influential Party members awaiting trial or suspended from the Party, yet you want to reduce the number of potential seats. In that case, can Tobby ensure he takes away some of their votes?"

"You are not sharp enough, Diesel. I want your contribution."

"Aaah, Your Excellency, those guys scare me. If they find out, they might kill me," he squeezed his temples, breathing heavily, and his heart beat faster. He later held his head in his left hand, almost shedding a tear.

"Are you with me or with them, Diesel?"

"I am with you, boss," Diesel responded timidly.

"Tobby, help this poor fellow," Runo threw his hand towards Diesel, looking away from him with frustration.

"It would be best if he works with the opposing candidates. Give them additional funds and campaign material. Assure them that they will have our protection for any tactic they use. Offer them inside intelligence to win. I will also do my part come voting time."

"Excellent, Tobby. Now Diesel, go out and get to work. I

want results," Runo commanded.

"Boss, we are under siege. We cannot afford this luxury," Diesel pleaded with a low and begging voice.

"You are weak-kneed, Diesel. Just do it. There is no room for cold feet," Runo said in a high-pitched voice, his face contorted and almost running short of breath. He was seething with anger and banged the desk with his fist.

"Alright, boss. I am at your service. I will do it. Wait for the positive feedback." Diesel threw his usual dry smiled and left.

"This chap is too slow, dull and downright stupid, yet my tribal heart rests with him. I know he will preserve my legacy. He will crawl to my grave for thanksgiving, wisdom and guidance. I know I can do all I want without him questioning me. Even from the grave is a possibility," Runo said in a soliloquy.

From the sidelines, Tunga had already launched his campaign to replace Simo in their home constituency. Runo could predict a Tunga and Great Crocodile pact ready to jettison him from power. It was not a welcome threat, and Runo quickly persuaded Simo to stay. He told him that Sabi was going to incarcerate everyone under instructions from the former coloniser. Retirement was, therefore, not an option at this juncture. That is how Tunga's political ambitions were completely derailed. Sloppy Man pulled out of active politics. His chances of winning were slim following the betrayal of the people from his home constituency.

Veterans of the war against Douglas felt that they were the biggest losers when the constitution was rejected. Their promised farmland entitlement was gone, and they could not afford to sit and wait. Twenty years after the war had been too long a wait. It was now time to take matters into their hands. They organised and embarked on a farm invasion process. Their leader, Clever Militia Man, who kept his head clean-shaven all the time, was very militant, had eyes popped wide open, had an angry look and never smiled. He had a very able deputy who always sported a straw hat. Digging Man was his non de guerre. He was a Security Officer but had to abandon his job to join the farm invasions. Runo had other issues to attend to; therefore, he did not have time to support them or chase them away. He let them fulfil their appetite for land. Besides, all regional leaders had agreed to take back land and were waiting for an opportune moment to pounce. Runo advised them that the time was ripe and action was necessary. Neri derailed the process on advice from his handlers.

After his conversations with Tadpole and Diesel, Runo did not waste time. He called Mudadi, Dumi and the Great Crocodile. It was a late night meeting at the Presidential Palace.

"Gentlemen, this is a high-powered meeting. There is no authority in this country greater than this gathering, which by the way is not taking place. The enemy is standing strong against us. We are in great danger, and the nation is likely to go to the enemy. We must fight back and not let the pen take away our privilege. I am open to any means fair or foul we can use to win this plebiscite," Runo sounded serious and concerned while using hand gestures to emphasise his point.

"Don't restrain the people from invading farms on account of the disappointment from the constitutional loss which guaranteed them land. Support the veterans in their process and take the glory. Let the general public join in and overwhelm the farmers. Offer the farmers no protection. *Ita nakirezvo mbudzi yatunga bere!* This will be a brilliant step in creating a bright future and awakening the consciousness of your kind. Remember, we are still waiting for a response from our regional colleagues. This should force them to act. Besides, you will be showing our former coloniser your true colours after they threw you under the bus with that letter abdicating their responsibility," the Great Crocodile easily offered a solution.

"Great Crocodile, you always come in handy. We can cripple Sabi's financial power base in an instant. It's done. This is a crisis, and we shall not debate about it. If we win this one, each one of you could end up with 100 farms. That is more than any enemy has ever owned." Runo took his third step in the right direction, firmly gaining control of the future of his people.

"We still need to work on our constituencies, Mr President. You need to use other resources for any other business," Dumi suggested.

"You are my senior members. If we die, we die together. If we survive, let's survive as a Party, as a family, together. I need more of your help for the good of the nation."

"Is it possible that we can sleep over the issue and think of alternatives?" Mudadi asked, knowing very well that he would lose many friends as he had received his education from the colonial master's country.

"Time is of the essence *saka kuramba nyama yechidembo hunge une yeshuro*. We must implement the outcome of today's meeting until we have an alternative position," Runo responded.

Within a few days, peasants were out on the farms, fighting to get land and assisting the veterans. Runo never answered the call for order by the former coloniser. Daily, farm owners were being driven out without any sympathy from the government. Sabi's financiers were being tossed out daily, and their financial base was eroded. They, therefore, cried foul, saying that there was a dearth of the rule of law and there was anarchy in the Nation. The former colonial power supported them and took their word, typically demonstrating that a black man was not a credible witness. They had always wanted to maintain the colonial rule of law to protect their interest, not those of the natives. Runo received international condemnation and, therefore, decided to legalise the farm occupations. Peasants from another regional country joined in the farm invasions. Their leader was paid handsomely and chased them from the farms like rats. Neri, whose country had one of the worst land ownership patterns in favour of colonial orphans, stabbed Runo in the back once again and went against land expropriation. He received huge sums of money and accolades from former colonial powers.

The peasants got token allocations along farm forests and not the arable land that the white farmers were utilising. Runo reserved the prime arable land for his friends and, in other instances, had hoped that the invasions would stop so that he could give back the land to the whites. A law was quickly drafted to designate farmland where the government had interests. He hoped that the whites would capitulate and join him. He accused the farm owners of being cry babies who had been illegally holding on to land at the expense of the majority. Land that had been stolen from the local people at colonisation for no compensation. Some sought legal recourse because they had title to the land. Runo justified land invasion, likening it to someone who had finally found their lost property. Even if that property had been sold and resold, the sales remained illegal. He invoked painful historical memories that resonated with the people. Most people who felt aggrieved by land expropriation by the colonial powers joined the Runo bandwagon. The tables had been turned, and there was hope for Runo to salvage something from the elections. This became his strongest selling point to justify his stay in power. Marujata took advantage and occupied several farms, a plantation and a game park. Officially, the first family grabbed twenty-one farms, and no one was able to ascertain the unofficial number. The country was put under sanctions by the world's leading nations. These nations always showed cowardice, instead of attacking any nation while at full strength, they opted to suffocate it with economic embargoes and sanctions, financial terrorism and piracy. Bank accounts of a targeted country would be frozen and money confiscated. All significant international transactions would be followed up and confiscated. The vulnerable would not have access to healthcare through withholding and blocking social funding to incite a revolt or uprising. After a decade of suffering and decline, they would then attack. Sanctions on Runo's nation followed the advice of their adviser who had been asked by members of his senate to make recommendations.

He then advised them to consider economic sanctions to destroy.

Other leading nations also followed suit, which worsened the economic woes. Poodle went on to enact legislation that restricted Runo's travel to his country and the continent. He started negotiating with some neighbouring countries to station his troops in preparation to attack Runo's nation. The same legislation was replicated by other nations.

Runo fired back in anger at his next rally. He had no kind words for his arch-enemy and his country.

It was an elusive template of democracy and human rights, and many failed to comprehend its level of abuse.

Back home, the unfortunate to suffer under the restrictive travel ban were the authentic Runobvepi family members, as they were assumed to be members of Runo's family. Meanwhile, most of Runo's family members remained unaffected as they carried different surnames.

Sabi was happy, elated and gratified by the imposition of sanctions. He knew that once the people had lost jobs and were starving, they would turn their anger on Runo and vote with their stomachs. The sanctions bill was an obscene document invoking democracy to destroy democracy. The terms of the sanctions bill were diabolical, a promotion and an incubation of lunacy. It was simply a profound lack of human decency by both Sabi and those who imposed the sanctions. Provisions of the sanctions bill advocated for the return of land to white owners who were termed the rightful owners. Global powers were accorded the right to change the rulers of the nation. All international companies were restricted from trading with the nation, which in turn meant most businesses were going to close and destroy the nation's economy. No lender was permitted to extend financing to Runo's nation or even consider offering debt relief.

When Sabi was confronted on the issue, he denied the

existence of any sanctions and called them restrictive measures instead. These were only meant to punish Runo and nobody else. Sadly, his supporters believed him. Sabi became a true lapdog of the great powers. When evidence of the sanctions book was presented to him, he said that Runo called for the sanctions due to his bad behaviour. A mad dog, a disgraceful puppet and a stooge, desperate for power, were slowly forming in Sabi. He had lost his morality for political expediency. With guaranteed backing from the world powers, he knew he could say anything about Runo, the Revolutionary Party and the Nation, without any serious consequences. Sabi had turned himself into a wheelchair-bound paraplegic ready to be pushed around, shoved around, force-fed anything and submit to be modelled into any character form as leaders of other nations wanted of him. People assumed he was brave, not realising that he was using borrowed robes. He turned his Party from a Movement of Democrats to a Band of Stooges. Sabi went on to encourage military intervention to assist him and his political party in removing Runo from power. He opted for an Open-War-Torn-Democracy to replace a Peaceful Democracy but was perceived as a Dictatorship.

Farmers who lost farmland mounted legal challenges through the highest court in the land, claiming that the farm occupations and land designation under the newly enacted laws were illegal. The court was inundated with innumerable farm litigations, resulting in the judges working around the clock to clear the cases. In the end, a blanket ruling was passed, declaring the move on farms illegal. Runo was dealt a huge blow but refused to take it lying down. He chastised the judges, accusing them of serving the interests of their white kith and kin, and therefore, he ignored their judgment and declared it null and void. He could not let beneficiaries of land robbery get the last laugh.

Runo had started another war and was working on finding ways of changing the composition of the judicial bench. It became clear that once the terms of office for the white judges had come to an end, no renewal would be considered. Besides the term of office, Runo was working on the individual judges closely, monitoring them for any errors that could warrant sacking them. Frustrating them also became part of the game to achieve quick resignations. Ziva enjoyed the moment, reminding Runo of his advice nearly twenty years back. Runo would have none of it and shut Ziva from accessing the media, labelling him as a failed politician who had nothing to offer.

Sabi and his Party had every reason to tell their financiers and the Western world about the dearth of the rule of law and the wanton disregard for property rights in the nation. It was, therefore, imperative that more funding was made available to enable them to unseat an illegal regime bent on trampling people's rights. Runo, however, was never short of made-for-the-purpose responses. He asked anyone, including the international media, who wanted to pin him down as a dictator who disregarded the law, where the law was when his people were being enslaved, colonised and dispossessed of their land. That question was repeated over and over again until he had asserted his position that the onslaught on his leadership was nothing more than a racial question. It was reduced to just a fight between black and white, with whites getting undeserved sympathy when they had ignited the whole issue given their colonial past.

Poodle, the leader of the former colonial power, was concerned about his kind losing their assets, access to resources, loss of economic power in Runo's nation and, most importantly, the loss of influence by Poodle's government. Runo went on to invoke the painful liberation war era memories telling the opposition and Poodle that the elections that they were so fond of and financing the opposition to win were a product of Runo and his rebels. Besides, Poodle had never been in good books with Runo since he came to power. He had never appreciated a black man calling for equal treatment and being on the same footing as their white counterparts. Runo, therefore, made sure that it was out in the open that the right to vote was achieved after a lot of blood had been shed and after thousands of lives had perished. It became apparent that Runo and his Party were, therefore, the only ones qualified to talk about democracy, human rights and elections in the nation. If Poodle and Sabi had anything to contribute on the matter, it would have been appropriate for them to consult first.

When the farmers took their cases to a regional court, Runo did not hesitate to revoke the principle of reconciliation that he had extended to the white community at Independence. Any further attack on Runo pushed him to inflict more damage on the rights and privileges of the whites. In line with Runo's pronouncements, it became apparent that whites had no legal claim on land in the nation, and the best they could get was a negotiated settlement. The more they alienated themselves from Runo, the more they lost their cause. Runo was prepared to suspend even the constitution to buttress his stance. He, however, wished he had accepted Great Crocodile's constitution with entrenched land rights for the indigenous people. At one rally, Runo was visibly angry on the issue of land redistribution and promised to take a tougher stance in pushing all white farmers out of the farms.

✱

Poodle worked with a leader of a neighbouring country, formerly led by Kenny, to accept some of the farmers. In return, the country got debt relief and a lot of financing to spite Runo and show the people in his nation that the West was very amenable to good leaders. One aspiring legislator from Sabi's Party warned this country about the downside of a bad decision they had taken instead of supporting Runo. Sabi censured him.

All accused officials were released on Runo's instructions and started campaigning for the elections. Corruption allegations were buried in an instant. Runo identified one heavily bearded energetic man to assist in the election campaign. It worked wonders. Mandebvu For Hire greatly pleased Runo. He travelled across his constituency and was later made available for the nation. Anyone who wanted assistance invited Mandebvu For Hire. Many people who had turned away from Runo, however, were not convinced. All they wanted was hope for the economy, not some cheap campaign rhetoric. Mandebvu was, however, generous with the truth. He told Runo point blank that he had to work extra hard because the people were no longer interested. All they wanted was a change. A shadowy organisation called *Chipatapata* was then formed to terrorise people, replacing the tired concept of using the youths. It operated from the capital and would be sent on missions throughout the country. Mandebvu banned all opposition press from his territory and all neighbouring constituencies. All visitors had to be vetted, and the opposition was banned from campaigning. He became a star attraction on the evening main news bulletin. His dancing antics, a pot belly, a hoarse and thundering voice, and an intimidating oratory speech.

Sometimes he would bring a hired crowd to his rallies, burning their opposition regalia, confessing and rejoining the revolutionary Party. In some instances, a rented crowd would surrender opposition affiliation cards for burning. The worst case was when he brought a group of men with their hands tied. It was alleged that they were caught after having been sent to his farm for sabotage by the opposition. On that day, he had a computer claiming to be recording the details of all people. He claimed to have acquired high-tech software that would help him know which political Party a person would have voted for. Mandebvu's tricks never seemed to end.

A spike in numbers for non-governmental organisations

was recorded. Local lawyers and political activists got sponsorship from Poodle's country and those allied to him. Representatives of these organisations appeared regularly on international news stations talking about lawlessness, state-sponsored terror and lack of property rights, among other allegations against the nation. To ensure funds kept flowing in, they had to be creative in their work and association with Sabi's Party. Several terror videos were released to the international media. Many of the financially savvy made their money with these organisations. Financial statements were engineered as most of the money was spent on travel, subsistence and four-wheel-drive vehicles. Nothing was spent on the supposedly suffering masses. Their daily bread was to create a negative image of the nation and groom people to hate their nation, become pessimists and non-productive while waiting for a saviour from outside the nation to uplift them from tyranny and poverty.

Despite the odds against him, Runo did not stop his hatred towards some of his colleagues. At the Presidential Palace, he invited Diesel and Tobby for an update one day.

"What is the progress, Diesel, my boy?"

"It has been very insightful, Boss. I am enjoying every bit of it," Diesel smiled and squeezed his hands.

"Good, Diesel. Now give me an update. Am I going to succeed or not?" Runo wanted positive feedback.

"Mudadi realised that he was going to lose and sent some hired thugs to kill his opponent. Luckily he survived but is still hospitalised. Mudadi might just turn the tables because of this development."

"How about the Great Crocodile and Dumi?"

"They are greatly intimidated by the Great Crocodile, and he might just scramble a victory. Dumi has no idea what is going on. We are the best of friends and his loss is guaranteed. If Tobby comes to the Party, then his ego will be battered and bruised."

"Thank you, Diesel. Go and get Mandebvu's services to

cap your final campaign with a bang. He will give you the much-needed morale."

"You are welcome, Boss." He continued smiling.

Tobby, who had been listening to the conversation, remained with Runo, and Runo asked him.

"Tobby, how can we ensure that there is no trace that this chicken is fire-grilled?"

"You may need to accept a lower haircut, Your Excellency. The Great Crocodile's situation does not bode well for you."

"How much of a loss would that be?"

"You may have to take home less than 60%. In this instance, we just hop over the line and justify the narrow win to opposition funding and enemy machinations," Tobby looked concerned. Runo's request had reached the breaking point of his capabilities.

"Break it down to me, Tobby, how this will work," Runo rested against the back of his chair with his hand on his cheek.

"We create a pattern, Your Excellency, which is unquestionable and will ensure that you bag the heads of your enemies."

"Go on, Tobby," Runo was relieved.

"Like constituencies, we lose; like constituencies, we win, with just a few exceptions. Mudadi is in an odd setup, and we may need to leave him with his victory to avoid losing this one completely."

"Wonderful, Tobby. I see Sabi decided to be overzealous and throw his hat into the ring in his home constituency. Do we have an answer for him as yet?"

"He is an endangered species, Your Excellency."

"Make his loss big, Tobby."

"It is settled, and I may not even need to pull a fast one on him."

"Good. Now go and craft the numbers so that we can review the losses before election day."

While Runo had nightmares over the opposition's gains

and the prospect of never getting the international support he had always received, he was content about how he could potentially consolidate his power base at home. His friends had deserted him and joined hands with Sabi. Even the leader of the former colonisers, the Poodle, would publicly state that Runo had lost the mandate of the people and should give way to a new leadership. For the first time in his political career, Runo faced unprecedented pressure both at home and abroad. The Poodle went on to suggest credible electoral reforms and allow an independent electoral body. Runo would have none of it, but it became evident that his age was not coping with the crisis he was facing.

At every public gathering, campaign rally or televised interview, he never missed the opportunity to call Sabi a lover of white racists and a puppet of the former colonisers and slave masters. He would warn everyone against selling out the nation and reverse the gains of independence. Runo was particularly passionate about how he was determined to drive out every racist white man from the country to consolidate the gains of independence. Every time he mentioned the name Sabi, it became clear he was shaking with fear and anger. All he wanted was time to get his revenge, but this time it seemed an impossible task. He engaged church leaders from all the churches he had promoted since independence. These were sponsored to attend all rallies, funerals and other public functions to boost morale and sway public opinion.

Poodle made a deliberate publicity stunt on the conflict between Runo and Bellyman soon after the nation's independence. He used it to Runo's disadvantage, passing all the blame and accusing him of gross human rights violations. Poodle ensured that he omitted any facts or realities that could implicate the Bellyman. He made it seem as if the Bellyman, his party members and the rebels were standing by, watching helplessly as Runo's army was weeding the garden. Poodle wanted the people from Bellyman's region and all those with access to the nation's news station to vote against Runo. It became clear which nation had been the greatest benefactor of the conflict between Runo and the Bellyman. The issue was instantly converted into a major selling point for Sabi as well. A new daily newspaper serialised Bellyman's memoirs, adding to Runo's misery.

Violence escalated. Youths rampaged and harassed the elderly at every turn. Two new names became associated with the election period and the violence attached to it. Either Sabi's Hooligans or Unknown Assailants would be mentioned in any violent incident. It was easy to tell who the Unknown Assailants were and why they could not be mentioned by the state media. The international media concentrated more on the violence around farms. Some of the footage they produced were typical movie-style videos. It was difficult to comprehend how any sane individual could perpetrate violence to the extent of doing it in front of the international press. It was very clear that the Poodle wanted Runo out of power at any cost. Besides, he also wanted to ensure that Runo's human rights record was tarnished beyond repair.

Sabi, on his side, tried hard to tarnish Runo's electoral image as someone who had never won any election but was relying on his rigging machinery. He, therefore, encouraged anyone seeking change to vote in huge numbers to overwhelm Runo's rigging mechanism. Sabi also claimed to have studied the rigging process and convinced the public that they should not be apathetic to the elections. In his quest to undermine Runo's rule, Sabi used his newly acquired financial muscle to sabotage water reticulation and electricity supply. He would hire employees to close gate valves in bushy areas and break water pipes in such areas too. This made it difficult for local authorities to account for water shortages or water cuts, but the public blamed Runo for creating a health hazard. Power cuts in high-density areas became a daily phenomenon, making voters more than prepared to see Runo's back.

The power cuts meant fewer funds coming into the treasury and, therefore, an incapacity to continue providing the service. Fortunately for Sabi, his brother-in-law worked in the electricity distribution control centre for the national power company. This made it easier to implement the power cuts religiously.

A few days before the elections, Runo devoted time to campaigning for his Party in a televised speech. All electronic media was owned by the government. Runo, therefore, made sure that for two and a half hours, everyone was subjected to his torturous speech. He devoted a good half hour talking about the Poodle, denigrating every aspect of his life and zeal to impose his will on Runo's nation. Anyone without the full history of the impending election would have assumed that the Poodle was an opposing candidate due to the excessive reference he got in the speech.

On announcing the results, Runo made sure his enemies' results were the first to be announced to make a great impact. Some of the results were announced before the counting had even been finalised. A few results from the capital city were announced to set a trend, and then Tobby jumped to Dumi and announced a crushing defeat. The Great Crocodile had a marginal loss. Diesel managed to win by a very slim margin of three votes. He survived by a whisker.

People were particularly interested in Mandebvu and Sabi's constituencies. Mandebvu had thoroughly intimidated his people, giving him an easy victory. Sabi lost completely, as his constituency was in Tobby's odd pattern. Besides, Runo wanted to send a strong message that Sabi was just a *Zizi risina nyanga* (an owl with no horns). Sabi's blossoming political career became doubtful. This is what Runo had always wanted. Some of the results were announced before the tallying had been done. In one example, the results were announced while a delivery truck was still on its way to the vote-counting centre. Everyone got lost in the excitement that the opposition had a good show. The headlines after the announcement of election results were, "The bigger they come the harder they fall."

Dumi was disappointed and, in his anger, announced that he was prepared to step aside. This gave Runo a good platform to announce his new executive. Runo's exuberance could not be contained. He would say in a soliloquy, "The Great Crocodile will never bother me ever, ever again. I will offer him a small consolation but an embarrassing one. This victory has been worthwhile as I have finally crushed him below the belt. He will never get out of this political dungeon. Mudadi had to resort to dirty tactics, but I will feast on him too."

Sabi cried foul, alleging that Runo had rigged the results and even contested them in court. His supporters' gullibility was disgusting as they believed him hook line and sinker in the same manner they had believed he was capable of stopping the rigging machinery.

Chapter 15

Runo was quick to announce his new executive to spite the Poodle's calls to include Sabi's people and work towards a common goal. He did the exact opposite to renew his public political sparring with the Poodle. It was his infamous reputation not to take any public advice positively. He was known to do the opposite diametrically. In his vengeful style, he was quick to tell the Poodle that he accepted no order from an obscure figure from a former empire that he roundly defeated but could not let go of its imperialistic tendencies. He called the Poodle just but a little man and a gay gangster. This was especially after the Poodle had used his gay activists to harangue Runo on every international trip.

One of the notable executive appointments was the inclusion of the Great Crocodile. He was assigned to some newly created rural-based ministry. He would have said, "I got you now," in public but it was going to ruin his gentleman's reputation. Some ministries were split into three, others in two. In the end, the executive was extremely bloated and costly for an ailing economy. Runo did not consider any calls to take corrective action. He did not want any of his Party members joining Sabi, hence the numerous appointments of executives and their deputies. He wanted to keep his team satisfied to avoid being enticed where, in the end, they would dish out Party secrets. Instead, the large cabinet was attributed to the fact that it was a war executive to counter the Poodle and his efforts to recolonise the nation. Tadpole was made the Party and government spin doctor, to everyone's surprise. People assumed that he had failed in both the constitutional and election campaign roles and, therefore, deserved the boot. Everyone was wrong. Some had published caricatures of Tadpole crying hard, filling up a stream in anticipation of an obvious demotion. They completely failed to read the situation and the political relationship between him and Runo. After the appointment, the cartoons changed. A famous one on Tadpole had him hopping from smaller chairs to higher and more prestigious ones and eventually eyeing the praesidium.

It turned out that four legislators who had won the elections from Runo's Party had sodom roots. One was even caught in the act soon after and had to apologise, then quit his position in shame. Many people were left wondering if Runo himself belonged to this club. If he did not, then how did he associate with members of such a club when the public already knew about the status of these individuals?

The Pidogori man released *Mamvemve* summarising the decay and ruin in the economy of the nation. He also released a special song for Tadpole in *Mkoma Tadpole*, pointing out how this man, full of hot air, was destroying everything good. The Dancing singer released *Yingwe Bani*, describing how Runo was an untrustworthy spotted leopard and likely to die soon due to old age. Both singers had to skip the borders into exile, fearing reprisals from Runo. They realised that with Tadpole's ill-mannered approach, he could pronounce any irrational breach of a yet-to-be-enacted law, and the two could rot in jail. Another once obscure artist, the Coughing singer, who had suddenly struck rich pickings and attained worldwide fame, also joined the bandwagon. He released *Ngoromera*, a song denouncing the use of a raised fist in any setting, which coincidentally was Runo's Party symbol. He was not well read and, therefore, was not aware of the meaning of this solidarity, unity, strength, resistance and black power symbol. Instead, he assumed it represented violence. This Coughing singer had been under a lot of pressure from Sabi's fans to publicly declare his political allegiance. He was too much of a spineless jellyfish to do so. Besides, he did not want to ruin his newfound fame, preferring to get favours from both sides. The majority could not infer the implication and meaning of the song. Though well crafted, the song did not become a hit. Runo was not bothered by the criticism. He was back in the driving seat; therefore, he would always play the Pidigori man's *Chidza chepo*, singing along with his finger up and dancing to the tune. His favourite part from Chidza Chepo by Thomas Mapfumo was:

Vakomana ini handiende (I shall not leave) hiya hoo
Honde Honde
Makandiwana ndiripo(I am here to stay) hiya hoo
Muchandisiya ndiripo(I shall still be around when you are gone)
hiya honde
Honde honde,
Hiye hiye hiya hoo
Honde honde vakomana ndarambawo(I refuse to go)
Honde honde vakomana,
Hiye hiye hiya hoo
Itaiwo zvamunoda hiya hoo,
Yowerere hiya hoo
Honde honde, hoiye hoo vakomana
Makandiwana ndiripo hiya hoo
Honde honde vakomana ndarambawo heiye hiye
Vakamona hundibvume hiya hoo
Honde honde vakomana ndarambawo heiye hiye

At times, he would add the names Great Crocodile and Sabi after the phrase, *Itaiwo zvamunoda (Try whatever method)* – *Croc naSabi.* Even in the shower, he would belt out the tune. The song gave him great comfort and assurance as he truly believed himself to be a *Chidza chepo.*

Chidza chepo aptly described Runo's life tenure presidential wish and the fact that he was not in a hurry, nor was he ever going to leave office. Anyone could try and remove him, but all attempts were going to fail because Runo was a *Chidza chepo.* True to the song's message, Runo had no plans to leave office.

To please Runo and aid in his fight against Poodle, Tadpole hired a rambunctious singer. Play-it-Alone was his name. Rough around the edges, free-spirited and indocile, could not nearly sum up the singer's character. He did a piece that likened Poodle to a pit latrine. It was played over and over on the radio and television. The singer was given endless opportunities to belt his piece at many gatherings. The Poodle was ruffled by the song and, in his infantile temperament, started deporting immigrants from Runo's nation. Runo knew that he had scored a diplomatic sucker punch.

Tadpole helped Runo craft and enact a law preventing any gathering of people without police approval. It did not matter the nature of the gathering; everything had to be cleared by law enforcement agencies. Sabi's Party activities were seriously affected because Runo would receive a schedule of their meetings in advance. He would then decide on which meetings or rallies to disrupt, disprove or sanction. Tadpole further influenced legislation to gag journalists on what information they could or could not publish. The law criminalised any perceived abuse or breach of the law.

The Great Crocodile was interviewed about his loss and subsequent token appointment. "Token appointment? You are completely off the mark," he shocked them, and every reporter laughed at the Great Crocodile's response.

"Why do you say so when your new ministry is pointless and aimless and any common man in the street will confess to the same facts?"

"You are delusional, madam. Look at the Party results again and open your mind," he calmly responded without even looking at any of them and got everyone curious.

"What is so special about your Party results, Great Crocodile, that no one finds fascinating?"

"I am a man of vision, and that makes us different," he continued without directly looking at any of them.

"Is that so, Great Crocodile, when you have been demoted?"

"Of course, my lady. The majority, if not all, of our constituencies are rural based."

"Is that special, Great Crocodile?"

"One thing for sure is that we have a rural power base as a Party, and I, my lady, have been entrusted to interact with and fulfil the needs of those people. I am suddenly the most important person as far as grassroots support mobilisation is concerned. Winning any future election will be based on my performance and relationship with the people. I am, therefore, grateful to the President, His Excellency Runobvepi, for this honour and privilege. It is rather a promotion instead of a demotion."

The scribes could not help but cheer and marvel at the Great Crocodile's wisdom.

Runo, who watched the interview later while at the Presidential Palace, was furious and completely lost his temper. He shouted at his family and security detail around him.

"If I cannot kill him, sideline him or destroy the public confidence in him, what else can I do?" He took a lampshade and crushed it against a wall. He picked up a fish tank and tossed it onto a pillar, and made a mess of the floor.

"Should I send him to a firing squad?" He stared into the eyes of one guard who had shown a willingness to help him out as the others had given him space to vent his anger or kill himself if he so wished.

"No, no, no, I am not a failure," he stomped his feet. "I can have him arrested any day and lock him up in prison. I will personally handle the key or throw it into a river, but on what charges?" He rested against a pillar, showing signs of fatigue and stress. This time he went around the room,

"Should I poison him? Make him disappear? What is he? A superhuman? Why should I always play into his hands? Why? Why? Why?" He shouted as he stood in the middle of the room, holding onto the heart side of his chest. Runo tried a few steps, losing control, staggered, turned round and fell onto a chair with the back of his head hitting the woodwork. Eventually, he collapsed onto the floor and fell silent.

Runo's health team was summoned, but he seemed not to have a pulse. Everyone was afraid of making any decision, whether to pronounce him dead or hold the decision until the Party had met. His deputy, Simo, was called in, but he was as helpful as two sore thumbs. He was overwhelmed by shock and the prospect of facing the Poodle and Sabi. Finally, the Great Crocodile was called in. At that moment, a very weak pulse could be detected, but was not promising. He ordered Simo to act in place of Runo while he airlifted Runo to a foreign hospital.

Some of the horrified staff talked until the incident leaked to the press. Other leading news stations speculated that he was dead or was almost on his deathbed, and Sabi was likely to triumph in an election to be held thereafter. Those opposed to Runo and those advocating for reforms rejoiced. "Finally, the nation was poised to have a great future with the only obstacle and curse to the nation removed by an act of God," the international press pronounced. Two weeks later, Runo recovered and returned to the country. The Great Crocodile had played down all rumours of Runo's death or sickness and had attributed his absence to a diplomatic emergency in the far east. Tadpole was left to handle the press offensively. Runo's return was marked by more rhetoric and political sparring with anyone who wished him dead. Sabi, who had waited with bated breath, had to forget about an imminent ascend to power and wait for a proper election time. Runo did not forget about his hatred for the Great Crocodile. He wanted to limit the scope of his ministry and, therefore, he had to assign him other duties. The ministry remained because he knew he would have lost if he had abolished it. The Great Crocodile realised the power games were on once again.

Marujata and Runo called in one of their bankers, Bullman, for a meeting. She had been shocked by the health scare and needed to shape her future of abundance quickly. Bullman was also head of the biggest bank in the country after the colonial banks had been reduced to minions by the locally licensed banks. The colonial banks that used to hold Runo at ransom were collectively managing close to 10% of the nation's deposits and loans from over 70% they used to command. Runo had achieved his goal of pushing these institutions into the ground.

"Bullman, you have been my trusted banker for a while now, and I think it's time we had a frank conversation."

"Your Excellency, everything is safe. You don't have to panic."

"I don't panic over such matters, Bullman. If I can stand my ground against the Poodle and the whole world as well as Sabi back home, why should I panic?"

"I assumed that maybe you no longer trusted me, Your Excellency."

"Runo, just tell him what we want." Marujata was impatient.

"Don't worry, my roommate. We will get to it."

"Name it, Your Excellency. I am your faithful servant."

"We have a few properties. Real estate, you know. Farms, to be precise, and we need to equip them and start viable projects."

"I can handle that confidentially, Your Excellency. Name the projects you want."

"Something big, Bullman. We need long-term financing, but we cannot shoulder the financial commitment as the First Family."

"That can be arranged, but I need your support," he said with hesitation.

"What are you afraid of, Bullman?" Marujata interjected.

"It's a public company that I lead, and these publicity requirements may compromise my standing and position. How can you help me help you?"

"Stop fretting, Bullman. My men shall talk with the auditors."

"Thank you. Everything shall be done as you please."

"Well done."

Everything they needed was accomplished, and Bullman had the protection he had asked for.

Mandebvu For Hire, who had been appointed to the executive, had also found his way to the Party supreme committee. The man was appointed to be in charge of the Party's educational campaigns, membership and staffing of Party structures. He was tasked to purge all sympathisers of the Great Crocodile. Instead, he started a Party and regional cleansing exercise. Hearts were broken, families lost their source of livelihood, and many were threatened with job losses for simply sharing the same origins as the Great Crocodile. Mandebvu For Hire, unfortunately, had a short stint in the limelight. He died tragically in an accident while on a Party mission. It was a great loss to the Party, and he was mourned like a true hero, but equally, those aggrieved had every reason to rejoice. His replacement was very enthusiastic that he recorded a song invoking the war memories. It became an instant hit that even those from across the political divide involuntarily nodded, danced, sang along and embraced it.

The fortunes of the Party were slowly changing, but the economy did not improve. Many people left the country in search of a semblance of a normal life. In a very short space of time, nearly a million people had emigrated. Hunger was stalking every citizen due to non-production on the farms. Senior officials were holding on to too many farms speculatively without any production taking place. The food import bill ballooned and depleted the scarce foreign currency in circulation.

Runo routinely went for his medical checks abroad, costing the economy a fortune with each trip. All measures to control and contain competing foreign currency use were futile. The informal market picked up at a great speed, accelerating economic collapse. Senior officials used the opportunity to export any available resources and externalise all foreign currency earnings. They exported cotton seeds, sunflower seeds and many other inputs in the manufacture of cooking oil, forcing all oil expressers to suspend operations.

Queues were forming randomly, and one had to join a queue every day at least, be it for fuel, cooking oil, or sugar; the list was endless. Still, no one revolted. New farmers who had been allocated land did extremely well in producing different kinds of crops to fill the void left by their white counterparts. However, these farmers never got to enjoy the fruits of their sweat and realise their dream of feeding the nation. Runo's friends quickly invaded their space as soon as the crops were ready for harvest and chased most of the farmers away.

No one could stop them because they had Runo's backing. Once the crops had been harvested, they would move on to the next target. In other instances, the motivation to invade emanated from the infrastructure on the farms. These friends would take possession of a fully mechanised farm and sell off all equipment. Unfortunately, most of these farmers used their resources and life savings or sold their houses to carry out farming activities. All was lost, and they had no one to turn to, unlike their white counterparts, who still had the backing and support of the powerful nations. The suffering of these new farmers was worse than the treatment given to white farmers. What followed were years of little cropping and poor harvests, but Runo did not care. The only guaranteed way of securing one's land was not to farm or just utilise a small portion for subsistence to avoid arousing the interest of Runo's vultures.

Calls for early elections to remove Runo and appoint a more competent individual were initiated. Runo never listened. He blamed everything on the Poodle and unwarranted sanctions for promoting a regime change agenda. While the explanation was genuine, he had done nothing on his part to improve the governance framework or the economic policy framework. He wanted total control and centralised authority that all institutions had to rely on his call. Devolution and autonomy of decision-making were not welcome because his looting scams were going to be affected.

A war broke out in a country where a former ally of the world's leading nation was going to be forcibly removed from power. The leader had boldly taken a stance to sell oil in an alternative currency instead of that of his former ally. This was considered economic espionage as the move was going to weaken the leading nation's currency. To stop him in his tracks, he was falsely accused of having weapons of mass destruction by his former ally, a world bully. At this stage, his country had gone for over a decade under debilitating economic sanctions to weaken his grip on power. His country's resources were only supposed to be sold in exchange for food and nothing else. No evidence was presented and no resolution to annihilate him could be obtained from the United Nations.

The process and option to remove him were, therefore, undermined owing to just a savage determination to vanquish him. For public and diplomatic support, the leading nation brandished him as a dictator and dangerous man possessing weapons of mass destruction. The headline news was awash with the story and some made-up pictures of his untoward behaviour. His nation was eventually invaded, and he had nowhere to turn because all his friends had been threatened. Leading world news stations had embedded journalists on the battlefront. They gave detailed updates in the press on the events from the battlefront. Sophisticated military equipment was on display to the extent of explaining the sheer capabilities, properties and advantages of each tanker, jet or firearm on the news. Sales of military equipment by the bully skyrocketed, and the financial haemorrhaging effects of the war were inconsequential.

News reports focused on what they termed beautiful sights of operation shock and awe. The night skies were lit by bombs, rockets and bullets, with targets being razed to the ground. It was taboo to talk about casualties or display pictures of victims in a sorry state. This shocked Runo, and it made him assume that the same could happen to him. Therefore, he wanted to sway public opinion. He started televised debates on the morality and legality of the issue. Mudadi was a panellist on the first show. Runo wanted him to rekindle the good old days when he used to be a good foot soldier. He had also hoped that Mudadi was still interested in the games they used to play. His health was failing, and the assumption was that he would not go against Runo. In a shocking turn of events, Mudadi was candid but also emotional when his turn to comment came.

"People of the world must never tolerate dictators. I bemoan the urge for dictatorial tendencies, and I strongly feel such dictators must be weeded out of society by any means necessary. Let me restate, by any method, fair or foul. It is not a matter of morality or legality but the principle against evil people. It does not matter if a dictator is the legal head of a nation, but the fact that he is one must compel the world to topple that person in good conscience. We cannot hide behind legal processes to justify that which is evil, as we see criminals being acquitted by the justice system. The time has come to warn anyone who wants to rule for life by oppressing his people, never mind that he could be winning elections. This war is a wake-up call and a warning to all dictators," Mudadi emotionally responded without looking at the moderator or the camera.

The moderator of the show tried hard to change Mudadi's line of thought. "Mr Mudadi, this was an illegal invasion against all international statutes."

"It's the principle, as I have mentioned, that if you are one and have overstayed your welcome, then one day you will pay for your sins."

"Are you not worried about the dangerous precedent being set akin to the days of slavery or colonisation?"

"Precedent or no precedent, the important message is for dictators to watch their step because they abuse the public trust. That is no different from slavery or colonisation except that dictatorship is disguised behind an electoral process."

The moderator had to avoid him for the rest of the show, fearing for his job and life. Mudadi was never brought back on the show again. The show itself suffered a reputational risk because it was looking for a certain opinion only. Several series had been planned, but due to the Mudadi glitch, the show had to be cut short. For some unknown reason, Mudadi's health continued to deteriorate further.

Chapter 16

There was an earth summit in a neighbouring country, and Runo realised that he had been presented with an opportunity to elaborate his side of the story to the world. He had unquestionable and immune travel as sanctions had seriously curtailed and confined his globetrotting routine. He seized the opportunity and attended the gathering against the odds of the international press offensive. He surprised everyone by attending as the expectation was that, as a culprit on human rights, bad governance and his presiding over a near-dead economy would make him shy away. His attendance in itself proved that he had a good story to tell, solid ground to put up a defence. A defence against an international onslaught on racism, lawlessness, and not respecting property rights. Runo stood tall among other leaders without wavering. He was ready to attack the Poodle. This was the only way to clean up his record. When his turn came to present, he did not disappoint.

Runo got a standing ovation as he walked off the podium. He was a different man by the time he finished his speech. The world accommodated him and understood his side of the story. The Poodle left the hall, knowing that he was not going to get a good exchange with the other leaders. Another presenter also accused the Poodle of undermining and being oppressive to Runo and his nation, buttressing Runo's offensive. A representative of a leading nation tried to overturn Runo's side of the story but was booed by the delegates. Runo had won. He returned to his nation in high spirits, having scored a diplomatic victory. The nation cherished the moment. However, reality soon dawned that despite the diplomatic score, they were still hungry and jobless. It was back to the usual again. Runo never changed his economic policies; he was more concerned about his profile. Each time his international rating was high, he wanted everyone to rejoice with and for him. He forced everyone to feel it and celebrate with him. While Runo had become an international hero, back home, it was a mixed bag. The speeches at international fora were a welcome development because they were directed at a common enemy. However, his policies for his people remained disempowering in stark contrast to the international image he portrayed.

The Poodle, however, did not stop. He could not let Runo win on a silver plate. He, therefore, continued to churn out stories undermining Runo in the media. Farm invasion videos were aired over and over again to tell the world that Runo was not the man he claimed to be. The economic malaise was attributed to bad governance, corruption, farm invasions and the murder of farm owners. Sanctions were justified as self-inflicted and a direct result of Runo's bad actions. It, therefore, became an endless struggle. Poodle went to open an asylum platform for anyone from Runo's nation who needed a place to stay. He had to ensure Runo's human rights record was recorded as the worst in the world. He even influenced Neri, a now-retired leader of a neighbouring country, to chastise Runo. His word, as a world-renowned statesman, was going to help the Poodle's agenda. When Neri complied and rebuked Runo, he got a very candid and unmoderated response, with a personal attack and a call on Neri's followers to rethink about his reputation.

Runo was not done. He needed another forum to fight the Poodle and prove that he was of impeccable repute.

To worsen Runo's woes, Poodle masterminded a censure

of Runo by the Queen's club where wealth was supposed to be common to all. Runo felt the embarrassment of a club where he was just an insignificant cog with no power or benefits. He, therefore, withdrew his membership to stop the Poodle's power and influence over him and his nation.

Poodle further asked his Queen to strip Runo of the honour she had bestowed on him by conferring him a knight of her empire. His Queen acquiesced to his request. Runo felt stabbed by a million knives, but reality dawned on him that he was walking on thin ice. He had come full circle and was forced to embrace the hard truth that he did not need the Queen's Island, its approval and recognition to be a man.

Simo, Runo's deputy since the nation attained independence, died and was buried in a huff. There was no celebration of his life akin to Bellyman and Lady Amai Marunjeya's funerals. He was interred like a dog and nothing compared to a decent burial of a pauper. Tunga had already died, and Runo saw no threat in doing anything untoward. Runo had a public international event to attend. He could not wait to defend his poor record against the onslaught from the Poodle. The people of his nation were not a priority. He planned to compensate by short-changing them once he had scored yet another diplomatic victory. The event was the United Nations General Assembly. When the moment everyone was waiting for finally arrived, he did not disappoint. He appealed for international sympathy with a hard-knocking speech that endeared him and resonated with every oppressed group in the world, and he became a respected international icon.

Runo received a standing ovation, bringing the house down for several minutes and disrupting the proceedings at the General Assembly. His presentations at the assembly became a trademark event from this moment on. People looked forward to his speech every year. On his return home, he ensured that people were bused from across the country to celebrate his victory. Business at the capital's international airport was brought to a halt. It had been swarmed by an unprecedented number of people for Runo's celebration. He was mobbed by the crowd, and he only managed to address them after almost an hour. People were singing, dancing, whistling and drumming. For an entire month, the presentation was screened on primetime television. Everyone in the nation believed that Runo was invincible, untouchable and infallible for him to walk freely after poking the bullies' eyes. They didn't realise he was one of them and had not only done a lot of good work for them but continued to collaborate with them. Sabi was pushed to the back seat, overshadowed by Runo's exploits on the international scene. A comparison began to emerge on the scene in terms of the ideal traits of a statesman who should, at any time, lead the nation. Sabi became a desperate alternative and stood to benefit from a protest vote only if Runo continued with his economic mismanagement.

Professor Reverend Banner died after his release from prison. Runo's Party and the government did not honour him, and neither did any senior official attend his funeral. Asked why they had taken such a hardline stance, one elder told the press that Professor Reverend Banner had done things that disgraced the nation. It became clear and real that Runo and his team meant what they said and said what they meant to those belonging to the Rainbow movement. The funeral became a non-event. On social media, however, people made jokes about Simo having written, complaining bitterly to God. He allegedly was bitter that happiness and peace in heaven had become rare commodities owing to an undesirable element that had been added to their fold. Every man had to be vigilant, fearing an attack from behind, fearing sodomy by Banner. Even in sleep, each man had adopted a standing position, following the footsteps of a sheep due to the terror from Banner. Simo's plea to God was to resurrect Banner and keep him among the living. The joke went on for several months before it eventually faded.

Perturbed by his superfluous verbosity, a neighbouring country named a road after Runo and invited him for the official opening ceremony. Runo had to attend to maintain a clean international image. He did not disappoint with his speech. Even the press was impressed as Runo endeared himself to the local people. His speech was punctuated by long, complex sentences punctuated by commas and semi-colons and broken by hyphens. This had the effect of engaging the listener, taking him or her from the beginning to the middle, where sentences were broken, and then to the end, when the listener – confused and entertained – was supposed to link up the three parts of the sentence to make the meaning.

It was beyond everyone's comprehension, emotion and belief that Runo could deliver such a sweet and heartfelt message of appreciation. Truly, he was the hero they had read about, watched on the news and talked about on the streets and in bars. He wooed them beyond their wildest imaginations. That was his deceptive nature. Tadpole once said that Runo lacked pity and didn't have any human feelings, *akarasha moyo achisiya ndove*.

In reality, Runo cherished the suffering of his people. He, however, was very pretentious in public that his people could not discern truth and fact from his neatly couched, calculated and well-thought-out words and statements of deception.

Stick Man also died, and Runo delayed announcing whether this former rebel leader was going to receive the highest honour. After five days of waiting, the family made their burial arrangements. At that point, on that date of burial, Runo called for an executive meeting to decide on the Stick Man's status. While the burial was taking place, the verdict was delivered that the Stick Man was a traitor and, therefore, not deserving of any recognition by the state. He did not receive a hero status or even a state-assisted funeral. The decision had Runo's hand written all over it: revenge, vindictiveness, insecurity and immaturity.

Chapter 17

A clergyman, a bishop, Bishop Mukanya, was very disheartened by how Runo was running the economy. He detested Runo's overstay in power and, worse still, the Chipatapata group. A week would hardly go by without Bishop Mukanya mentioning something negative about Runo. He was extremely critical of his presidency. Initially, he called for Runo to relinquish power. Even in his church sermons, it became a permanent feature. Newspapers widely covered his criticisms and sometimes insults of Runo. His calls fell on deaf ears. Over time, he became a regular on many foreign television stations. Sometimes he would have his interviews in the company of youths he claimed were members of Chipatapata. The youths, he claimed, had killed, maimed and raped.

Bishop Mukanya, however, never answered one simple question on why he kept the company of murderers instead of having them arrested. He could not even account for how he had managed to locate the murderous youths. His efforts to have Runo forced out of power yielded no results. After a long time of trying to have Runo removed from power by the international community, he had a rethink of his strategy. Bishop Mukanya engaged in prayer for God to terminate Runo's life. He urged all Christians to pray for Runo's death. Bishop Mukanya even recommended that President Runo should be excommunicated from the church at the very least.

Runo mocked him at every gathering for his evil wish. Public opinion was swayed in favour of Runo, but Bishop Mukanya was not deterred.

Runo realised that he needed to retaliate and finish him off with a strong blow. He got good tidings that Bishop Mukanya, despite his vows of celibacy, was living a normal life like any other mortal man. A fake electrical fault was staged at his church and residence. Clever 'electricians' installed a surveillance system to monitor him. Each time Bishop Mukanya got to the press with his usual Runo stories, he got no response. When enough evidence had been gathered on the Bishop's lifestyle, Runo gave the Bishop a chance to redeem himself. The Bishop refused to meet him or even talk. Bishop Mukanya's assertion to Runo's emissaries and the press was that he did not want to be tainted by associating with an evil and sinful man. One day, after Bishop Mukanya had made bad utterances about Runo, his dirty linen was screened on national television. Viewers were warned that the news content for the day was only for adults. Gory details of his affairs and having a nice time with different women became public. The rest of the print and electronic media was also awash with the revelations. Despite the revelations, Bishop Mukanya remained defiant. The press quickly interviewed him soon after the videos and pictures had come to light. One lady was very patient until she got a chance to talk to the Bishop.

"Archbishop, are you going to resign over your scandal?"

"I am not involved, neither have I been involved in a scandal." The Bishop was defensive and hostile.

"Everyone has seen the videos and pictures, Bishop. Why do you say you are not involved in any scandal?"

"That is an invasion of my privacy, and I need to sue whoever planted those cameras."

"Do you confirm those pictures were taken at your parish?"

"That is the reason I need to take the people who did it to court."

"Are you admitting to committing adultery?"

"No."

"How are you going to face your congregation now that they know the kind of shepherd you are?"

"The church is an institution of sinners and, therefore, there is no need to judge anyone."

"Is that an admission that you broke your vows of celibacy?"

"I never said that."

"Archbishop, is this a matter of semantics considering that you were caught with your hand in the cookie jar?"

"This is just a diversion from the president's economic mismanagement, daily murders and corruption."

"Given the turn of events, will you continue calling for the ouster of the president?"

"That is unquestionable. I will not stop because I have to be the voice of the voiceless."

"What do your superiors think of your escapades?"

"This is a personal matter that has nothing to do with the church."

"But you used the church premises, church congregants, and church resources to achieve this scandal?"

"You must learn to separate individual behaviours and the church."

"Yet those individual behaviours collectively make up the church's moral fibre."

"If one breaks a rule, it should not be deemed a church norm."

"Not if it is practised by the leaders."

"I don't have time to waste with you neither do I report to you. Please leave my church."

Runo influenced one of the ladies' husbands to sue Bishop Mukanya to further soil his reputation. Bishop Mukanya surprisingly went to court and never wanted to give an apology to the public, to Runo or pay an out-of-court settlement.

There was too much pressure from the church hierarchy since its image was being tarnished because of one man's ego. Bishop Mukanya was, therefore, forced to resign and relocated to another country. Runo was finally free after recording yet another victory under his belt.

Another general assembly cemented Runo's position in the international arena. He was on a roll, clearing everything in his path.

Again Runo's narcissistic behaviour never allowed him to deprive the people of celebrating his victories. Some people detested his propaganda, but Runo could not help it. No matter how small his achievements were, he forced the national broadcaster to air his most influential and successful presentations repeatedly. Television programmes would be suspended to accommodate his presentations even long after the event. Sometimes the presentations would be advertised with the caption "By public demand". This was all made up to make the people believe that their leader was a darling of the nation. He needed to remind the people that he was the man in charge. His fortunes, however, were not as bright back home as he still presided over a nation synonymous with hunger, chronic unemployment, high inflation and poor economic management and performance. This was, however, the least of Runo's worries. Power was his only love and lover; he was faithful and addicted. Runo's voice resonated more with the oppressed of the world.

Back home, it was more of the same old song, a song everybody would have loved to avoid singing but without a choice. A song that nobody dared change, revamp or discard. That song whose sacredness was as man made as religion. A sacredness nobody dared put to the test. A false sacredness that would be taken as truth and divine over time owing to fear and intimidation. Runo unofficially anointed himself life president and declared the nation a one-man state. He became an obdurate democratic despot due to his guided and violent democracy both in his Party and at national elections. The man had mastered and perfected the art of acquiring legitimacy, illegally and by foul means. It was a test case to centralise power by abolishing key posts in the Party and combining them under one man to avoid dissent. He was not only one of a kind but the only one of his kind.

The Great Crocodile saw an opportunity once again to rise to the top. A vacancy had arisen at the top following Simo's death. It was an opportune time to try once again. He had to but this time with cards very close to his chest. His campaign was very low key and calculative. He ensured that all Party members with voting powers would go for him. The Great Crocodile further went on to influence the outcome of any election of any candidate who could influence his rise to power. The votes for the deputy position were based on provincial affiliation. Out of ten provinces, four representatives were on his side. Three needed to choose representatives. He supported his preferred candidates, and they won, so his tally moved to seven. From the remaining three, he managed to secure two. Once he was voted as the party's next in command, it was going to be easy for him to secure the appointment to replace Simo.

Runo was against the Great Crocodile getting anywhere close to power. When it became clear that the Great Crocodile was the automatic choice, he changed the landscape. This was a man familiar with making the rules as he went and applying them selectively. Runo was a judge who almost always overturned a jury's verdict to suit his own desired outcome. He, therefore, started to purge all provincial leaders with only a month left for the Party congress. Every provincial leader in the Party who was known to be close to the Great Crocodile lost his job. Several charges were laid on these leaders, making them ineligible to vote. Runo hand-picked his preferred candidates to lead the provinces in an interim capacity. While some of the leaders were dismissed, suspensions were common, and others were simply cowed into submission. Jabu, a provincial representative helped by the Great Crocodile to win, was also an aspirant to lead war veterans. He was suspended by Runo on the basis that his war credentials were questionable and in doubt. Runo still realised this was not enough as the tables could turn against him. He, therefore, suspended the process while waiting for an opportune time to strike. The Great Crocodile lost in another subverted non-democratic process. He did not complain and took it like a man. Knowing his fate was sealed, he had to wait for yet another chance, never giving up hope, making sure his ultimate goal was to lead both the Party and the nation, eventually. It was easy to find comfort in the Davidian trials and tribulations at the hands of a heavenly disappointed Saul. In the short term, he knew his chances were not even mathematical but worse than passing through the eye of a needle; still, he was prepared to wait.

Igi, the local government minister, worked with some business maverick, Fine Lips, a close associate of Runo, to annex all prime land in the city. This land was reserved for future developments. Ownership was changed either into Igi's investment vehicle or into the businessman's trust. A huge piece of land earmarked for a school and shopping mall development in a leafy suburb was taken over by Marujata. She immediately fenced it to stop all activities that were taking place. Igi later forcibly acquired farms close to the city's residential areas and turned them into residential housing. Any farm owner who refused was threatened. The general public was influenced to occupy any farm or open space close to the city. Igi assigned touts to collect cash from anyone who was allocated a piece of land on the invaded farms or open spaces. Some of the touts allocated themselves land first and later to the masses. It was a cash cow for Igi, and Runo never cautioned him. The communities they created, in some instances, were under the control and influence of these touts. Immorality was rife, but no one bothered to correct the anomaly. Runo was very pleased and, therefore, he never lifted a finger or called Igi to order. Runo went on to build a mansion on his Party's property in a prime location. He had hoped to change ownership after assuming total control of the Party.

During the same period, a very educated employee in the service of the government was approached by an international university and promised a lot of funding to construct a twinned University. He assumed that it was going to be easy to get land allocated to him if he met Runo and advised him of the development. An unexpected heartbreak was experienced when Runo referred him to Igi to finalise the deal. Igi, in turn, demanded a substantial shareholding, a shakedown and board representation. The deal collapsed.

Chapter 18

The first term of office for the head of the Central Bank ended. He was against Runo's economic policies or lack of them. At that point and being his nature, Runo was overwhelmed by the need to control each institution. Such an opportunity was rare, and he quickly made use of the chance. The term was, therefore, not renewed. He took his time, giving the public the idea that he was vetting all potential candidates and wanted the best for the country. In the end, he simply appointed Bullman, his Banker. After the appointment, Bullman was very ambitious and made sure he tamed inflation and threatened to name and shame corrupt individuals. He became feared and wielded more power than any of Runo's executive members.

Runo, having had a good distraction in Bullman, called in Tadpole to the Presidential Palace one evening for a chat on the Great Crocodile.

"Tadpole, it's not enough that we have clipped the Great Crocodile's wings. He has a penchant to rise from the ashes. How do we avoid the vote he had set his eyes on and snub him on the appointment?" Runo was worried and looked dejected.

"He trusts me, Your Excellency, and thinks we belong. I should be able to hoodwink him, but the key is on who else we have on the table."

"It's an obvious choice since Sloppy Man still bothers me because I owe him a favour."

"He is too sloppy for the appointment and might cause trouble, Your Excellency."

"I don't intend to work with him but only to pacify him!"

"It can work, Your Excellency. Heli is clueless and confused. She is a perfect toy for the project," Tadpole smiled from ear to ear.

"Heli lacks academic discipline, Tadpole. She cannot even write her name. This woman could not even pass her general certificate of education examinations and had to implore us to localise the system to enable her to make it. That worries me, Tadpole, and our detractors would have a party. I think I have used her enough times in my tenure."

"It's not a tragedy as yet, Your Excellency. *Hatisvori chambere parwendo tisati tafamba nayo.* She can earn her certificates by default, and she won't even think of challenging your presidency."

"How will she comprehend the material?" Runo was far from being comforted.

"Remember, we control everything from high school examinations, and we have plenty of universities too," Tadpole implored Runo.

"Tadpole, you are such a darling, but the time factor is not in our favour." Runo nodded with a hidden smile.

"You have nothing to worry about, Your Excellency. It's a Party matter, and the constitution is silent on the period. You may delay the appointment as much as you want and cancel the elective congress."

"Perfect, Tadpole, but how do I justify her appointment?" Runo leaned forward in his chair.

"We can always bring in the emotive gender perspective, and this should earn you some points on your reputation. Women are the majority, and we need their sympathy."

"That is music to my ears, Tadpole. What shall we do if he revolts? How do we defeat him?" Despite the joy in his heart, he put up a sad face.

"Treason will be the charge, Your Excellency."

"If he doesn't take the bait, what do we do?"

"I have to be closer to him now than ever, Your Excellency. He should trust me with his life. Then I can lead him on a wild ride."

"What have you got on your mind, Tadpole?"

"I will facilitate the revolt if he doesn't take the bait. We can arrange everything and trap him. Heads he loses, tails he loses, Your Excellency." Tadpole was exuberant that this was the Great Crocodile's last moments of his political career.

"I hope this is the last time I will have to talk about him. After this, I should be alone at the top without any threats."

"Trust your protege, Your Excellency. I can deliver the greatest victory of your political career."

Turtle Man continued to be elusive, and Runo's patience had been stretched to the limit and wearing very thin. Charges were laid on him and the directors of his company for not complying with regulations. Turtle Man was cornered but found cover in the law. He won his case easily in the courts. The case was thrown out of the courts due to the frivolous nature of the allegations levelled against him. Runo thought of other ways to decisively grab the company, but nothing solid was coming up. Finally, an illicit trail of foreign currency dealings was uncovered. Before persecuting him, a law was hurriedly put in place that would force him to give up the company or face jail time. Once the law was in place, it also happened that an allegation of Marujata being a close friend of Turtle Man surfaced. An intrusive officer of the law wanted presidential recognition and spilt the secret. Runo was very patient. He approached Turtle Man with the two files.

"Turtle Man, you have been a thorn in my flesh for a long time, and we must settle our differences here and now." Runo showed a stern face.

"I like you, Mr President, and could not do anything to hurt you." Turtle Man looked helpless.

"Yet you refuse to share ownership."

"That was a deal, and I expect to receive something from you to close the chapter."

"Must we always be dealing with your childish games instead of making progress, Turtle Man?"

"I don't understand, Mr President."

"You leave me no choice, Turtle Man. It's all or nothing."

"How is that possible, Mr President?" Turtle Man was sweating after noting a very different negotiating atmosphere.

"Look at this, Turtle Man, and tell me what I should do. Illicit financial transactions carry a heavy sentence under this new law. You also have this personal matter, which is not even negotiable. You disrespected your president and defiled his bed."

"I beg for your mercy, Mr President. Please be merciful."

"Forms will be availed for you to sign away your rights, Turtle Man. We shall not negotiate any further."

Turtle Man fainted under pressure, and Runo left him alone unattended. When Turtle Man regained consciousness, he never waited for anything or anyone but went straight to the airport and flew out of the country. The press was filled with news of his fugitive status, and people speculated on the affair but never on the big prize. Marujata wanted pressure off her back and accused the intrusive law enforcement officer at the centre of her storm with Turtle Man. She accused him of soliciting payment in kind and groping her behind. The law enforcement officer lost his head after being thoroughly tortured, and he departed mother earth unceremoniously. Rumour had it that Marujata was notorious for soliciting friendship in exchange for payment in kind. Those close to her knew they were in danger. If at all she grew an affection towards you and you spurned the advances, then you knew death was assured. If you accepted her proposal, then Runo would have a go at you. It was, therefore, a no-brainer that the law enforcement officer had displayed his principles at the wrong time in his life.

Bullman, who had grabbed the headlines and hogged the limelight, was being touted as Runo's heir apparent. Instead of this being a good diversion for Runo, he was instead unhappy with anyone threatening his position. In his last leg of establishing good relations with international lending institutions, Runo made sure that he failed, although he knew that failure was obvious and a given. The sanctions imposed on the nation went against Bullman's project. It seemed that he was illiterate, as the document was readily available for all to read. The international financiers he wanted to please were never in his corner. Runo also made pronouncements contrary to what Bullman was proposing. The outcome became a familiar ending. Bullman came home with his tail between his legs. There was only one saviour of the nation, and that was Runo. Bullman was not supposed to cause a possible political threat to Runo. Once the failure had been publicised, a bitter Bullman was interviewed and opened his heart and soul, blaming the international lending institutions for banishing the country to poverty. He bemoaned the violation of trust. Bullman had handed over all secret documents and plans to the institutions. He had even raised money to pay instalments that were due by dubious means. Bullman realised that these institutions wanted to see carnage on the markets and a failure of the economy to set an example to anyone who wished to work without their helping hand. Runo went up to him to offer a comforting hand.

"Bullman, my boy, you have done very well to reign in inflation and arrest excessive money supply. I must thank you *Mushaya chiraswa* (every part of you is useful), *vemushenjere* (the one with a penis), *vemuhwezva* (the one with a penis), *vanotunga nenyanga yemberi* (one that uses the penis), *vakatakura masvada* (one that carries balls/testicles)," Runo looked genuinely thankful and sympathetic to his junior by addressing him with the recital of his totem praise poetry.

"Thank you very much for the compliment, Your Excellency.

Well appreciated, *Mutinji wahwera* (dangling labia), *Gunuuswa* (the passage underneath the grass), I shall always do my best."

"There is, however, only one problem you have created. A situation you have created for my colleagues and my support base."

"What problem, Your Excellency?"

"They cannot survive, and we have nothing to give to the supporters. We need something to lure them to the Party. They have to vote for us."

"It's a small problem, Your Excellency. Owing to my efforts, the economy will rebound very quickly, and employment will rise very soon. You will not be able to thank me enough for what I will have done for you and the nation."

"Yet when the time comes, you and I will still be poor. We will be on equal footing with the rest of the nation. Is that good for power, Bullman?"

"The nation will be progressing, and your profile will be strengthened. The IMF and World Bank would beg us to be part of our success story."

"People have very short memories. We need to feed only those that will stick with us and forget the rest."

"We are public servants, Your Excellency. We must create an enabling environment for our people and sacrifice for the good of the nation." Bullman thought a lecture to Runo was the best way to win his heart and mind.

"Power over the people is more crucial than power from the people. Forget about your dreams and vision for the future, and work with me."

"I would have betrayed their trust, Your Excellency." He still didn't get the point.

"I appoint and disappoint. Let's shape the future I want."

"Your wish is my command, Your Excellency. I shall do as you please." Bullman realised his mistake.

"Welcome to the fold."

"For public scrutiny and for governance issues, how can

you help?" Bullman responded while nodding endlessly.

"Everything you do will get my blessing."

"How about the payback?"

"Assume you are now my Prime Minister. You can deal as much as we require and print as much as we need."

"How about inflation, Your Excellency?" Bullman asked timidly, afraid of stepping on Runo's toes.

"Be innovative rather than be a slave of bookish economics."

"It's a one-way street, and there can be no arguments on the consequences."

"How did you raise your last instalment to the IMF?"

"It was an illegal transaction, and I will never repeat that, I promise."

"If you do it again and again, imagine what you can get for you and me without a trace."

"How much are you looking at, and which of your inner circle shall I assist?"

"You don't understand, Bullman."

"What do you mean, Your Excellency?" Bullman was still trying to catch up.

"It's never enough, at least until the people start complaining. Only then will we change course. Remember, no cold feet."

Bullman became the most hated man in the nation after Runo. Investors flocked to the stock market, fearing losing money in fixed interest-bearing instruments. Bullman did not take it kindly because his source of finance had been affected. He, therefore, took a swipe at the stock market whenever there was a bull run, describing it as exuberance. He would approve banking licences for his friends. When deposits reached a certain threshold, he would borrow even up to 20% and leave his friends to do as they pleased with the balance. The bank would then liquidate due to non-performing loans. This would either be voluntary or forced. When bank management denied him an opportunity to take a loan, their bank would be closed overnight and an announcement to withdraw their licence made at a later stage.

At one point, there was a serious shortage of foreign currency, and he directed all banks to surrender their foreign currency accounts to the Central Bank. It was said that he needed to monitor any abuse or unnecessary allocations. The money disappeared, and nobody had the nerve to ask for a reimbursement. In one of the worst cases, a bank employee stole five million dollars and transferred it to a few accounts abroad. The bank executives noticed the anomaly and followed the money trail. They uncovered everything. Before arresting their employee, they approached Bullman to assure him that they did not break any law. They were, however, not sure how Bullman's office had authorised the transfer because externalisation of foreign currency was a serious offence.

When Bullman had listened to their story and the plans to have him arrested once they left his office, he stopped them and made them wait. He went to another office and made a few phone calls. Once safety was guaranteed, he rejoined them and assured them that he would support them in the case. The employee had disappeared from the office when they got back. Police were contacted and every effort was made to trace him. By the end of the day, they discovered that the employee had left the country on a hired private jet. On arrival in a neighbouring country, he made a connecting flight overseas. One of the bank executives was frustrated by the level of corruption and resigned. Bullman never made any comments.

When the case made press headlines, Runo ignored the serious offence. When inflation ran amok and notes were being printed in values of millions for change, billions and trillions for the purchase of groceries, Runo did not care. Still, these notes were unable to cope with hourly price changes. When value and prices were beyond known mathematical terminology, numbering frightening levels, the currency was revalued by lopping off the excessive number of zeros, after which new notes would be printed. This process even affected exchange rates, creating multiple rates depending on whether cash or bank transfers were used. Even hard currencies were affected depending on note values. Small notes attracted a marginal exchange rate, and the pattern would change as the note values increased. The rates even depended on communities where higher rates were obtained in big cities and affluent suburbs. Poor neighbourhoods, high-density areas and smaller towns had lower exchange rates. Runo still forced Bullman to maintain a low official exchange rate. This exchange rate enabled Runo's friends to become millionaires overnight, and without working for it. These friends would have a preference in the allocation of foreign currency at the banks. Once they got the currency, they would trade it at the parallel market and get local currency transferred to their bank accounts. They would repeat the process until they reached unimaginable levels of foreign currency. It was said that most of these friends started with only a thousand dollars of local currency, which they turned into a million in foreign currency in less than ten transactions. The only sane-minded people in the mess turned out to be Kombi drivers who refused to accept any new notes printed by Bullman or accept the crazy rates dictated by the lazy people on the streets determining exchange rates by the minute. They instead started running their stable system with acceptable notes and prices, whether local or foreign.

It was not only the Great Crocodile among senior officials who despised how Runo handled the affairs of the nation. The head of the army, Fox, was secretly calling for Runo's retirement. He had stated that each one of his generations had either died or retired, and for the good of the nation Runo should also leave office. He was also bitter for having been involved directly in political matters when, on several occasions, he had been used to intimidate Sabi. Whenever Sabi's popularity surged or when the country was close to elections, Runo would assign General Fox to hold a press briefing. He would read a statement to the effect that he would not salute any leader without a credible war record or history because this is what made the nation achieve independence. Runo did not appreciate Fox's point of view and wanted him out of the way. In addition, he had suspected him of plotting a coup d'etat. Runo could not afford to have another election with a growing list of troublemakers among his ranks or lose his life when the obvious was brewing right before his own eyes. Getting Fox out of the way meant weakening the Great Crocodile's support. Promising Fox a higher post meant creating rivalries between Fox and the Great Crocodile. Runo's task was easy because he only had to deal with one individual. He invited Fox to the Presidential Palace one day.

"Fox, my General and Commander of the defence forces, you are one true and loyal soldier in this nation. I admire that."

"Thank you, Mr President. I hope to keep you happy."

"How can I reward my loyal soldier, my one true soldier?"

"Is it necessary to talk about rewards when I am the Commander-in-Chief?"

"You could do much better, Fox. Open your eyes."

"What do you have in mind, Mr President?"

"You are aware Simo, my deputy, was from your constituency, and it has been a while since he died."

"Yes, but what does that have to do with our discussion?"

"I feel it would be an honour and befitting to bestow that privilege on you."

"Is that a problem since you have the power to appoint and disappoint?" Fox was sceptical.

"Protocol must be observed, Fox. This is politics. It's different from the army."

"What protocol?"

"You are still a soldier, and it will be viewed as a military takeover."

"What are you saying, Mr President, in plain language?"

"If only you can retire, and then I will appoint you from civilian life. Your successor will be of a lesser rank, and I will hold the title of Commander-in-Chief of the Defence forces in trust for you."

"It seems noble, but what are the timelines."

"I cannot give a timeline because this is politics, but I can only promise that the job is yours."

"What other guarantee can you give? Even a girl will get a love token as a promise for a marriage."

"In politics, we simply have to trust each other. My word should be sufficient to carry my honour. I trust you. That is the reason I want you close to me and no one else."

"You are very old, Mr President, more than twenty years past the normal retirement age. I am quite old, too, and should be attaining retirement age in the next three years. Don't you think we should give way to the next generation?"

"I think you miss the point. You are my best soldier, and we have both come a long way from the war years. We are the guardians of this nation. The people still have a lot to learn from us. Look at Sabi and how he is already prepared to reverse the gains of our hard-won independence. Join me, Fox, and together we can do great things."

"If you say so, Mr President, it's a deal."

"You will not regret this, Fox."

Fox retired from the army the same way Sloppy Man did but with a much better promise. The promise of becoming the nation's deputy president, while Sloppy Man had only been asked to stand for election as a member of parliament. After winning the election, Sloppy Man was to be considered for a ministerial post. These Nations, his deputy, took over the post but not as Commander-in-Chief. These Nations was believed to be a cheat and a failure; besides, he was believed to have a commandeering leadership style due to a lack of grey matter between his ears. Runo preferred to work with him because he believed that this man was not likely to cause any threat to his rule. The nation was shocked by Fox's retirement, and the news made headlines for a few weeks. People talked and speculated, but in a short space of time, everyone had forgotten about it. Fox waited for three months, and nothing materialised. Those suspected to have been working with Fox to topple Runo died one after another in the most bizarre of circumstances. Talk on the streets was that these soldiers, of Captain rank, had been killed in advance but were being kept in a mortuary. When it was convenient, death would be stage-managed, then announced, and a body released or placed at an accident scene. Preferably, this was being done at a biweekly interval. Fox was exposed and did not have a backup plan, knowing very well that his friends were all dead. Fox cursed himself for the loss of his men. After three months, he approached Runo to try and manage the damage he had suffered. Runo was evasive, dismissive and elusive.

"Why am I still languishing in the cold, Runo?" Fox was bold and serious.

"Greetings, my dear friend, Fox." Runo tried to neutralise the anger

"Why did you not keep your end of the bargain?"

"This is a republic, Fox, with parliamentary democracy. Everything has to be scrutinised."

"What is your point?"

"Everyone in the executive was elected, and it's difficult to justify your appointment. Believe me, I have analysed every possible method, but it won't work without breaking the law. Even the Party structures have to approve."

"What's the bottom line, Runo, without wasting time?"

"Elections are due in five months. Why can't you wait to get elected, and then your appointment will be guaranteed."

"I just cannot believe we went through all this without you consulting first. Once elected, how many more hurdles will still be in the path?"

"None, no more; it becomes automatic. But you cannot

just blame me because you were party to this agreement."

"It was your proposal, and I expected better from you."

"We cannot weep over spilt milk. Let's take it in the stride like mature men, Fox."

"My opinion of you has changed, Runo. I see you in a different light."

"Your views shall change as soon as we start working together."

"*Totenda dzamwa dzaxhwera nebenzi*, Runo."

Fox was very frustrated, but he was powerless without any command of the army and no other position of influence in the Party or government. His trusted friends were gone, and he had nowhere to turn to. Fox rued why he had not consulted the Great Crocodile before going into a deal with Runo. He had been outmanoeuvred by Runo. Runo knew that any threat from Fox was only academic. He, however, let him participate in the election as a consolation. Fox had many hurdles, from very little funding and support from Runo to a formidable opposing candidate from Sabi's Party. Besides, there were several other independent candidates in his constituency, which was very rare in the nation. Fox had no strategy to deal with this further hurdle that he was facing. Runo never entertained him during the election period for any assistance he needed. Banking on the Party and Runo's reputation to win the election was not sufficient due to the economic damage the country had suffered. Short of any election trick, Fox was doomed.

He lost the election by a painfully narrow margin. Runo's job was done. Fox had no basis for making any demands. His fate was sealed. Fox had been outfoxed. It was yet another victory for Runo. Great Crocodile knew that *chiripo chariuraya Zizi harifi nemhepo*, but this was not his fight.

Chapter 19

After a few months, Runo announced that there would be a quota system where women would be represented in the nation's government and party's praesidium. He and Tadpole had set up a few teams to endorse the decision once the pronouncement was made. Hired teams from each province would somehow quickly embrace the idea and hail it as a victory for all women in the Party and the nation. From the onset, it was clear who the intended victim of this policy was, and rumours on street corners became rampant. The Great Crocodile did not give a dissenting opinion as the rule awaited formal endorsement. Besides, he knew the Runo train was violent. In this instance, it was a direct challenge by taking away an opportunity from the rightful winner. Despite the Party's trend and Runo's reputation, the Great Crocodile had hoped that a vote might be allowed in an open forum. It would have been blatantly arrogant to deny an obvious vote again according to Party established and practised norms. True to Runo's devious nature, the matter was handled in a very opaque and dubious manner that even the Great Crocodile was baffled. Runo requested the women to quickly vote and elect a woman candidate without the public knowing that such an important event was taking place. Heli, Runo's favourite and pre-anointed, lost. Runo had to use his power and guided democracy to ensure the right candidate won. A lady, once a member of Collar Man's Party, who had won the election had to surrender her victory. Once the hurdle was over, he quickly appointed Heli before the Great Crocodile could even dream of mounting a challenge. The Great Crocodile held his peace and went along with Runo's wishes.

Tadpole was very vocal on realising that the Great Crocodile did not pick heads in his political gambling phantom casino. Left with no choice, he wanted him at least to pick tails as a last resort. The Great Crocodile remained lukewarm in his response, forcing Tadpole to mobilise most of his supporters. To finish off the Great Crocodile, Tadpole arranged a forum to oppose the appointment of Heli. In the first forum meeting, the Great Crocodile did not attend, but some of his supporters and sympathisers were present. Tadpole did not tire in his quest to utterly destroy the Great Crocodile. He then prepared a final blow and decisive meeting in his home town. The Great Crocodile snubbed him again, suspicious and wondering why Tadpole should be aggrieved on his behalf, more than the Great Crocodile himself or anyone else. After the meeting, all supporters of the Great Crocodile were suspended.

Tadpole was left unscathed. Runo and Heli teamed up to purge all business associates of the Great Crocodile on a variety of charges. Knowing Runo's heavy hand, they all skipped the country. Most of the businesses were placed under liquidation arbitrarily or under government administration. These businesses were key to the operations of the economy, and employed thousands of employees, with extremely beneficial value chain effects to several downstream industries. One such business employed six thousand employees and exported more than 60% of its products. Another business was the third largest insurer, owning several buildings and investments in the nation. Also closed were a key and only iron smelter which was in the Crocodile's home town to weaken his base. It employed over five thousand people and supplied the whole nation with steel products. The iron and steel company was a key business for the nation, saving millions as an import substitution anchor.

Runo had always employed his close allies as head and also directors of the company. These were used to siphon out funds using a foreign subsidiary unit. He kept a close eye on the company to the extent of having a closed-door meeting with the Chief Executive once every month. Even when its fortunes were waning, the nation's executive could not recommend the sacking of the man. They were too scared to make any moves, knowing he had more power than all cabinet ministers combined. Closure of the businesses destroyed any potential of the economy rebounding. The Great Crocodile then approached Runo.

Runo looked at him and mocked him before any exchange of greetings.

"*Ko zvaunenge woita mafunga mafunga pavete nzuma ichifunga chakadla nyanga dzayo.* It's written all over your face. Do something." Runo laughed at the Great Crocodile to distract him. He felt he had finally destroyed Great Crocodile's political career and any ambitions he had.

"Do you believe that your selfishness might end in this lifetime?" he said calmly.

"I am a respected leader of the nation and an international icon, Great Crocodile. It's an unfounded allegation you are levelling against me when everyone has put their faith and trust in me."

"You never did anything positive for this nation. Your only interest is to perpetuate your stay in power. This man you have sidelined, the other eliminated, that one pierced with a sword, and the party is always in turmoil at every turn."

"*Mvura bvongodzeki ndoogarani,* besides, the people love me Great Crocodile, and there is no doubt about it."

"Really? How come you never allowed the Party to exercise the option to re-elect you since we gained independence?"

"People use different methods to test their popularity, and you cannot force me to be subjected to a Party election."

"She cannot even spell or write her name, let alone aspire for your office, yet you cheated her into believing that she could be part of your succession plan!"

"You betrayed me, Great Crocodile."

"Look who is talking. Do you even know what betrayal is or means, Runo?" Great Crocodile responded without blinking or looking at Runo's face.

"It's the ways of power. What made you think you could pull a fast one on me?"

"*Mucheri wembeva mutevedzi wemwena.* I use legal and ethical methods while you, on the other hand, are a dirty player."

"I could not let you kill me silently with the constitution, and now I got my revenge, Great Crocodile. *Bhuru rasarira shure rasarira shamhu!*" Runo was on top of the world and feeling safe.

"A constitutional coup was the best medicine for a nut job like you. You destroyed the best piece of legislation just because of your personal and selfish ego. When will you grow up?"

"It's time to quit. I have crushed you and your accomplices (showing a clenched fist). Your eternal bags must be in minute fragments and smithereens (emphasising with gestures). Hopefully, you will get a good doctor and a caste to piece everything together (showing a provoking smile). *Ava mangongomera mupasha wapfura musoro* (and he laughed). You are finished. I am now alone at the top with no challenge. As for you, *afa nemavanga enyora haachemwi*, no one, absolutely no one, will weep for you. You have already been eviscerated in the press and left for the vultures to finish off. You invited this misery upon yourself. I have the power, and there is nothing you can do to me," Runo sarcastically smiled, then laughed, beating his chest.

"They say, *zilajalika muuzumi* (it happens in life) but *Rukova gwizi kuyambuka unokwinya nguwo. Asika kutatarika humira zvaunoona, saka uchasvora mbodza neinozvimbira* (in a very calm and controlled voice). That's why we say, *ashunya agwa.* You can dash all my hopes, but my spirit will remain raised. Enjoy while you can, but you must feel ashamed. How do you justify purging people selectively for the same crime? If I make this fight public, do you think you will be able to live in this country again?"

"*Atsinzina rega atsikwe.* I know you won't quit, but I am determined to destroy you completely. You no longer have a constituency, and your financial sympathisers are gone. Do you think it's still worthwhile to fight?"

"*Chikomo shata divi, rimwe ritambire pwere.* You are too short-sighted, Runo. You will never realise your shortcomings until you get trapped in the pits you keep digging. That Sloppy Man will let you sink as long as he is safe. *Uchenjere kuiboba nekumux-hwe.*"

"I will cross that bridge when I come to it, Great Crocodile. Don't cry for me because you have worse troubles to deal with. About the Party congress, I will crush anyone who wants to bring other ideas to the table. You better warn your friends and be careful because I realise that *chinotaura ndechiri mumusungo, chiri muriva chinoti denga rawa.*"

"As an aside, how many national economic development or business development policies or discussion platforms have you enabled or held since you came to power?"

"I am a political leader, Great Crocodile, not a business manager."

"That response should not surprise any sane thinking person. That's what you are, Runo. With you, the fortunes of the nation will never change. You are a curse to our nation."

"*Heee, lokhu la lokhu,* I know a case of sour grapes, Great Crocodile. Go home and reflect on your loss. I cannot give you the comfort you need. This is my nation."

"Look at the state of our farms, Runo. How long can the economy sustain non-productive multiple farm ownership by you and your friends?"

"*Kakara kununa hudla kamwe.* At least my friends are happy, and the enemy has been expelled. My stay in office is guaranteed. I am the real McCoy."

"The idea was to make our own choices in terms of what we can grow for local consumption and export. You have destroyed all agricultural markets, and all rural folks have to rely on tobacco, which is seriously damaging the environment by cutting down trees for curing..."

"It's their choice, provided my rule is not affected," Runo cut short the Great Crocodile's narrative.

"Enjoy your win, Runo, but your puppy must have realised by now that he was a baby *aitumwa kunotinha zhou*. He is all smoke and no fire, all froth and no beer, that I wonder why you employed him under the circumstances. The boy barks, barks and barks all the time."

Runo knew that he had only scratched the Great Crocodile. Very soon, they would have another duel yet again, and he needed to close all loopholes. If only he knew what form the threat would take, he could stand ready, but the Great Crocodile was unpredictable. The purging of the Great Crocodile's associates ended to avoid falling prey to any moves he might have planned.

Tadpole felt it was time to face his boss and admit failure. He made a late evening appointment at the Presidential Palace to ensure there would be fewer prying eyes.

"Your Excellency, I am sorry I failed you."

"What in the world are you talking about, Tadpole?"

"The Great Crocodile did not take the bait. Purging his friends is not even shaking him. It seems nothing ever happened. What is he? A monster? A god? He is too calm, Your Excellency."

"Hold on, Tadpole, slow down and stop crying. The fatality of failure has never been confirmed. Therefore, there is still a redeemable position."

"I messed up, and I don't know if you are willing to forgive that easily?"

"You probably are not so smart, Tadpole."

"Why do you say so, Your Excellency?"

"I thought you knew that he is the ultimate opponent one can ever face and win. His instinct is beyond comprehension. His calculations are beyond measure. His resurrecting abilities are amazing."

"It seems you gave me the task when you knew very well that I was going to fail. Why did you do it anyway?" Tadpole looked relieved.

"You disturb the water to catch the fish, my dear Tadpole," he said while gesturing and smiling. "It was an excellent effort."

"Where to now that we are back to where we started?"

"We have moved some steps forward. Tomorrow is another day. It will take him time to rebuild his attack. We made considerable progress, Tadpole, given the opponent we are facing."

"What do I do next?"

"You have to continue on your destructive path."

"Is it necessary when he does not follow?"

"We play the devil's advocate. I may need to get rid of you so that no one suspects you are my puppy."

"What happens if I am out?"

"You strategise. Study him as much as you can. When I recall you back to the Party, you have to be ready to destroy him completely."

"Time is not on our side because of your age."

"You have to be patient. Even to my dying day, I have to sleep with one eye open because of the Great Crocodile."

"We make him seem immortal. Why could you not destroy him all along?"

"I tried everything since the war and even sold him out for a train derailing incident, hoping they would kill him. It didn't work."

"I can't believe this has been going on for so long. How has he been fighting back and living alongside you all this time?"

"He saved my life and my job several times without thinking twice about it."

"Why does he do it when he knows you are probably his worst enemy?"

"From the goodness of his heart, Tadpole. It's unconditional for him, and I hate that with a passion."

"Why not embrace him, knowing he is that kind of person?"

"I believe that if ever I am to lose power, it will be to the Great Crocodile, and I cannot stand the thought of giving up my throne as long as I live. They say, '*Sakunatsa ndiye sakubaiwa*', and I guess I was born to love and embrace that phrase. Some things you just cannot seek to comprehend or explain." He paused. "You cut your hair but shave your beard. It's an offshore investment if you stash your money in Guernsey, Isle of Man or Cayman Islands, but money laundering if you stash it in one of our neighbouring countries or the far east. Just imagine the top customers of a cigarette company being rewarded with the possibility of suffering from lung cancer. Back home we say, '*Shiri yakangwara inovaka dendere neminhenga yedzimwe*', and I need you to comprehend that statement (patting him) or at least that *Unodiridzira rugare nemisodzi yevamwe* like what the white man did with slavery, colonisation, religion and continues to do today."

"In that case, *toita mununura ndakapinga, kuita zimhuhwa riri mundove* (with emphasis), we can use Heli to our advantage."

"She cannot help our cause. The best she can do is report for duty every day."

"It's not her but you going in public, propping her and asking her to aim higher. She now has our certificates, remember. Therefore, we should take advantage."

"You have a point, Tadpole." Runo nodded in agreement.

"It can also help us to get his reaction and plan for our next step."

"Goodbye and good luck, Tadpole."

To justify and prop up Heli's image, many projects for the benefit of women were tabled and funded by the state. The projects were designed to uplift the livelihoods of women by deliberately empowering them financially. Such projects cut across the whole business spectrum from farming to manufacturing. There were funds for fish farming, crocodile farming, ladies' care manufacturing and many more. Heli registered a company in each of the sectors that had been funded by the government. Her companies sucked out most of the funds provided, and a few of her friends took the balance. After six months, no one talked about the projects, their success or failure, the number of people empowered and whether the women had started repaying the borrowed funds. It turned out that this had been one way of siphoning money from the system. No reporter dared to follow up on the projects, and in his usual style, Runo never cracked the whip on the much-hyped projects that he had funded. Beneficiaries of the funds were later rewarded with a debt relief concession, which was decreed by Runo.

The emissary from that country that put sanctions on Runo's nation saw an opportunity to annihilate Runo's Party and government. He approached the Great Crocodile, intending to have him team up with and strengthen the opposition. From thin air, he appeared at a very unlikely place, knowing a formal meeting had remote chances of ever happening. It was at his farm where the Great Crocodile was cooling off during a weekend. The emissary had made a great effort to disguise himself as a colleague of the Great Crocodile to gain entry into the premises. He then drove down to the fields where he met him. Great Crocodile immediately noticed the anomaly and asked him to do away with the disguise.

"I apologise, but I had no choice. I needed to see you."

"Why must I trust a secretly serving diplomat?"

"Some important tasks need personal attention without the involvement of third parties. I come in peace. Please hear me out."

"How altruistic are your intentions?"

"We need people like you on our side. As a potential future leader of this country, we need a working relationship with you. We can even assist with your safe ascension to your desired position."

"There is only my country and my side. Your side is irrelevant and of no consequence. Everything I need, I have it figured out."

"Your leader and Party have treated you badly. Surely, this is a moment you should open up and let us save the day. Work with us and the opposition."

"In my language they say, *Kurumwa netsikidzi rambira mumba ukatizira pazhe unorumwa mhino nebere.* Leave now, go consult on what that means and make your peace with it. *Chaunoda chii pahuku yomweni?*"

The Great Crocodile continued with his farm inspection.

Runo was determined to prove that he was popular and shame the Great Crocodile. In addition, he knew the Great Crocodile's fate had sowed seeds of discontent in the Party, and he wanted to stamp his authority. Some people were busy calling for all positions to be elective at that year's Party congress. Stamping his authority was imperative, and he needed to do it at any cost and silence all members of his Party. He looked for someone with energy, someone vulnerable, someone desperate for power, and someone fond of publicity. Jabu, a former ally of the Great Crocodile, did fit the profile. He sent for him, and a driver did bring him in a luxury vehicle. This vehicle was then allocated to Jabu. Runo said to him:

"That vehicle, you can use as your shopping basket."

"Thank you, Mr President. I am still not sure how I end up being rewarded when I am supposed to be on suspension." Jabu was worried.

"It's a small thing, Jabu, and I hope you like it."

"You are very kind, Mr President; I like it."

"I understand you have a shelter issue?"

"True, Mr President. That information is correct."

"It is being sorted; therefore, do not agonise about it."

"I appreciate your kindness, Mr President." Jabu was excited.

"Back to business, Jabu. I have a task for you at hand."

"Name it, Mr President." Jabu was willing to do anything to get back into the fold.

"I know the Great Crocodile wanted your support and had assisted you to assume leadership of our dear Freedom Fighters."

"It is a fact, Mr President."

"You shall get that post back."

"I appreciate your efforts."

"You, however, have to earn your stripes, Jabu. I cannot just appoint you without anything convincing for the public. I love your energy and stamina."

"Thank you for the compliment, but what is it you ask of me?"

"Many people have been left with doubts and questions about my legitimacy owing to your debacle and all the adventures leading to some congress resolutions being proposed. People want to usurp my power and authority."

"That's treasonous, Mr President. I am here to help."

"You shall have a million man march, Jabu. You have to coordinate people from around the country and deliver a record-breaking crowd to shame detractors of the revolution."

"What will be the message, Mr President?"

"My endorsement as the sole leader of the Party and cancellation of any resolution that was not sanctioned by me."

"Leave it to me, Mr President. Your faithful servant shall deliver."

Jabu did a perfect job for Runo but was very shameful to himself and the nation. No one ever believed a million-man march was possible, nor did it matter in a republic where elections were supposed to be a determinant factor for genuine leadership. The message was clear; only guided democracy was welcome, and no one dared to face off with Runo. After a month and a half, Jabu had travelled the length and breadth of the nation. Peaceful threats were employed to gently coerce bus owners to avail their buses for the march. Genuine allegiance to Runo was tested, with all true supporters obliged to dutifully support Runo's cause. Runo could coerce, intimidate and terrorise his fellow countrymen. He was a legitimised obdurate serial terrorist. Jabu led the people in the streets of the capital, destroying and seriously harming business turnover for the day as he led the people to the Party's head office. He handed over the crowd to Runo after giving a brief address aimed at opposing any resolutions by the Party against Runo. Runo used the occasion to prop himself up and intimidate those Party members who had doubts about him. Given the impetus from the march, Runo got his way by bulldozing and intimidating every Party member. He then set his agenda for congress. Jabu received his due rewards for perpetuating a geriatric to hang on to power. Being a politician or affiliated with politicians became the only gateway to a good life as the economy had been wrecked. Opportunities were only available to those in power.

Chapter 20

Bullman's unorthodox and visceral monetary adventures blessed by Runo never brought any positive fortunes for the nation. Every citizen was critical of his policies, and inflation broke new ground to snatch an unprecedented and unbeatable world record. Runo always came to his rescue by blaming bookish economists for their analysis and recommendations. He blamed them for offering no practical ideas to save the nation and working with the enemy to stifle economic growth, bringing poverty to innocent people of the nation. Bullman and Runo played several financial innovations to line their pockets and convince the public that they were trying. Every monetary experiment ended up in a disaster until it was clear that there was no way out, and Runo's tactics had completely failed. Food was scarce, and supermarket shelves were empty. Farms were not producing anything meaningful for the nation.

Runo's friends were not working the farms, and some of the farms were held in trust on behalf of senior leaders or their yet-to-be-born children and grandchildren. A few of Runo's friends who were producing for export externalised the little foreign currency earnings they made. Banks ran out of foreign as well as local currency. Runo introduced price controls as a way to tame the embarrassingly high inflation. This worsened the situation for the citizenry, with all products finding their way onto the informal market. Tadpole remained highly critical of Runo's appointment of Heli, but no action was taken against him. People assumed that Tadpole was invincible and was the new kingmaker in the Party. Instead of Runo changing course, he went on to play more of his political games to secure his position. The first gamble he took to get foreign currency was an electricity supply deal. He promised some regional leaders that since he had many rivers in his country, he could build hydroelectric stations and supply them with electricity. Another option was a thermal power station, which the nation had but needed repairs. Some trusted him and paid funds to assist Runo. Several publicity stunts were made about appointing reputable and world-class companies to undertake the work. Contracts were signed in front of cameras. Headline stories were awash in newspapers, giving the impression that the nation was about to turn out of the poverty corner. That is the last time Runo ever talked about the power projects. Contractors were never paid to enable them to commence operations. By the dishonesty displayed in the power deal, Runo alienated himself from his regional and neighbouring peers.

Runo did not stop in his attempt to destroy the Great Crocodile. He had a complete file on the Great Crocodile's ventures and decided to trap him using hazy evidence of a newly discovered precious liquid from the ground. He called in his trusted tribesman, Diesel, to lure the Great Crocodile.

"Diesel, my boy, I have sleepless nights because the Great Crocodile will not relent or die. I need you to finish him off."

"How do I do that, boss?"

"I have set him a trap, and I just want you to ensure he sniffs the peanut butter therein."

"What's in the trap boss?"

"I know the Great Crocodile loves shiny things from the soil. There is a possibility of a precious liquid found in my hometown."

"How much is involved?"

"Don't get too excited, Diesel. He must know its bottomless."

"Is it in order if I survey the area first?"

"Do what you have to do, but I would like you to do a convincing rumour that will push him into the trap."

"If it's not adequate after the survey, should we still go ahead?"

"Diesel, that is not your problem. You and your team must secretly break the news to catch his attention. Once he responds positively, then his career is finished."

"I will try, boss."

"You have to do it, Diesel, and if you need assistance, use as many Party elders as you can."

"Let me execute it perfectly for you, boss."

"Go on, Diesel."

Diesel gathered intelligence and fell in love with the feedback he was getting. He gathered a few seniors to assist him in uncovering the mystery. When they arrived at the site, they were welcomed by a hostile spiritual lady. This lady would not allow the team to do any survey because there was a price attached. She told them that they were on sacred ground and needed to take their shoes off, to which they complied. The lady used a small branch to sprinkle the precious liquid on them, after which they were led to the outlet of the supposed liquid nozzle. She hit a rock several times, and a hidden bouncer poured a drum of the liquid, which started gushing and oozing from the stone. Diesel and his team were led through the liquid shower to get a necessary bath as their quest had been accepted. A press team that had accompanied Diesel captured everything on camera. The press team had been put together by the Great Crocodile. Diesel was very excited, but no work was to take place before a handsome sum had been paid to her. She also demanded an audience with Runo. Diesel ensured the story made headlines, and he went to Runo with his head high. Runo was embarrassed and furious at the development.

"Diesel, Diesel, Diesel. Why are you always disappointing?"

"You will be happy once you let me explain."

"Explain what, Diesel?"

"It's a great find, and once we comply with her demands, the fortunes of the nation will turn."

"Precious liquids do not miraculously appear from a stone. It's a science you must understand."

"It was all so real, boss. You need to see it for yourself to believe."

"Wake up, Diesel. She was my project. You are such a perennial failure."

"Do you think the Great Crocodile will take the bait?"

"Did you check the press, Diesel?"

"There are wonderful pictures of the find. I had hoped the nation would be overjoyed."

"It's embarrassing to hear that from you. There is no precious liquid, Diesel."

"I am sorry, boss. You should have told me. I didn't realise the Great Crocodile could trick us."

"For how long, Diesel, should I babysit you before you learn to walk on your own?"

"I can put a warrant for her arrest, boss, to save us from this debacle."

"Do it. It's the only sensible thing you have ever said throughout your entire life. However, you have to warn her first so that she can run."

"If that happens, we will not be able to find her and punish her."

"You are too slow, Diesel. Let her run and pretend to chase until you finally catch up with her. Let all the papers know to divert attention."

"Thank you for saving my life."

To distract people from their misery, Runo forced a deal to acquire two baby aeroplanes for intercity travel. The deal involved him getting a piece of the action as usual. He sidelined the need for servicing the better rewarding long-haul routes. All he wanted was something to uplift his name from the fledging fortunes of his political career. When the two small planes arrived in the nation, Runo arranged a big bash where he delivered a long speech on how the country was going to progress with the purchase of the tiny planes. The bash took an entire afternoon, and it quickly turned into a circus on social circles and social media. To the majority of voters, without enough information, Runo had made an impact.

People got desperate as only those capable of crossing the borders had the power to feed themselves and the nation. The currency became worthless, and government employees started to abandon their posts as salaries had been severely eroded by inflation. Even Heli felt it was criminal to continue on the destructive path. An election to select a president for the nation was due, but Runo realised that he had already lost before the exercise began. Heli and some members were secretly campaigning against Runo. He again intimidated his people and forced them to change the law. The presidential and parliamentary elections were aligned and harmonised. This strategy forced the Party to work as a team. Tadpole decided to stand for elections without Runo's approval. Due to the public confrontation, Tadpole's constituency was declared a gender empowerment seat. Only a woman could represent the Party in that constituency. He challenged the decision and was expelled from the Party. The Great Crocodile established a safe constituency for himself. Heli, on advice from the Sloppy Man, did not campaign for Runo. She influenced more of the Party members to work against him. They wanted to let him fall to establish a coalition with Sabi and start a new chapter in the politics of the nation.

Huge deposits of some precious liquid were discovered in one African country. A plan was hatched to siphon the resource at no cost. The resolution was to forcibly remove the leader and replace him with their lapdog. Young and excitable men were paid handsomely to achieve the task under the tutelage of a world-infamous terrorist and mercenary but misnamed coup mastermind. Among the crew was a son of Maggie (former leader of Runo's nation's coloniser). Two planes were chartered for the task. One had the leader in waiting with his crew, and the other with the soldiers of fortune, or mercenaries. The plane with mercenaries made a stopover in the nation to collect weapons.

Based on intelligence, the mercenaries were all incarcerated and heavy sentences were imposed. Maggie secretly flew into the nation and paid Runo a handsome sum to secure the release of her son. The world's leading nations fought tooth and nail to have the leading mercenary released. He was their point man and sweeper whenever they needed to eliminate a stumbling block. Runo instead threatened to extradite him to the country where they wanted to commit atrocities. He wanted more money in exchange for this highly prized mercenary, and he did demand a sizeable sum, which the leading nations were not prepared to part with. Leading news stations went on a mission to discredit Runo, his government and his Political Party for his stance on this mercenary. Chief among the reasons for fighting for his release was humanitarian grounds and the fact that his family missed him. People got confused about how people who claim to be on high moral ground could fight for the release of a mercenary. The excitable young guns who were on their first mission were later released after a year, but their leader remained behind bars. This was one of those rare moments where Runo made the right call in favour of his people and held the world powers to ransom.

Sabi and his Party worked hard to ensure electoral reforms were implemented. A senior Party female member was pushed by Sabi to be friendly with the Head of the only influential regional block. This enabled Sabi's Party to force Runo to accept certain standard regional practices. In this instance, Sabi wanted transparent elections free from any manipulations. He, therefore, pushed an agenda for electoral reforms adopting the regional standard. The regional bloc, which the nation belonged to, approved the request and asked Runo to implement it. Hesitantly, he did. It was a small loss for Runo after every neighbouring country had supported the reform. Tobby's responsibility was taken away, and a new team was put in charge. Runo, therefore, went on to change the winning rules from a simple majority to more than 50%. He persuaded a few contestants to join the race so that he could split Sabi's vote and render the reforms meaningless.

The election campaign was one-sided, as Runo had nothing to offer except his war history and sanctions mantra. Sabi got massive funding and distributed Party information and regalia throughout the nation. Although he had nothing to offer in the form of a political agenda, people preferred him as an alternative to breaking away from Runo's bad policies. The only positive contribution he had made to his political relevance was advocating for sanctions, which, in addition to Runo's incompetence, were adding to the economic collapse. Owing to the food shortages, many donors were in the country to assist communities. Sabi worked with the donors towards election day. They concentrated on Runo's electoral strongholds and collected people's identity documents a day before the elections.

This was an exercise to record those in need of food handouts. It had become a custom that Runo's supporters got food handouts first. Weeding out these supporters from the polls was, therefore, ideal for influencing the election results. People's identity documents were only returned to their owners after the elections. It was a smooth operation, and most of Runo's supporters were unable to cast their votes. The results were not in Runo's favour. Runo's new election commission team did not know how to handle the negative results. He quickly fled the country in secret when he got to know about the results. An election commission team, still in shock and paralysed by the results, did not know whether to announce them or not. After a media blitz on the glitch, the Great Crocodile discovered that Runo had abandoned them. Runo feared for his life, knowing how cruel he had been to Sabi and everyone else. The Great Crocodile quickly phoned Runo.

"I told you so. Heli has been a disaster, just like I predicted that you would be hoisted by your own petard."

"This is not the time for a lecture, Great Crocodile. I could be put behind bars or be hanged in public."

"You need it because you left everyone exposed, and there is a power vacuum due to your foolishness. "

"I had to leave because we are finished."

"If you don't return, I will announce your retirement and take over."

"No, not my reign and my people, Great Crocodile. I will do anything to have it back."

"Talk to me because I am in charge."

"I am the constitutionally and democratically elected leader."

"If you are as you say, why are you in exile?"

"Please understand, Great Crocodile. Let's talk."

"I will accept you on two conditions."

"Name them, my Lord. I always knew you had a great heart, Great Crocodile."

"Stop the patronage, otherwise the deal is off."

"Please, Great Crocodile, have mercy. My family is still young, and my roommate is the only breadwinner her family has ever known. Please, help an old friend."

"Come home, Runo, so that we can negotiate with Sabi. I will talk while you keep your foul mouth shut."

"If you promise my safety, I will be back by sunset."

"You have to go by my rules, Runo, because you have no choice."

"It was just a slip of the tongue. Forgive me."

"One more thing, you will have to get rid of Heli. She is a liability to the Party."

"I understand. We can work on the finer details when I return."

The Great Crocodile did not announce the results. He waited, moderated some, and when he had a reasonable result, he then invited Sabi for a discussion. Runo sat in attendance, and so were all other senior officials invited from the defence and security forces.

"Welcome, Sabi, your delegation and all senior officials here present. This meeting is confidential. No one has to know what transpired because it's not happening. For the glory of the nation, we had to arrange for this meeting. Sabi, you may be wondering why you are sitting alongside your greatest enemy. From my perspective, we are brothers, although we may have political differences or otherwise. As mature people, we must accept that we have a responsibility to the nation. It is the sole reason why we hold our respective offices. Does anyone have anything to ask before we continue?"

Tiny Mind, a delegate from Sabi's Party, asked, "When will the election results be announced?"

"We are here for a common goal, and we cannot begin our discussions without talking about the elections. That aspect has to be respected."

"We have heard that we should never salute Sabi, yet we find ourselves in the same room talking about common interests. Is there a problem?" an army commander asked.

"Political campaign rhetoric and reality are different things. If we meant what we said, we could not have facilitated this meeting. I would request everyone to loosen up and treat each other as a friend, a brother or a neighbour, which we are in any event."

"I think we are ready to progress," Sabi suggested.

"Very well then. The first thing we need to know is that the election ended in a near stalemate, and the results will be circulated shortly. Banya, if you can give confidential copies to every delegate of the meeting."

The Great Crocodile allowed a few minutes for everyone to digest the results. He then continued.

"It is obvious the most contentious one is the presidential vote, which may need to go for another round to determine the ultimate winner."

"What do you request of this meeting, Great Crocodile, now that we know my Party did very well?" Sabi asked.

"Our country is in great economic turmoil, and any election exercise is going to drain the treasury while the people will be suffering. We must talk and find common ground as one family."

"Are you talking power sharing, Great Crocodile?" Tiny Mind asked.

"Exactly, my friend."

"What would be the terms?" Sabi asked

"We can have suggestions, but I was hoping that His Excellency, Runobvepi, retains his post. Sabi will be his new deputy, and the executive will be shared between the parties. The results and our agreement will then be announced simultaneously."

"Sabi, I don't think you need any further negotiation. The deal is clear, concise and fair," Tiny Mind suggested.

"Take the deal, Sabi, it's good for everyone," another of his delegates, Ian, suggested.

"What will happen to Heli?" Sabi asked.

"That is the very reason we did not include her in this meeting. We wanted to progress. She would be retired with full benefits."

"Great Crocodile, what do you benefit from all this?" Sabi asked again.

"I am the moderator. I was not in the pracsidium and don't see the reason to bulldoze into it. As a lawyer, I believe in legality and constitutionalism."

"If there are no objections to the proposals, should we reduce everything to pen and paper?" Banya asked.

"It's up to Sabi and his team," Great Crocodile left it to Sabi to decide.

"No violent objections from me," said Tiny Mind.

"I agree to the deal," Ian seconded Tiny. Every other member of Sabi's team agreed.

"Gentlemen, let's shake hands and drink to the dawn of a new chapter in our nation." Great Crocodile invited everyone.

"To the dawn of a new chapter in our nation," they all raised their glasses and drank to the progress they had made in a very short space of time.

"I wonder why we were squabbling for so many years when we could achieve so much progress in such a short time in one room. You played some magic, Great Crocodile. Thank you," Ian remarked.

"You should be the next leader of this nation, Great Crocodile," Tiny suggested.

"Only if it is the will of the people," responded Great Crocodile. Runo was thoroughly unhappy with the praise that the Great Crocodile was getting.

"I envisage a change to allow our colleagues in the diaspora to vote shortly." Sabi was dreaming of the future. No one responded because they felt this was not the occasion to talk about such proposals. Great Crocodile diverted the conversation as he introduced family issues into the mix for the gathering to loosen up some more. Runo was already working on ways and means to make Sabi walk away from the agreement. He felt he was slowly getting back into the game and made a crazy remark.

"I hope, Sabi, you won't take vengeance on our police." He was referring to an incident where the police had been instructed to manhandle him. The Great Crocodile dismissed the gathering to diffuse any possible tensions. He knew he had passed up a great opportunity to take over the reins, but due to legitimacy issues, it was not the right time.

In a few days, an agreement was crafted. Sabi's team perused through it and was happy with the contents. The people, however, were unhappy with the delay in announcing the results, but neither Party was worried. On the day of signing, Sabi did not turn up. One of his foreign advisers and main sponsor had told him that there was a high probability he could have an outright win in another election. Everyone tried hard to convince him to give up his ego and respect the interests of the public. Runo was angry at the prospect of losing and forfeiting his privileges by sharing with Sabi. He was, however, opposed to the deal, knowing that Sabi had the upper hand. At every opportunity, he had sent some of his allies to take a jibe at Sabi to force him out of the deal. Internally, Runo was happy with the development. The prospect of a ruling Party presiding over a winning Party was not his ideal and preferred situation. An upper hand was what he had always wanted. He knew the Great Crocodile would save the situation and, therefore, he could play any dangerous game. When what he had anticipated eventually happened, he called the Great Crocodile for a discussion, almost in tears.

"Great Crocodile, Sabi has reneged on his promise. This is your baby because I have run out of ideas."

"Tell me something new, but is it your sworn statement that you abdicate your role?"

"No, not at all, Great Crocodile. All I am saying is that we are in a mess, and I want you to clean it up as the person who has been de facto in charge."

"You play too many old and stupid tricks, Runo. That is your problem. It's not my fight."

"This is not the time for arguments. Our backs are against a wall."

"Your back, not mine, Runo."

"Why are you so extremely calm in the face of danger?"

"You keep messing up, Runo, and I always have to come to your rescue."

"Must you take advantage of this situation, Great Crocodile?"

"I have never done that before. If it happens now, I cannot say that I didn't learn from the best."

"People are different, and you should not necessarily give

me a taste of my own medicine. You are not me. Your upbringing was different."

"Your upbringing is not an excuse. It's just your evil heart, a tribal heart, a tribal prejudice, yet your parents were never from this nation."

"You go too far, Great Crocodile. Let's finish the task at hand."

"At your age, I wonder why you can't let go. Is it worthwhile, Runo?"

"Please help your Party, your nation and your old friend."

"This is just for you and your selfish interests."

"*Anebenzi ndeanerake kudzana anopururudza*, Great Crocodile. It's not in your nature to let someone perish while you watch."

"Is that why you take advantage of well-meaning people?"

"Great Crocodile, I am sorry for whatever I have done. Help me." Runo knelt and shed a tear.

"I know you don't mean anything you say, Runo. *Ndoo misodzi yebere iyi.* That is the reason this nation is in a big mess."

"What I could, I did, Great Crocodile. For instance, the land and keeping this nation free of perverts."

"That wasn't even your initiative. You only usurped the programme because it served your interests."

"I have stopped many parastatals from downsizing, which could have pushed many of our people into poverty?"

"You should be ashamed of yourself. The parastatals must be commercialised and operate profitably with an optimum number of employees, paying their taxes and dividends instead of the government pumping taxpayers' funds out every year."

"I have ensured that our indigenous people are empowered so that they get shareholding in white-owned companies."

"*Zvokwadi ura mapako hunozvara mbava, mhondi, nemuroyi.* It's just your friends you are proposing as partners in those companies. Why don't you let each company choose a viable partner? Besides, the law is open-ended because your hand-picked ministers have the final say in every deal. The intention of the policy is, therefore, in name only. If you were serious about it, you could have started with all government departments and parastatals, putting a policy that they should not deal with a company that is not compliant. Everyone will comply over-night."

"Must we continue debating while everything remains at a standstill? Will you help and do me this great favour, Great Crocodile?"

"Only for the glory of the nation, Runo, and don't forget that."

At that point, Runo smiled and clenched his fists with his eyes closed. He knew the day had been saved and said, "Thank you." He then tried to hug him, but the Great Crocodile pushed him away.

The results were released, but people were not convinced that they reflected the truth. Too many ideas and rumours had circulated, giving the impression that Runo had tampered with the results. Tiny Mind published his version of the results, which resulted in him being arrested and put in leg irons like a career criminal. Runo's security was unleashed and instructed to be as brutal and inhumane as possible on Sabi's people.

Runo's gamble on changing the constitution had worked because Sabi had failed to secure the necessary majority, and now the Great Crocodile was going to deliver the majority that Runo craved. It was necessary to have this exercise while people were in their confused state. Runo instructed the Great Crocodile to push for security personnel, the army with These Nations (one of his friends assisting in the background), and vibrant youths into all centres that had supported Sabi. They quashed all dissenting voices by any means necessary until Sabi realised that he was fighting a losing battle. In one incident, a soldier approached the rural home of one Sabi Party campaign manager who was making rapid gains. His mother had just been buried, and he had left to process the records at the Birth and Deaths Registry. The soldier was frustrated that he could not punish this man. He, therefore, shot several times at the grave with his rifle in a stern warning that this was exactly how he would meet his fate if he continued. Sabi withdrew his charges at the eleventh hour to plunge Runo's win into a void and illegitimate result.

Another financial bonanza was created for non-governmental organisations. They took advantage of the violence to call for extra funding. They purported to be building shelters around the nation for victims of political violence. The numbers of victims were highly exaggerated, and financial floodgates were opened from the heavens of the non-governmental organisations. Rent-seeking opportunities were created in the process besides just enriching managers and owners of non-governmental organisations. Those consulting on behalf of or approving the funds for the organisations got a shake-down for their contribution. Donors were happy to be working against the government and usher in a new leadership. Little did they know that their contribution was for the destruction of the nation, not otherwise. People associated with the opposition despised their nation more, and the idea of destroying everything to start again from scratch became more appealing. Anything positive was dismissed without any due consideration. The lawyers were opposing anything and everything. When they lost in court, they alleged unfairness and state capture. The only acceptable verdict became a ruling in their favour, and this cancer caught up with Sabi's Party.

Corruption was not only associated with government officials and non-governmental organisations, but the private sector was in the lead. Financial and investment experts were some of the culprits. They created fictitious financial instruments to dupe the public and investing institutions. No laws had been created to deal with this emerging line of crime. Even company executive officers could call for share rights issues and use the money to boost their benefits. There were no consequences for such high-level crimes, and many got away with it.

Runo was happy with Sabi's decision as he cruised to victory uncontested. Once he achieved his victory, he had two things on his mind. Revenge for two things: the loss and humiliation at the hands of Sabi. Having secured his constitutional legitimacy, Runo was free to rule as he pleased. First of all, he intended to keep the Great Crocodile away from the centre of power and rule uncontested without anyone eyeing his position. Secondly, he had to crush Sabi and destroy him once and for all. He needed him closer. Runo failed to recognise that this was not his victory; he was going to operate on a borrowed mandate and power. Gleaning from the Great Crocodile's notes on a coalition government, he realised that it was a great idea. It was a wonderful thought because no business was going to invest as long as Runo was in power, and no financial assistance was going to be considered. The economic situation was going to remain bleak. Runo decided that it was time to consider talks and a unified government. This would buy him time to work on destroying Sabi's reputation. At least with his victory, Sabi was going to occupy a less influential post. He bypassed the Great Crocodile and asked a friend from a neighbouring country to assist in the negotiations with Sabi. Runo asked his friend to include other insignificant Parties to undermine Sabi's significance. This was also going to reduce the Great Crocodile's role and significance while uplifting the credibility of the talks to a legitimate and international level. If Sabi was not careful, his reputation was going to be ruined at the first hurdle and in the eyes of the international community.

The Great Crocodile did not delay warning Runo. He visited him late at night at the Presidential Palace without even making an appointment. Runo knew his nemesis did not have any kind words for him but was not worried because he was now firmly in the driving seat.

"Don't you think it's time you start making appointments, Great Crocodile?"

"I see. You want to avoid me?"

"What if I am busy?"

"Not at this time of the night, Runo. At your age, I don't think you can still perform any marital duties."

"A cock crows at any age, Great Crocodile, that's why we say *Jongwe rinofa richi kukuridza.*"

"You may please yourself with all the lies in the world, but I could not believe that."

"I sense a hostility in you. What is the problem?"

"Unbelievable. Your stupidity never ends. You are negotiating with Sabi on your terms and have even taught Tabo to despise me."

"You are way off the mark, Great Crocodile. The economy needs political stability. It's all for the good of the Republic."

"Since when have you cared about the economy or anyone else besides yourself?"

"Our people are suffering, and changing course is necessary."

"Political and economic confidence hinges on your absence from office. Once you are out, everything will fall into place."

"I cannot leave at such a critical moment, Great Crocodile. I love my country and my people," he emphasised by banging on the table.

"If you love them, would you have sentenced them to this level of poverty? They have become beggars, street vendors, economic refugees, and money changers, and millions have been exiled by your ineptitude."

"I made education available for them, and the choice is theirs to become beggars or refugees. It is out of my control."

"Have you ever asked yourself why they are leaving and cannot make ends meet in their nation?"

"I am the President and will not be drawn into such a trivial issue."

"You are hopeless, and that statement is a reflection of your failure, but I know why you are doing this."

"What evil intentions do you think I have, Great Crocodile?"

"You want your revenge on Sabi, and very soon I see Tadpole coming back to do your dirty job. Isolating me is another, while you hang on to Heli, who could never stop stabbing you at every turn."

"I cannot let people walk all over me and get away with it. It's immoral, and you need that quality in your life."

"I can read your mind like an open book. Once Sabi is finished, Heli will be so close to him, hoping for a marriage of convenience. She cannot read the signs, and his last victory is all she can think of, and she hopes she can unseat you."

"She could never think that."

"It's not about her but the Sloppy Man." Great Crocodile smiled sarcastically.

"I know him, but he is too slow and sloppy. He doesn't worry me anymore."

"You still owe him a favour, and he wants to use that to his advantage."

"It's an old favour. Even if he spills the beans, he will implicate himself more than he can tarnish my reputation."

"I note that he is ready to be on your plate for breakfast because he poses no threat but remains too much of a distraction."

"I like you, Great Crocodile. You behave like a leader of this nation, but unfortunately, I cannot let that happen."

"Go on with your games, Runo, but don't say I did not warn you."

Chapter 21

Sabi was lured into Runo's trap and got a token offer after lengthy and gruelling negotiations. Runo incorporated a splinter group from Sabi's Party in the negotiations. This splinter group was led by known Runo secret operatives. The operatives' leader was popularly known as Agogo. These were professionals in their respective fields but doubling up as agents for Runo. They had failed to destroy Sabi's political party from within. The reason for including this group with a negligible number of representatives was to neutralise Sabi's influence and undermine his support. It had taken six months of negotiations, and the results were not worth the publicity, resources and efforts. Sabi had hoped to get public sympathy or international military assistance. A secret deal arranged by the Great Crocodile was far better than the crumbs Sabi eventually received. His tactics proved a weak intellect on his part. At the ceremony to celebrate the signing of the pact, Runo was the last to speak and never showed respect for Sabi and one of his backers, a leader of a neighbouring nation. This leader was in his sixties and single, and many believed that he was from Sodom. Runo showered praise and later told the crowd that he was not referring to this leader but his father. He took a jab at Sabi and later told the crowd that everyone had to come to their senses. In this instance, the noise-making parties had finally come to the table and signed an agreement to allow the nation to move forward.

Tadpole was brought back into the fold soon after the signing of the power-sharing pact. He immediately started to feast on Sabi and his political party. None of the secret files on his personal life were spared. The phrases *open zip shut mind and open mouth shut mind* became synonymous with Sabi. All his intimate adventures became a daily public media display. To show the public that Sabi's post was ceremonial and of no value, Tadpole employed art in the form of song and dance. He formed a women's group and gave them songs to sing about Runo being the only one in charge and that Sabi must carefully take note. The first of these songs humbling Sabi was *Nyatsoterera*. Another song mischievously chronicled the hierarchy of power in the government, which reflected that Sabi was not even in the top three; the song was *Team*. These songs were played repeatedly, but one could not say that there was a lack of talent on display in composing the music. It was so brilliant an effort that people wondered why Tadpole was wasting his career in politics instead of considering being an artist. However, besides the entertainment, Sabi's supporters were outraged by the musical connotations and complained. Feminists were quick to point out that the women's dances were demeaning to the women folk. Tadpole was interviewed on the matter, but his response needed no effort, and anyone could have done the same.

"People say you are abusing the media by playing your music every time. How do you respond to that accusation?" a reporter asked.

"Firstly, I don't have a musical group, and the proof is in the open for everyone to see. You never hear my voice. I don't work with the group or even produce their music. Secondly, their music is being played by public demand, and you cannot accuse me of influencing people's musical tastes," Tadpole responded.

"The women's dances are not in sync with religious norms,

yet you let our national broadcaster air them all the time. Don't you feel morality should be promoted?"

"As a woman, you must be ashamed of attacking other successful and hard-working women. In addition, their dances are part of our cultural heritage as passed down from generation to generation. What you want to do is replace who we are with foreign concepts reflecting a colonial mentality. You should be profiling these women and promoting their brand of music instead of being negative and creating evil out of good things."

The reporter abruptly ended her questioning feeling dejected, low and disappointed at having asked something so clear and simple. Tadpole had won, and his music continued to be aired by the national broadcaster.

*

Mudadi and his wife died six months apart, succumbing to that menacing chronic pandemic. Fox died soon after. They were all honoured by Runo, but it was clear his path to a life presidency had a few hurdles removed to his advantage. A currency from a leading world nation was introduced to replace the worthless local currency that no one had confidence in any more. This currency flooded the market in record time, and people were delighted by the magical development. Little did they know that a rebel Bako group in one African country was being funded through their nation. Sabi, whose party member was the finance minister, removed bank withdrawal limits and any limits on cash movements at any point. This allowed the rebel group's foot soldiers to withdraw their cleaned-up cash of any amount to fund their clandestine movement. It was this dirty money that made financial analysts, investment managers and politicians tout the coalition of Runo and Sabi as a match made in some dreamland.

To clean up his act, the leader of a world-leading nation,

that bully, had to put up a brave face. The Bako group embarrassingly abducted schoolchildren. There was an outcry around the world, and the leader sent his wife with some civilians onto the streets to demonstrate for the return of the children. As if that was not enough, he went public about it and gave a press statement accusing the leader of the nation fighting the Bako group of not doing enough. His team went on to press for that leader to show support for his people and go to the battlefront in solidarity. The idea was to have him killed once he stepped into that war zone. He was a master of deception, and that is how he ended up in that top position. After failing to remove the leader from power through the Bako group, he funded the nation's opposition political party in the next elections. The world's leading newspapers and television stations were also pushed to support the opposition political Party. Eventually, the opposition political party won. The outgoing leader's crime was the formalisation of operations for key industries in his country, which meant that the world's leading nation could not continue to loot resources. He had also proposed to diversify the country's reserves and hold them in different currencies. For that, he paid dearly with a rebel insurrection and eventually lost his job.

Most of Sabi's colleagues were caught on the wrong side of the law, but Runo didn't rebuke them or arrest them. This was the leverage he wanted, but he did not hide the incriminating evidence from the offenders. He wanted them to know that they were at his mercy, and he easily achieved that goal. These offending executives sometimes openly praised Runo, to everyone's shock and horror. One of the young lads (who used shoe polish for hairstyling) from Sabi's party, was lured into Runo's clutches, became a business partner, and promised future leadership and his education was fast-tracked using the Heli style template. The rest of the pack never even criticised the regular exorbitant medical bills incurred by Runo as he sought medical assistance abroad. His trips were so frequent that it became questionable how one could survive for so long, spending more time in a hospital bed than in the office. It would seem that some underhand deals were at play under the guise of medical trips. Based on the marriage of convenience, the economy was on a rebound and public confidence improved. Anger towards Runo by the public waned, giving him a new lease on a political shelf-life. He even got credit for the improved economic fortunes. Tiny Mind, however, remained vocal despite a mounting pile of offences. He was also getting a heads up from the world's leading nation and, therefore, he believed that Runo had no power to arrest him. Instead, Runo took advantage of the fact that Tiny Mind was a serial divorcee. He set him up for a biological killer blow with one of those chronic pandemic-carrying girls from Runo's closet. She did a good service to Tiny Mind and biologically destroyed him. He later realised it and unsuccessfully tried to sue her. Runo changed the law, and Tiny Mind was stranded.

Son of the Great Lord died and was replaced by Cowboy after a few months of Runo holding the position as bait. Runo wanted to use the vacancy to fish out ambitious individuals. Things always worked in Runo's favour as he had a few individuals clipped. At this point, Runo had managed to surround himself with family and friends. A brother had been appointed Deputy Chief of Police and another as the Head of the Agricultural cash crops marketing board. A brother-in-law at the Electricity Authority, another at the Roads Fund, a nephew leading one ministry, Cowboy, his deputy and the list was long.

A great find of gems made headlines, and many people flocked to search for the precious stones. It turned out that this was not a discovery but a fifty-year project where an international miner had been secretly shipping out surface-based gems. The miner, together with that other world bully, had never bothered to make the find public. These two were, therefore, enjoying the spoils at the expense of the natives of the nation. No expensive mining equipment was required; therefore, they decided to employ people to pick up the gems for the duration of their exploration contract. The contract had been renewed a few times without any scrutiny and was up for renewal again. This renewal came under fire due to too much scrutiny, which forced the termination of the contract. The minister involved, Runo's toy boy, had been fingered in shady deals with the miner. Not willing to let go of the lucrative gems, the company used local community-based people to continue picking up the stones. Weekly trips were being made to collect and pay for the gems. The practice grew as unemployed youths joined the fray until the whole country knew of the secret.

Heli was the first senior official to claim a huge portion with her estranged man, the Sloppy Man. They fenced their portion and started shipping rubble filled with the gems to their separate abodes for gem selection. The two even forced Runo to give them a concession on the entire gem field on the basis that they had bought the claim from a former owner. Runo was disappointed that the two wanted to muscle him out of the deal, and a fight between them ensued. Runo finally tried to formalise operations, but Heli had had a good harvest. After formalisation, all informal operations were closed off and sealed.

Obi, a well-known money-siphoning conduit for Runo, was appointed the Mines Minister to specifically oversee the gem extraction. Runo had a few companies on his behalf. He had a good take on the mineral as helicopters would fly in after every few hours to collect the loot. The production figures were never made public as all gems were sold in secret, and Runo stashed the money away. Heli was doing the same too. There was a public outcry, but Runo and his team never bothered. Defence, Security and Law enforcement were each given a contract to extract the gems as well. Finally, staggering amounts were alleged to have been realised through gem sales. Amounts more than the country was earning over five years. A few people were fingered in the deals. After a while, it turned out that Marujata was also part of the scam, and the authorities went quiet. Nobody was arrested or prosecuted for the stolen money and gems, although the operations continued in their shadowy state.

Some businessmen were keen to add value to the gems and, therefore, they started a project to cut and polish them. Heli realised that this new project was going to ruin gem sales on the alternative market. The men were, unfortunately for them, accused of many economic crimes. They were arrested, tried, rearrested, and charged, and the case dragged on for years until the project was completely derailed and eventually abandoned.

Heli became a shamelessly corrupt individual. Obi was summoned to a hearing by legislators on corruption. He admitted to illicit deals taking place directly by senior officials and was prepared to name everyone involved. Word was sent out quickly by informants to Heli. An emissary was quickly dispatched to the House of Assembly gathering, to collect Obi, by Heli. Obi had to excuse himself and attend to the Vice President's call. He returned later to continue with the hearing but denied ever having admitted that there were corrupt activities. The press extensively published all the corrupt activities that were taking place in the nation. Due to Heli's involvement, she didn't have any kind words for the development. At a Party Executive meeting, she stated that the exposures being promoted by the press on underhand dealings were the work of subversive elements trying to destroy the Party from within. Individuals and the press were silenced. After that statement, she went on to sell gold worth more than a hundred million dollars in a private transaction. Runo never reprimanded Heli or took steps to fire her.

Runo wanted a share of all mining operations. He took advantage of an open-ended indigenisation policy. Bossy Boy, a recruit by Runo, was put in charge and a Ministry was created for him. Compliance for each company needed a consultant to make proposals and recommendations in terms of the indigenisation guidelines. Bossy Boy had exclusive rights to refer a consultant, whose cost was not less than ten million dollars for each company. Once the consultation stage was done, Bossy Boy would then recommend suitable local partners. In addition, local communities where the mines were operating needed to benefit through community share ownership schemes. Bossy Boy also had authority over the community share ownership schemes. Money paid for these schemes never reached the intended beneficiaries as dear Bossy Boy would siphon all the funds. Despite the public complaints, Runo never said a word or rebuked his Bossy Boy. Instead, Bossy Boy continued to get accolades from Runo.

He was later transferred to the Wildlife Ministry. It did not stop his controversy as many animals were dying mysteriously or from cyanide poisoning, minus their valuable ivory. The blame was passed on to senseless and reckless poaching. People were curious, though, why he never solicited help from the well-trained army of the nation. The poaching continued until it became apparent that senior officials were involved. Due to the fear that the racket would be exposed, the activities stopped. By that time, irreparable damage had been done to the country's wildlife.

Still, Runo did not stop. He wanted to lay his hands on every lucrative mineral in the nation. To achieve his goal, he employed his brother-in-law as the Mines Minister and took control of the master exploration map for the nation. He tasked his new Mines Minister to reserve all the areas with key resources that he wanted. For all areas with existing mining claims, he forced the owners to utilise them or lose them, even if these were reserve claims. One of the biggest miners in the nation was hauled before the courts and forced to cede their land to Runo. All remaining precious mineral reserves held in the government vaults disappeared mysteriously under Runo's convenient arrangement into his hands.

The nation's major highways were in a sorry state, but Runo refused to offer contracts to construction companies that proposed to build and operate the roads before transferring them to the government. He kept on pushing for grants and loans for government to be able to construct the roads. Finally, the government received a loan from a regional bank to dualise one major highway. Runo awarded his company the contract and only resurfaced the road and took the spoils for the project. He awarded a friend from another country a tender for another highway. This friend did not know road construction and did not even have a construction company. He only had to register one for the project. The project cost was set at three times the value with the hope of subcontracting a competent organisation for the true cost and then sharing the balance with Runo.

There was one courageous leader, a Colonel, who had aided many liberation movements for several African countries and beyond. He had also done a lot of work assisting the persecuted natives in that world bully's backyard. In turn, the bully persecuted every recipient of the courageous leader's assistance or those who facilitated the assistance. The courageous leader had even stopped unfair competition and trade between African nations and their former colonisers, which would have seen the collapse of African industries. In his home country, he used key natural resources for the benefit of all citizens. This pushed his country's Human Development Index to be among the top in the world. For all his good deeds, he was passionately loathed by the continent's former colonisers. What he was doing was unacceptable. This man had even proposed a single African currency and had single-handedly put together a hundred-and-forty-two-tonne gold package to support the currency. This was going to threaten that world bully's currency and interests. Another former coloniser was supplying its former colonies with currency, goods and services accounting for over half of its annual revenue. It had forcibly made them sign an agreement for the continuation of colonial rights and control of revenue. This new development would have bankrupted this former coloniser.

According to their rules-based order, an alternative financial system was regarded as trespassing and was punishable by death or through a violent coup. These nations, therefore, hatched a plan to bring him down. Firstly, they befriended and fished him using a lady of African origin. They then persuaded him to invest in their nations, which he did. They later put a script to their international news stations about his alleged dictatorial tendencies before funding a rebel group. A gang of like-minded predatory hunters came together and pounced on his country. Runo was one leader who expressed his anger and displeasure at the development to the extent of closing an Embassy that had shown its support for the gang of predators. Our dear leader, Runo, for all his wrongs, had made the right call in this situation once again. He was vindicated when the courageous leader was gunned down like a dog in the street, without any trial. After his death, the predators confiscated his investments and the gold stocks as well as all-natural resources for themselves. The rebel groups that had been used to fight him were left to fight among themselves for leadership while all wealth was being siphoned out of the country. The country became a failed state in an instant, despite being endowed with one of the most sought-after resources.

To consolidate political power and shake off Sabi, Tadpole introduced a youth policy as well as a gender policy. The two legislative bills were tabled before parliament for debate. Research had been carried out that the youths were the majority in the voting population while women had a higher population compared to men even for voting. Runo, therefore, forced all his legislators to support the two bills. Sabi realised that he was going to lose political mileage, and he followed suit. Some of his members were not amused by his behaviour and labelled the bill as diabolical and likely to destroy the moral fabric. Sabi fired them for telling the truth. The public was not given a chance to air their views on the bills due to the political objective of the pieces of legislation. During the same period, Marujata slowly began to enter the public space. Her introduction was through some charitable work she was doing on a farm she had invaded. Every dignitary who visited the nation was taken for a tour of this facility and the project that Bullman had spearheaded. Great Crocodile felt it was necessary to call Runo to order. He requested a meeting through formal channels to give the impression that his intentions were pure and harmless. When he got to Runo's office, he was very humble and relaxed but his words were not.

"Greetings, Supreme Leader."

"May I remind you that our nation is a Republic and, therefore, we cannot have titles such as that which you want to assign to me." Runo was furious despite his love for supreme leadership. He took it as an insult.

"It's a convenient Republic on paper but in practice, it's not. We have no elections for our leader in the Party, and the first family takes precedence and centre stage in all publicity issues. This inches our nation closer to a dynasty."

"Which publicity stunt?"

"Your wife is a typical example."

"My roommate has done a lot of good charitable work for this nation. You cannot blame her for being a role model."

"If she does a lot of good deeds, as you claim, helping the underprivileged, is there a need to put the camera in front of her all the time?"

"What can I do for you, Great Crocodile, because I don't have time for your insults?"

"Why are you dividing our nation, our families and our people? Now you are even going ahead empowering children and disempowering parents." He didn't look him in the eye but sideways.

"I have done no such thing, Great Crocodile. Educate me on your accusation or allegation,"

"Why did you find it necessary to enact a women's rights and children's empowerment bill?"

"It is vital that they enjoy their freedoms as much as we do. We should not oppress them."

"When have you found time to oppress them? For the past five hundred years, we were under slavery and colonisation, leaving no time to make our own rules or deal with our lives as we wish. There is equal pay for equal work, extended maternity benefits, and equal opportunities for work and education with an added empowerment incentive for women. What else do you need these bills for?"

"It's the trend around the world, and we are signatories to the relevant conventions."

"Don't you feel we are being distracted? The gay agenda, women's rights, children's rights, what other convention are we going to approve? We are playing to their tune and focusing on issues that do not concern us."

"How would they be distractions?"

"Is there an international convention on the freedoms and rights of our people or reparations for the inhumane treatment we suffered over the centuries?"

"Is it a bad thing for women and children to have rights, Great Crocodile?"

"Yet when they have those rights, a sword would have been set between parents and children, creating animosity and a breakdown of the family structure. Let's not take their agenda and make it ours."

"Your concerns have been noted, Great Crocodile."

"Have a nice day, Runo."

Chapter 22

The Sloppy Man continued to interfere with government policy and operations. He wanted continued immunity in all his deals and preferential treatment too. He became a close friend of Sabi as well as all his foreign friends. In a sudden twist of events, Sloppy Man died mysteriously, and an inquest was held. Nothing conclusive was reached by the inquest, and his death was forgotten from the public sphere in a very short space of time. Heli's dealings, however, did not stop. The indigenisation policy was put in place for the agricultural sector which resulted in many poultry projects taking place. Many people took up egg farming and poultry production. Heli realised that she could import chickens with her friends at a very low price and sell them cheaper at a huge profit. She went ahead and brought in several shipments. The law was changed in an instant and her shipments flooded the market forcing the new entrepreneurs out of business overnight.

Cowboy died but was not replaced. Runo wanted to juggle things around until a suitable related body could be found. There was none close by and, therefore, talk of a replacement became taboo. He remained with no close ally at the top.

Runo approached the Great Crocodile after it turned out that Heli and a few of her friends had enlisted foreign assistance to push him out of power. He had run out of ideas on how to deal with Heli because he had always portrayed her in a good light before the public. Now she had the money and had access to all security apparatus in the country. He badly needed help, not just a public charade by Tadpole. He went to the Great Crocodile's home under cover of darkness.

"Great Crocodile, forgive me. I have given you nothing but trouble since the war ended, yet you are the only person who has helped me survive this long. Your loyalty is unquestionable."

"When you talk like this, I know you normally want a favour. Talk and be frank with me, old timer."

"From the bottom of my heart, I mean it." He gestured while holding the heart side of his chest.

"Great betrayer, do you want to crush me or use me yet again?"

"I only approach you in the gravest of situations. You must understand how special you are in this country's political matrix."

"Stop your ineffectual diplomacy, and just tell me what you want. I have no patience for a worn-out ghost like you."

"Hear me out, Great Crocodile. Don't be dismissive of me." He looked remorseful

"Talk then, and hopefully, you eventually want to tell me that you cannot carry out your duties because of old age and failing health."

"Never, Great Crocodile. I was born to rule and can never be a civilian."

"You don't need my assistance then. Go figure out how you can declare your life presidency and let's see if the people will embrace you like their king."

"Great Crocodile, I have had a good run. Do you want me to be tossed into the streets like a dog? Have mercy."

"I told you to talk, but you keep on barking, rumbling and begging with your nauseating failing speech, motion and health. Don't you feel you need a walking stick or wheelchair to avoid falling in public as you always do?"

"No, Great Crocodile. I don't need your temper, but I appeal to your understanding and friendship."

"Friend? Not an impudent old fool like you! I would have never gone through all this hell if I had a friend in you."

"Great Crocodile, hawks are circling and my seat is at stake, my reputation and my legacy will be soiled. True, I agree that I am aged, of failing health, and frail. At least let an old friend die in peace. Help me achieve that, because if she takes over, your career is finished too."

"*Zvokwadi muroyi munhu, kubaiwa anochema*, what a sudden turn of events." He laughed. "However, I am not afraid of that comforter. She is no threat to my ascending to power."

"Remember, there is a constitution. We have to bequeath a good record to our successors."

"That is not my worry or fight, Runo. Your continued stay in power is a problem for me and for this nation. If she topples you, then half of my problems will be gone, and people will know that you were never that good. I will have the last laugh if a simpleton like Heli gets you. *Ndosaka ndakataura kare kuti panomera muxhwe panonyeredza, zvino nhasi wazobvuma woga kuti chingoma chamusinzwi chakazoguma nataisireva. Nhasi wazvikokera mhepo yakatakura mamera.*"

"Help an old friend. I swear by that very sacred passage that gave me life that I will hand over the reins to you."

"This is just for your convenience, Runo, and nothing concrete. It's good that Heli and I now have a common enemy."

"I do not need to create perpetual enmity. Help me. You know when I involve my mother, I will be sincere."

"Everything you do is for your selfish gain. Any witch, murderer, oppressor, serial killer, missionary, slave master, or anything evil is more sincere and better than you. *Unonyanya kutonga nedemo!*"

"I beg you. I will not let you down this time."

"Enough of your nonsense. Find someone else to help you."

"Please, Great Crocodile, I can even give you a clear timeline or even sign an agreement."

"You are desperate, aren't you?"

"Please (struggling to go down on his knees) assist."

"*Kudla chomuzvere hubata mwana*, therefore, it will be on my terms. Once she is out, I am in with your promise to leave gracefully, paving a path to my ascendance to power. I know you have been a nuisance. I will, therefore, help you, but let the elections pass first because you do not know how much sympathy she has from your public rumblings about her good character. After the elections, I will fix your problem before she can get too excited, but before we get to that, do you have the elaborate details of her plan?"

"Your wish is my command. The power will be yours, but at the moment we don't have the full details; that is the reason I need your help."

"*Baba angu shumba iwee.* If you are this inept, why cling on to power?"

"Please, just assist. That is the reason I am begging you."

"Without wasting time, just get the weakest link and use its deepest secrets to get the full story."

"Wonderful, I know the man to talk to, and everything shall be done today."

"Good. It wasn't that difficult, was it?"

"She is also colluding with Sabi not to have the election. What should I do?"

"Since when have you succumbed to public pressure? The election shall go ahead, and that's another offence for her."

"Thank you, Great Crocodile. I know you have a good heart. Let's shake."

"No way. I don't trust that withered hand of yours. I will come for you if you don't meet your end of the bargain, chop your head off and devour your brains."

The weakest link identified was Small Talk (this man looked like a replica of the Small Talk show host. The public decided to name him Small Talk as a way of mocking an executive member of the government), who was rumoured to be a son or brother to Runo. He was softly cornered and gently threatened with jail time for all crimes committed in the past. Runo called him to his residence and almost had a meeting with him in his private office. Before the meeting commenced, Runo was asked to take a call by his security detail. He left a file on the desk clearly labelled with the name of his victim. Runo did not return for an hour as they watched their victim on the security footage. After a while, their victim got curious and opened the file. The crimes detailed therein as well as a warrant of arrest, put him in panic mode. Sweat could be seen all over his forehead as he unbuttoned his shirt, panting for breath. Runo then returned for the final blow. His victim felt weak and powerless, leading to him revealing every little detail of Heli's plans.

An elderly son-in-law to Runobvepi, who had become Runo's uncle and a brother to Runo's mother, died. Runo went for three years before he paid his condolences. The reason given in the end was a tight work schedule. Many considered it a lame excuse. It became clear that there was no real sense of the relationship between them.

Ziva released a book exposing Runo's political life before the nation achieved political independence. He made headlines, and the book sold like hotcakes. It gave a different insight into Runo's life, with the people getting to know publicly for the first time that Runo sometimes stayed over at his girlfriend's place when Lady Amai Marunjeya was not around. This was a once-off dose that made people believe that Runo was human after all rather than the Demi-god image of himself that he had created. However, Runo's image remained intact due to the passage of time and the period chronicled in the book. It turned out that time truly heals and makes people forget too. It could also have been due to people being afraid to comment, fearing Runo's heavy hand. After the book issue phase and hype had died down, Ziva rejoined Runo's Party.

Towards elections, a new and compromised position constitution was still to be adopted. It had been crafted and agreed upon by all Parties but had taken too long to finalise. Tadpole and Runo made sure that the previous clauses that would have dispossessed him of power were disqualified first. This enabled Runo to continue in power, seeing him go past forty years at the helm. It also ensured that he would most probably attain his hundredth birthday in office. Farmers who lost out in the land expropriation exercise got a boost as the new constitution guaranteed their compensation. It was an unfortunate development since the original owners of the land had never been compensated for losing their land, loss of indigenous trees, pollution of the land with chemicals and loss of cultural sites. A simple calculation would have shown that the white farmers owed the native population even after their compensatory damages. This constitutional clause was a giant step backwards in restoring the dignity of native people. Sabi did not contest the document, and neither did all his Party members. Runo's Party also made sure that their internal Party issues were incorporated into the new constitution, especially having two presidential deputies. Sabi was happy with anything being incorporated, provided the number of constituencies was increased. All he wanted was to see an increase in the number of his legislative representatives if constituencies were split. He was not concerned about cost implications to the national treasury but his leverage as a Party. Eventually, elections were delayed to make way for a constitutional referendum. The numbers of people who voted turned out to be more than the registered number of voters, but no one cared because of the outcome. The results were in favour of the new constitution. Sabi was happy, and Runo could not contain his excitement over the new empowerment tool.

Sabi and Heli teamed up to have an election that was due, postponed. Heli knew that if Runo was to win, she would be at a disadvantage due to the legitimacy conferred on him, and her partnership with Sabi would have been broken. She, therefore, supported Sabi as he went again to seek the intervention of the regional bloc that the nation was a member of.

Runo convinced the bloc of the illegalities involved in such a move and the defeat of a flourishing democracy. Besides, he asked them why a leader craving to see a thriving democracy was bent on subverting the very same principle. Sabi lost his case, and elections were put back on track as had initially been planned. He, however, didn't stop his call as he looked for alternative ways to stop the election. To put the matter to bed, a civilian working in the secret service was hired to challenge the constitutionality of delaying elections. He petitioned the government of Runo in a court challenge. The courts ruled in his favour and proclaimed a sixty-day deadline that the government needed to comply with or be held in contempt. Sabi and Heli were devastated as elections had to proceed. Meanwhile, Tadpole was busy putting together an exclusive piece consolidating Sabi's escapades and all the pictures of the events and the women involved as well as their detailed profiles. Children born out of wedlock were also included in the dossier.

The revelations further destroyed Sabi's credibility over and above his ill-preparedness for the elections. His Party did not even have a manifesto or campaign strategy owing to complacency emanating from his last memorable electoral performance. He failed to read the electoral mood. Runo's Party was well prepared, and Marujata came in handy to assist her ailing husband, Runo, in the campaign. Public opinion pointed to the fact that Runo could not afford to go for the election owing to his failing health and age, as he could not stand at the podium for long without assistance. Runo would hold on to the podium for balance while giving a speech, and it was only logical that a person in such a poor state of health had no business in politics. The people were wrong once again. Sabi had, by this time, suspended and subverted his Party constitution. He had gone over the term limit provided therein, adopting Runo's reputation of making rules as he saw fit.

Sabi was handed the heaviest defeat since his Party was

formed. The embarrassment overwhelmed him, and he shamefully rejected the poll outcome as fraudulent. There was no evidence to back up his claim, and he withered into oblivion. A flimsy claim that ballot papers were preset to migrate ink from Sabi to Runo was the biggest joke Sabi's supporters conjured to hide from their humiliation. Heli was axed as Runo's deputy, accused of working with Sabi and of attempting to topple her boss. Her leaving office was smooth as she failed to put any defence, as expected. Jabu was also relieved of his duties for siding with Heli. Gem mining operations were revamped, and she lost her stake. Marujata's influence was growing with each passing day as she assumed decision-making roles and gave Runo directives. The ailing man, Runo, was simply following blindly without any fear of the possible consequences Marujata's decisions could have.

Tadpole, too, was happy to spoon-feed Marujata with venom. He had found a weak target. Weak in intellect and brain power. Runo appointed another deputy and the Great Crocodile to neutralise the Great Crocodile's power. Whip, was the other deputy. He had a pea-sized brain despite his huge figure and stature that was ready to compete for top national honours, both as the most vertically and horizontally gifted in the nation. The Great Crocodile encountered several accidents soon after his appointment. He survived, and people started questioning what it was that was happening.

In a desperate measure, Runo's other deputy also had an accident to divert and create a pattern. When accidents had failed, his office was laced with a dangerous drug on a few occasions, but someone else fell into the trap. Eventually, a huge boulder was placed on a ceiling above the Great Crocodile's chair and desk. They hoped that he would die peacefully in his office without any assistance. Unfortunately for his enemies, the boulder broke the ceiling and crushed the desk before the Great Crocodile got there. A hostile security detail was then assigned to the Great Crocodile, and he got rid of them to revert to his own. Runo never indicated when he would retire but continued as if everything was normal. He was being evasive and seemed to be going against the Great Crocodile in his daily dealings. Whip did not waste time abusing his office and newly acquired powers. Local beneficiaries of the farm redistribution programme faced a new wave of evictions as Whip offered the land to his colleagues.

Runo knew the situation was not ideal for him where there was only one grouping in the Party after the Sloppy Man's side had been dismantled or its shelf life had expired. Knowing also that it was only a matter of time before the Great Crocodile visited him, he put out an instruction never to entertain any meeting with him. He would always hallucinate about the Great Crocodile, asking questions, especially just after or in between his naps.

"Is he coming? Is he starting an insurrection? Hide me from this man; I still need my power."

His wife, Marujata, was taken aback by Runo's behaviour. She wondered why he was suddenly becoming hypertensive at the sight or mention of the Great Crocodile. It forced her to push her old timer. Eventually, he told Marujata about the deal with the Great Crocodile.

"Understand, my roommate. I have used people along the way. The abuse and deception have taken their toll on me. I had to ask him for a favour for the umpteenth time. Looking at my age, you can tell I am in no mood for another fight. I had hoped to rule until my dying day, but if it cannot happen, so be it. I can still die with the unfulfilled bucket list item, cold in my bed, one of these days."

She was gravely devastated and held Runo by the collar before pushing him to a chair close to the staircase in a rage.

"What deal did you sign with the Great Crocodile?"

"It's a gentleman's agreement. We did not sign anything."

"There is no deal then. Go and tell him."

"That is unreasonable. I don't have the energy to pick another fight."

"I have the burden of cleaning after you every time. In public, I am the shadow walking stick disguised as a loving mate. We have plundered, maimed and destroyed to preserve your power, but now you want to abandon me. It's not going to happen, old man." She slapped him, and he fell into a chair.

He rose and responded: "I am your husband, but you call me an old timer. That is very disrespectful, my roommate."

"I don't care, old timer. You shall remain in power and make sure you hand over the reins to someone subservient to me."

"That is not possible. It takes too many resources to achieve and will create too many enemies."

"I am not listening to your excuses. It's either you give me what I want, or I poison you and bury you in the freezer."

"You will still have your problems and could still die in prison. Why can't you let me appoint him? It should keep him happy and stop his power march madness as well."

"That is not going to happen under my watch."

She pushed him over the staircase, and the security detail had to rush to his rescue. The damage had already been done and, therefore, Runo had to be airlifted abroad for medical attention. There were rumours of his death, but he quickly returned and showed up with a great welcome gathering at the capital's international airport. The rumour faded away very quickly. Marujata's influence continued to grow because of Runo's backing. Whenever she wanted funds, she would either go directly to the Minister of Finance and threaten him or use one of her frontmen.

The most used frontman was the infamous and publicity-loving Fat Boy. Fat Boy would participate in several government tenders and win them against competent and serious business people. In addition to winning the tenders, he would be paid in advance. In other instances, a tender would be floated specifically for the Fat Boy and money paid in advance for services that would never be delivered. Once, a national paper tried to expose the rot and the staff responsible almost lost their jobs. Everyone retreated into their shells after the incident. Marujata extended her projects to various sectors. She had a construction company that would win many tenders because of her influence. Marujata had business interests in road construction as well. Many of her companies had no formal business agreements for shareholders. If a company won a tender and she owned 40% of the shares, she would ask for 40% of the value of a tender up front. Project expenses or running costs of the company were not her prerogatives. Co-owners of companies, therefore, suffered losses as they tried to keep their companies afloat and to fulfil tender requirements.

Once Runo had settled comfortably, the Great Crocodile came to him unannounced.

"Am I talking to the resurrected ailing old timer?"

"You should feel sorry for me instead of insulting me."

"A man's word defines him. What you represent is the total embodiment of evil. You need to die a traitor's death."

"I am bedridden most of the time, and you should be ashamed of making such comments, Great Crocodile."

"You don't need my sympathy, old timer, but to renounce your throne. You have stifled the nation's development for too long. Where on earth have you seen a senile invalid ruling a nation? We are being ruled by a relic, an artefact!"

"I wish I could hand over the power, but I cannot."

"It's as expected of a traitor like you. I now know how to deal with a betrayer of your magnitude. Look, Runo, I have an agreement. You sign off; then we are done."

"Unfortunately, I cannot. There are too many people with vested interests."

"I am not falling for your tricks ever again. All I want is your signature, and this ends peacefully."

"No, Great Crocodile."

"You deserve to die then." He prepared to toss him through a window.

"No, Great Crocodile, you are not a shedder of blood. Let me just die in office."

"That is exactly how I am going to help you achieve that goal."

"You will die in prison and lose everything you ever wanted."

"Have you forgotten that I will be in power after your demise? They will bow to me, and so will your corpse."

Runo pressed his emergency buzzer, and his security details came in a flash. They surrounded the Great Crocodile and threatened to shoot him. Marujata came running, too. The Great Crocodile had to let go.

Chapter 23

Marujata was quick to enlist Tadpole's assistance. She had a secret encounter with him, and with time, these encounters became a norm. Subtle rumours were pointing to an illicit fling with this man from Sodom.

"I know you hate the Great Crocodile with a passion, Tadpole. How can you ensure he falls by the wayside to guarantee your safety and mine?"

"What has he done now?"

"He wants the old man to hand over power because they had a pact."

"What pact, madam?"

"All the assistance he got was from the Crocodile, and it's payback time."

"We cannot allow that to happen for the sake of our future. I agree."

"Can you do it?"

"I must admit that he is a strong opponent, *kuvaraidza nguva kuteya zhou neriva chaiko*, but it's worth a try. *Matanda manyoro mazungunutswa ungangosiya nerine muchenje.*"

"You have to put your mind to it, Tadpole. The gravity of the matter needs total commitment. If we fail, he might hit back in just one blow."

"True. You could not have said it any better."

"I think you do understand now. Do it, Tadpole."

"Don't worry. I will provoke him to say something in public so that he can be charged with treason."

"You must be quick and firm to stop his madness. We cannot delay for long without raising public interest. I will watch your back."

Tadpole quickly identified three overzealous women to sing his song. They were duly rewarded. At each public gathering, they would accuse the Great Crocodile of harbouring presidential ambitions. This mantra was repeated a few times until the press asked the Great Crocodile to comment.

"Please refer to the person who told you that story or rumour," was the Great Crocodile's response, and Tadpole knew he was losing the plot. He encouraged the women to repeat the same mantra during the Great Crocodile's presence as well. Bossy Boy, a novice in the Party (also from Sodom and a conduit for siphoning funds), who had been put in charge of mobilising support, was roped in by Tadpole. He had intimate insights and encounters with Marujata. Even the elders in the nation had cautioned him on this immoral act. Bossy Boy's task was to destabilise the Great Crocodile's power base. He, therefore, accused a few people and had them eliminated. It worked in a few districts but hit a brick wall in several regions. Many fired back at being tossed around by a newbie in the Party and called for his sacking. The public insult strategy did not work, as the Great Crocodile never responded publicly. It instead attracted a negative response that resulted in the women losing their positions of power. Bossy Boy's position was also in danger. Tadpole and Marujata had to approach Runo over the matter to save their boy and their failed strategy. They had to disturb Runo's daily nap of resting his ageing bones that were unable to cope with his presidential duties.

"We are trying to help you survive the Great Crocodile demanding power, but it seems you are working against us," Marujata opened the conversation.

"I don't understand. What are we talking about?"

"Tadpole, give him the full story."

"Mr President, we are sorry to deprive you of your much-needed sleep to enable you to recharge your batteries. However, we are here to serve you and protect your interests. We could never allow anyone to take advantage of you or distract you from your God-given right to be the life president of this nation."

"You speak well, Tadpole, but what have you done to protect me this time? We have not spoken before, and never at any time have I given you a single task."

"I must know what is best for my president. You don't necessarily have to call on me each time."

"You still haven't answered my question."

"Let him finish, old timer. Stop interrupting. You are too old, senile, out of touch and cannot keep up with what's happening in this marriage, let alone the Party and the nation. Go on, Tadpole."

"The point, Mr President, is that those ladies who were relieved of their duties were doing you a great favour. Bossy Boy is also another pony on your side."

"Haven't these people been insubordinate to their seniors and have gone against Party protocol? Also, this Bossy Boy, as we all know, is from Sodom like you Tadpole and previously called for a youthful president. How does he suddenly become a saint?"

"It's a long story, Mr President. The people that Bossy Boy wants to remove were appointed by the Great Crocodile to upstage you at any vote and to sway any agenda at any time. We intend to ensure that we have people who are loyal to you."

"Don't forget, old timer, that the Great Crocodile wanted to crush you in this very house and remove you violently from power. You must listen and act quickly."

"What have you got on your mind, Tadpole?" Runo could see an opportunity to start another grouping opposed to the

Great Crocodile, and the timing to do it was now.

"We can start by guaranteeing your candidacy for the next election due in four years. Any opposition from the Great Crocodile will be treated as treason. Bossy Boy will accomplish the task by using the people that he has appointed in each province. You have to make sure the Great Crocodile does not attend any of your foreign assignments because he might outshine you. On every public address, make sure that you let everyone know that you intend to fulfil your mandate from the electorate. There is no agreement beside that, and you shall not go against the people."

"It's a good start. You must also recruit everyone opposed to the Great Crocodile so that you can have legitimacy over the other group, which is bent on subverting power. Let's have another conversation after the Great Crocodile's response or once we have achieved the initial goal," Runo concurred with them.

"Thank you for the mandate, Mr President."

Runo again became a shadow sponsor of a grouping opposed to the Great Crocodile.

It did not take long before two provinces declared Runo as their preferred candidate for the next election, although they had just concluded another. Two more followed, but the trend immediately stopped as other provinces were quiet and refused to make any statements. Bossy Boy accused some of the provinces of insubordination and recommended elections to find suitable candidates loyal to the Party. Runo was quick to endorse the idea.

Elections were quickly conducted but were condemned as not meeting the preconditions to make them free and fair. Either the same candidates opposed to Runo had won, or those imposed by Runo had lost. Follow-up elections were arranged, and the same results were achieved. It was repeated three times over in a year of squabbling until the exercise was abandoned. Bossy Boy accused the provinces of not following

Party protocol and promoting factionalism. A sparring game ensued until it was clear that Bossy Boy had lost credibility and control. In the end, he was not welcome in some provinces.

To break the impasse and discipline the defiant people, Runo was called to intervene. Runo was requested to attend a disciplinary meeting in one of the provinces to resolve the matter. This was Tadpole and Bossy Boy's solution to intimidate the people. Runo attended and was told the truth, which he did not want to hear either. The meeting ended in a stalemate with no resolutions, and Runo promised a second meeting to iron out the issues. The next time, Runo sent Tadpole to whip the people into line since he was too embarrassed to attend another meeting, which he knew of its outcome in advance.

It was Runo's decisions they were against, although they pretended it was his appointees' policies. Each time they complained of the incompetence and oppression by his appointed ministers, governors or parliamentarians, they were directly attacking Runo. He was silently livid and protesting against their candidness. It had been Runo's lifelong resolution to have the incompetent surround him to help elevate his image to infallible status. As expected, nobody attended as they had no respect for this man from Sodom. Bossy Boy was the next emissary, and nobody pitched up for the meeting either. Runo was furious but had no choice. The Great Crocodile was happy with the result but made no comments. He only kept secret communications with the people.

At his next public appearance, Runo never made his life presidential wish a secret. He stated, "Some are saying Runo is old, so he should step down. No! When my time comes, I will tell you." It was a bitter pill for the public to swallow, but there was no choice. He even made it clear that he was not going to allow the Great Crocodile anywhere near the centre of power when he said, "Some are even suggesting that I should hand over power because we also want to rule. I say to you, 'Is that the agreement we had with people in the last elections when I was democratically elected the constitutional leader of this nation?' The answer is no."

Runo called a meeting with his foot soldier, Tadpole. Marujata, as an interested party, was in attendance. He wanted a solution to neutralise the Great Crocodile's influence and regain control of the Party by whatever means. The mood was low. They seemed to be making funeral arrangements. Marujata had her hands supporting her head and her eyes almost in tears. Tadpole had his left hand supporting his cheek, while Runo had his left palm on his forehead and fist on his right cheek. They all looked defeated and decided to hit any target while hoping and praying for the Great Crocodile to stumble.

"Tadpole, you have been in this for a long time. We need control of all organs of the Party, put our feet down and make sure we have no dissenting voices. Give me some ideas."

"The veterans are completely opposed to you, with Wood Cutter and Warrior leading the chorus against your continued stay in power. The ladies are quiet, but we need someone who can push them to be totally behind you. At least we have a new boy, Novice, for the youth who can be on our side."

"We need a step-by-step approach, Tadpole, not to shoot in the dark."

"You can deal with these veteran leaders first, Mr President."

"I am in my twilight years, Tadpole. We cannot afford the luxury of a decade-long plan. If need be, let's have simultaneous or concurrent plans."

"I understand. That is the reason we ensured that, in your frail health state, you attended every gathering and arranged even your hoisting up to light up that flame at our Independence celebrations just to silence your critics. If you stumble at any function, we attack the journalists to ensure nothing is captured on camera. We have made special walkways on rallies to assist you in getting to the podium with ease. There shall be no wheelchair as madam will hold your hand at all times. We are ensuring that quarterly, you fly out for your medical check-up and health boost to ensure that what your body cannot absorb normally is injected into your bloodstream."

"Thank you for the care, Tadpole, but let's get down to business. Remember it's not quarterly checks but monthly as we have to cover up most of our gems sales trips as health checkups."

"Of course, we were digressing but only to buttress the point. However, you can tell us how we can deal with Wood Cutter and Warrior, Mr President."

"I will have them arrested and rearrested to intimidate them. They will capitulate."

"How about the rest of the team? We need to break them up."

"Find nice vehicles from a top vehicles sales company and have them delivered to the rest of their leadership."

"We don't have funds as a Party or government, Mr President, How do we pay for the gifts?"

"Buy them on credit."

"We still won't be able to repay the loans."

"Just get the vehicles."

"Then we won't repay them. Let's go to another group."

"We can have our dear lady madam Marujata leading the women."

"You have forgotten that she is not diplomatic, and we cannot afford her shouting at the people at every turn."

"We use that to our advantage. She will address those critical gatherings where some officials have to be dressed down. Besides, the previous premier lady once held such a position."

"There is no time to argue. That shall be done. What else?"

"We can probably run with these ideas for now."

"No, Tadpole, you are not that good. This youthful parliamentarian, Novice, craves power and recognition. He can mobilise a million-man march for me to silence my critics. The Great Crocodile needs several plans to overwhelm him."

"I like that, Mr President. The top post for the youths is vacant, and we can use this as a test and carrot on whether to appoint him. Everything he needs should be provided to drive him crazy."

"You forget that we also need money for all these operations. How do we fund them?" Marujata asked.

"Damn, I didn't realise it could be so costly to deal with the Great Crocodile. We cannot possibly achieve all this without upsetting not only the nation's budget but the economy as well. However, we have no choice, we're damned if we do and damned if we don't. What shall we do, Mr President?"

"We shall do it. By whatever means, I must fight anyone who dares to scuttle my lifelong anointment to rule."

"Where do we get the money, Old Timer? Your officials give me a hard time each time I want to collect money from them," Marujata intervened.

"We have parastatals, the Minister of Finance and the Central Bank Governor, my roommate. You have my blessings. I shall call them in for a lecture. The police traffic section is a potential money-spinning venture. I will make sure the head of police gives his people daily targets to achieve what we need and even stash some for our pockets."

"I will leave that to her," Tadpole responded, ready to leave.

"You are not an exception, Tadpole. There are various opportunities to get money from your Ministry too. See to it that you contribute."

"Very well, Mr President. I will do it."

Chapter 24

Wood Cutter and Warrior were arrested without following due process of the law. They, however, remained defiant. After a few legal battles, they were released but were very vocal about the anarchy Runo was promoting to save his job. They were arrested again and again until they were eventually expelled from the Party when it was clear that they would not vacillate or waiver from their position. Their wish was to oversee a leadership renewal in the Party and nation. Perpetual self-imposition by Runo was no longer tenable. After each court session or release from prison, they took an opportunity to chide Runo while the press was still around. Other veterans of the war came to their rescue and demonstrated against the injustice. They wanted an audience with Runo at the Party offices. Runo refused to attend to them and instead sent the police riot squad. The veterans bore the burden of smoking tear gas from innumerable canisters, pressurised and itchy water from water cannon bowsers, uncontrolled savaging from police German Shepherd dogs and endless whipping with police baton sticks.

Runo had decided to stoop very low in his usual style to desperately safeguard his position. His sadistic terror tendencies were on full public display. Novice and Bossy Boy were instructed to insult the liberation war veterans in any demeaning words they saw fit. They were even encouraged to question Wood Cutter's war credentials. Tadpole spread rumours through social media that Wood Cutter was only a Taxi Driver while in exile and never participated in the war of Liberation. The veterans decided to book a new venue to discuss their grievances and make resolutions. Before they could sit down to conduct their business, the policemen made a follow-up raid, pitilessly crushing them. Again, they dispersed and planned to come back once the dust had settled, but their leaders continued with the fight. A loud and foul-mouthed lady was immediately hand-picked and appointed to take over from Wood Cutter, but she had no followers. Tadpole asked her to blame everything on the influence of the Great Crocodile, which she religiously did.

Novice carried out a desperate campaign, bordering on insanity, to mobilise all the people for a great million-man march in support of Runo. He was doing it under Runo's instructions to silence the Great Crocodile. It was a repeat of what Jabu had done previously. There were endless banners, billboards, Runo's regalia, as well as press advertisements. On the day of the march, Novice threatened all schools and bus operators to cooperate. Anyone who refused was to be treated as a traitor and reported to the president. Schoolchildren were forced out of school to travel and attend the march in solidarity with Runo's continued rule. These school children had been instructed to report for school in civilian clothing.

The day was partly overcast, very cold and windy in winter. Due to the shortage of funds by the government and the Party, none of the people attending the march was offered any food. The address by Novice, Marujata and Runo commenced late in the afternoon. People were shaking and shivering, their noses dripping, but they had no choice.

Marujata praised Novice but had some very unkind words for the Great Crocodile. Runo cemented the idea that he would never betray the people by reneging on his promise to rule as long as they wanted him to. He indicated that he was touched by the support the people had shown to willingly and voluntarily organise a march in support of his leadership. He felt very humbled as an exemplary leader rather than someone who wanted to usurp power through unorthodox means. He ensured that daily broadcast schedules on Radio and Television were disrupted to give full coverage of the march and the address thereafter. Even the main evening television news bulletin had to be cut short to accommodate the day's activities. The crowd dispersed in the evening. Some buses ran out of fuel, and others broke down. Runo and his project, the Novice, never followed up on the welfare of the people. The bus owners had to send mobile garage repairers and food to help the cold and starving crews.

There were no positive reviews of the solidarity march from the press. There was no euphoria from the Party on the solidarity march showing a tired mood by Party members. There was no positive feedback from the general public on the solidarity march either. The winner of the march was Runo's political ambition as he got the illegitimate endorsement he craved, albeit from himself. Other collaborators like Novice gained financially, but their reputation and social standing were seriously affected by their shameless obedience to money. Runo felt that he had played into the Great Crocodile's hands yet again. The march did not make a thunderous impact or intimidate enough. However, there was a feeling that the youths were a better crowd than the sceptical aged crew.

It was back to the drawing board for the desperate crew, but they soldiered on with Marujata's appointment. First, she was proposed as the candidate for the women's wing of the Party. It turned out they needed to have her as part of the Party structures first. Runo imposed her in the capital. Party members in the capital rejected her and proposed an alternative region for her. Runo came out guns blazing, accusing many of the leaders. He had them relieved of their duties or arrested, and the appointment went ahead unopposed. Marujata automatically became part of the executive arm of the Party. The lady who was in charge of the women's wing had been persuaded by a quiet, reserved and often respected Party elder, a lady who had been secretly sent by Runo. She diligently performed her task, not knowing what other plans were being brewed behind the scenes. The elder was not aware of a potential whirlwind that could turn into a hurricane before the possibility of turning into a rampaging tornado. Marujata could now team up with Runo, Tadpole, Bossy Boy and the newly appointed Novice to influence all decisions. The stage was set to attack and crush the Great Crocodile from a solid front.

The loud and foul-mouthed lady upped her game and had several confrontations with the Great Crocodile. He ignored her anyway. At one meeting she even made a slogan,

"To hell with the Great Crocodile."

The Great Crocodile responded, "To hell with him."

She was confused and did not say anything further. A minister who had been appointed to be in charge of the veterans' affairs was not spared the humiliation either. She felt he was not bold enough to support Marujata's position and did not like her taking over as the veterans' leader. At the same event, the minister also did not have any kind words for the lady and Whip. He felt Whip was a sellout in supporting Marujata and working against the Great Crocodile.

Meanwhile, Bullman's successor, Prophet Jona, failed to find his feet from the day of his appointment. He was baffled by the way things were structured. People could withdraw unlimited cash amounts from the banking system; even a million was possible. If any bank limited the withdrawals, then one could utilise several branches to achieve their target. People were charged for depositing funds, and no interest was paid on bank balances. Many banks were undercapitalised, and depositors' funds were at risk. Any policy shift needed not to affect Runo in any way. Companies continued to fold, and government revenues were dwindling. Runo put up levies for roads and fuel. Millions of dollars were realised, but not a penny was used for its intended purpose, nor did the funds reach government coffers. Runo could ask Prophet Jona (stemming from the connotations of his first name, the public decided to prefix it with prophet, as the man from the bible and the feeling that economic practices were more of guess-work than well-accepted principles) to make funds available at any moment. However, it was clear there was no reasonable source. He was, therefore, forced to issue loans to finance the government's daily expenditures. This worked until the government could not repay the loans, so he had to come up with other innovative ways. The banks, who were the initial buyers of the loans, struggled to meet their customers' cash demands. Queues formed, and a run on banks became imminent. Runo forced Prophet Jona to issue an alternative currency to run parallel to the official currency. He intended to use the alternative to settle the position of the loans. Whenever there was a shortage of foreign currency, they could print and buy from alternative sources. Prophet Jona refused, and Runo called him for a meeting.

"Jona, my Prophet, how do you do?"

"How do you do, Mr President?" The Prophet hesitantly responded.

"You are not taking good care of my needs. How can I be alright?"

"According to any rules in the book, I have not strayed yet," The Prophet affirmed a principled stance.

"You realise that we have a mounting debt, and I need con-stant medical care abroad. My people need to be kept happy at all times; therefore, I have to travel with a huge staff entou-rage on each trip. If you consider my family, then you will understand my lavish lifestyle needs. What have you to offer?"

"The solution is simple, Mr President."

"Let me have the simple solution, Prophet Jona."

"Just cut back on the expenditure, Mr President, and you will endear yourself to the people."

"What people, Prophet Jona?"

"The people that voted you into office."

"No one gave me this job because I never made an application."

"Mr President, you promised the people, and you have to deliver."

"How long have you been in power?"

"Just a little over a year, Mr President."

"How long have I been in power?"

"Almost forty years, Mr President."

"Good. You must know how politics work. I cannot lose my privileges and power over the people due to some corporate governance issue. It's just a fad."

"In good conscience, we cannot do that, Mr President. It's suicide."

"I appoint and disappoint, my Prophet. My instruction is, therefore, supreme."

"We cannot repeat our mistakes of the past. People would think we are unreasonable."

"Imagine, Jona, that your wife spends 97% of her time with her boss either at work or having fun because they have an illicit relationship which has become public knowledge. You instruct her to stop working and be a housewife, an option that makes you happy. Unfortunately, you will be seen everywhere with her having fun. Do you think people might say you are unreasonable?"

"It's a personal matter." Prophet Jona was shocked by the example and how this matter had been made available and of personal interest to the president.

"Then you and I are in the same boat, Prophet Jona. Don't worry yourself and do as I instruct."

"Mr President, can I have time to think about this?"

"Suit yourself, Prophet, but you must remember to also allocate some funds for my daughter, who is having a baby in one of my favourite countries."

The following day, Prophet Jona's ranch was invaded by some strange individuals. They were busy helping themselves to everything that was on the farm. There was a break-in at his house, and a fire was reported at one of his companies. The signs were too visible to miss for a Prophet. He had to acquiesce to Runo's demands without any further debate. This accelerated the run on banks, but Runo did not care.

Many roadblocks were mounted on the country's roads. To drive across a town, a driver would go through a minimum of five roadblocks. Tourist activities were severely disrupted. Police stations had only skeletal staff available to attend to emergencies or accident scenes. They had no transport because police vehicles would have been used by those manning road-blocks. Policemen were stationed at stop signs, faded road markings and signs, where one or two traffic lights were not working, and road curves to ambush motorists. Instead of paying for fines at police stations, spot fines became the norm. Fines were introduced for any imaginable offence. Plain reflectors were introduced on vehicles and people were fined for not displaying these on cars. When all drivers had complied, diamond reflectors were introduced to replace plain reflectors. After a while, reflectors inside vehicle doors were also introduced. Drivers were fined for torn seats, flat spare tyres, non-display of a vehicle mass, cellphones on the dashboard, and anything the police felt needed punishment for the day. Identity particulars or car keys were confiscated for any driver without the required amount of money for the fines.

Any police teams not meeting their daily monetary targets during the day would work overtime, returning to their road posts overnight. Commercial passenger transporters, motorists and the public complained, but Runo ignored them. Nothing changed. Commercial transporters were the Police's easy access to cash. Every driver needed to pay a daily road access fee in the morning to avoid harassment during the day. The army temporarily halted the police routine when they beat up traffic policemen, but Runo was determined and he unleashed more of them on the road again. From all of Runo's money-spinning rackets and robbing of his people as well as the nation, it was rumoured that he had a stash of over ten billion in cash at his house. This was in addition to all his real estate and other local investments not paid for by his earnings, gifts and foreign investments.

Additional toll gates were constructed along all the nation's pothole-riddled highways. Several millions of dollars were collected each day. However, none of the funds were used to repair or upgrade the roads. A Roads Authority established by Runo would not give a logical explanation to the nation on the whereabouts of the money. None of the leaders was relieved of their duties for failing to account for the money despite growing public pleas. It became clear that the bigger share of the funds was for the benefit of the supreme leader, dear leader and life president.

There was very little influence from Sabi as his Party's footprint had faded; its structure was invisible to the naked eye, with only the name reminding the people that there was once an opposition with great potential. No one listened anymore to what Sabi or his Party members had to say. In addition, Sabi was believed to have been poisoned by one of his Party members in cahoots with Runo. His health was deteriorating at such an alarming rate that many wondered why he continued to replicate Runo's love for power. He had busted his Party's leadership term limit twice, resulting in several splinter groups, but he still held on. This was the situation that Runo wanted, and it gave him the space to operate freely without anyone posing any threat to his actions. He could afford to fight the Great Crocodile without any restraint.

It became increasingly evident that Runo would eventually fail in his fight against the Great Crocodile in the school of public opinion as the economy was suffering. His forgetfulness, mindless fight against his junior and support for a pack of feeble-minded individuals past their sell-by date were a cause for concern. Runo would never accept options such as retirement, pass the baton, succession, and time to leave the stage. Even his nephew, Cub, was forced into exile for advising him to pass the baton. His long-time spiritual guide had also died after she had proffered the same advice. With Runo, it was best not to give him unsolicited counsel, advice not in line with his vision or advice that would benefit the generality of his people. Runo was worried about the possibility of losing it all and needed any method to get his paws back on the leash. He called in Tadpole for a rethink and further attack on the Great Crocodile. Tadpole waited for more than two hours before they could meet because Runo could not wake up from his daily slumber. The meeting was scheduled to commence at eight in the evening but only started after ten. He had to wait because he had no option. His life depended on it, but he realised Runo was no longer a reliable bet. It was a matter of when, not if, Runo's life ended either peacefully in his sleep or by falling while attempting to walk. When Runo finally came, there was no apology for his lateness.

"Hopefully, you have built many termite mounds to distract the Great Crocodile."

"Not a chance, Mr President. He is still marching across barriers with ease. I don't think he is afraid of anything you say or do."

"School me, Tadpole. What is your theory?"

"Why don't we propose another candidate to shake him because you may be all too familiar to him?"

"Are you suggesting that I should leave my seat?"

"No, Mr President. We have to scare the Great Crocodile so that he can make irrational decisions. They have even made a song for him as the president-in-waiting. *Mdhara Vachauya* is the song, Your Excellency. Let me do it."

"If Diesel cannot show his mettle, I have to rule from the grave. He is such a weak character despite the post being his to take, but he cannot even make a move."

"You can rest assured I could scare the daylights out of him with the Diesel proposal."

"Too many people know your history as a traitor in the war and your Sodom origins. The last time you tried to be a war hero, all hell broke loose, and everything was exposed. Who else do you propose?"

"Your wife can be a possible contender with her vociferous and intimidatory approach. She could save the day rather than relying on Diesel. We want someone or something that can scare the Great Crocodile."

"Her fall will be quick. With a shut blind mind and an open wide mouth, she can never survive. Pretending to be my roommate and mother of my children is proving too onerous for her. Imagine how she will make it after I am gone with all the enemies she is making."

"Let me try the Diesel agenda first while Novice works on a countrywide tour. We could kill two birds with one stone. A campaign for the forthcoming elections and the succession issue while eliminating the Great Crocodile."

"Try harder, Tadpole. I think you may need to prepare a dossier in the executive meeting to soil his reputation with anything you can come across."

"I will do it, Your Excellency."

Novice worked on the rallies while Tadpole worked on sprucing up the public image of the preferred candidates. He wrote an instalment in a weekly newspaper on behalf of Diesel. Not many fancied Diesel and, therefore, the articles never got much attention. He then forced a guest speaker invitation at a political speaking forum. In his speech, he created a straw man as a political chameleon and chronicled how that straw man had turned into a traitor and was not deserving of any space in the political arena of the nation. That straw man was named the Great Crocodile. He brought in another who was a fine example with credible credentials and worthy of people's recognition. That ideal straw man was Diesel. Tadpole had wanted the release of Diesel's name as a successor to coincide with the commencement of Novice's youth campaign rallies.

Unfortunately, Diesel's proposed name came as a joke to the nation. People made unpalatable comments on the proposition and how Diesel was a pathetic choice of a successor. Tadpole's ego was deflated, and Runo could not even talk about Diesel because of the cold response from the public. His agenda for the initial campaign instalments had to be changed hurriedly. Even Runo's health check proved that his stamina was waning and he was not up for the task. At the campaign rally, Runo was supposed to make a grand entrance, waving and punching his fist in the air. Age restricted his impression, grand entrance, as well the pomp and fanfare. He crab walked into the venue, a stadium, his hand firmly held by Marujata. It could have appeared as a loving hand-in-hand, but she seemed overwhelmed by the heavy support he needed. He tried a couple of times to punch his fist into the air, but the feeble supporting muscles could not accomplish the task. It seemed he had only attempted to point into the air.

A teenage girl who had requested her mother to accompany her to the gathering asked, confused, "Mum, you always talk of young love. Does the same happen in old age that there is aged love?"

"Why do you ask my daughter?"

"I always see Marujata holding His Excellency Runobvepi's hand all the time."

"Are you impressed, my child?"

"I don't know."

"Why?"

"I hardly see old couples holding hands. Probably this is a perfect couple."

"No, my baby. He is too old to stand on his own. She, on the other hand, needs his power and money."

"But mother, she can employ servants to do that."

"She needs to make her presence felt and also for public grandstanding."

"You mean women can do anything for money?"

"Some women."

"Which ones?"

"You will know as you grow up if it's the immoral, the desperate, the evil or the lazy."

"It seems a big task, Mum."

Runo slept through all the other speeches and only woke up when it was his turn. Cameras were turned away each time Runo fully utilised his sleeping couch. Security details were ready whenever he stumbled to distract the public. He addressed his first rally with subdued optimism, holding on to the podium to avoid any fatal tumble. Even Marujata was not sure whether to engage her scornful nature or withdraw and adopt a lady-like stance. She, however, intimated that the only person entitled to name a successor was Runo and nobody else. It was time he did, and she was going to force him to do it. Novice, however, was very exuberant yet delusional, harping on about Runo as a heaven-sent angel. The show was unimpressive as some who had been force-marched to the gathering started trickling out of the venue before the speeches were concluded.

After the campaign rally, Woodcutter and Warrior issued a scathing attack on the farce of a rally and immature pronouncements by Marujata. They described the proposition by Marujata as a mathematical impossibility and urged everyone to strongly oppose any dictatorial or dynastic tendencies. They went on to print T-Shirts for all veterans with the following inscriptions on the front: "War Veterans of the Nation, Say no to Dictatorship & life Presidency, Family Dynasty, Corruption & Tribalism." This irked Runo.

The Great Crocodile realised that the battle to oust him was on, so he held a secret meeting with his close friends, These Nations and Fly Half. These two were in charge of the

Defence forces of the nation. They met at a farm, Fly Half's farm, far away from the city one afternoon.

"Gentlemen, the senile fox is at it yet again."

"Don't you suppose he will just fall off his perch and die any time now?" These Nations asked.

"He is as strong as a proverbial horse; don't be fooled."

"Why, then, does he take these frequent medical trips?" Fly Half asked.

"To sell precious minerals, trading in endangered species and externalising foreign currency. It's very plausible that he could outlive all of us."

"Any possibility of us letting nature take its course rather than fight?" These Nations asked.

"*Chakataira pasi ndechomunhu wose asi chiri mumuti ndechewagona kukwira,*" The Great Crocodile responded.

"Who is in danger at present?" These Nations asked again, realising that the stakes were high.

"Their prime target is me, but they will also cleanse the whole system if it so happens that they succeed. Just like you have to understand that *hapana chembwa Tenzi vararira mutakura.*"

"Should we prepare for a Party that can beat him in the elections?" asked Fly Half.

"No, not at all. *Chakachenjedza ndechakatanga, haungachenjedzi Nyamukuta kuzvara uchada.* We must have a foolproof plan and hit him once without missing. *Kuita ziita kamwe mimba yousikana.* Some of us gave life to the Party and continue to sustain it, yet this latecomer has personalised it. He wants to rule for life and eliminate any obstacles with brute force."

"What options do we have?" asked These Nations.

"He must be taught a key life lesson. Runo needs a taste of his own medicine."

"Do you want us to kill him?" asked Fly Half.

"No, no, no, there shall be no bloodshed. We have to be smarter than him."

"How do we pull it off since we have our backs against the wall?"

"Once his back is against the wall, the Party and the legislature will feast on him. Let's make him vulnerable and give him enough rope to hang himself. *Zvaarikuita manyengedza pfungwa efodla kuzadza dama nevutsi husingasviki kuguru. Ini ndava kutoti waniwa haachahli kufamba mudova ndichizivazve kuti zhira ine mhihwa ndiyo ine vushe. Zivai kuti kana rokwata roda kunoibva!*"

Chapter 25

Runo tried once again to take charge and destroy the Great Crocodile and stop him from his attempts to ascend to the throne. He was back to his usual mood. Instead of looking at the big picture, he was now busy focusing on Runo and only Runo as the great anointed in the universe. He called in Tadpole for a chat, at the Presidential Palace since he was spending most of his time in bed rather than awake and, worse still, at the office.

"Tadpole, you are moving too slowly."

"What have I not done?"

"The dossier, Tadpole."

"It's almost complete, but I need to verify certain facts to avoid falling into the Great Crocodile's pool or ruffling his scales. If I only manage to do that, then you know with the character of a crocodile that I won't be able to cross the river, drink from that river or even take a bath therein again."

"We don't have time. Forget about the luxuries. You shall present it this week at the Party's executive gathering."

"My pending case is another deterrent, Your Excellency."

"What case?"

"Remember you recommended that I take money unofficially, mostly for your use, and I utilised the balance in my constituency. The Great Crocodile wants to ensure that I pay for the crime."

"That is a small matter. Marujata shall exonerate you in public to scare away anyone who wants to convict you. Consider her to be your lawyer, judge and jury."

"Bossy Boy has been implicated and accused by Party members of being impartial and causing divisions. He is the only other effective arsenal we have."

"The same shall happen to him. That report which had been done on him shall not see the light of day. I will save him from anyone who wants him expelled from the Party. My roommate shall save both of you."

"The veterans are still not towing the Party line, Your Excellency. You need someone to whip them."

"Call on Diesel to fix it. I know that he is incapable of solving any issue without supervision or instruction, but we shall have him as the only senior on our side."

"Not a problem; I will go ahead with my part. If there are any issues, hopefully you will be able to spring to my defence."

"He will get the message from the mere fact that I will be giving you free space to nail him."

"We no longer allow any electronic gadgets to the meeting, Your Excellency. How will I make my presentation?"

"I will make an exception. I am the Party's centre of power and, therefore, I can make the rules as I go. I have done this for most of my career. Therefore, there is nothing to worry about."

"They will think you are a dictator, Your Excellency, by making the rules as you go and applying them selectively."

"I shall deal with whoever dares to offend me."

"The matter is settled then. I will attack."

At the meeting, everyone objected to Tadpole bringing in his baggage, but Runo never paid attention and let him go ahead with his business. When Tadpole's turn came, Runo pretended to sleep or conveniently turned his chair into a sleeping couch. Tadpole went on to make every frivolous accusation and unfounded allegation about the Great Crocodile.

Each time someone or the Great Crocodile wanted to interject, Runo would wake up and allow Tadpole to finish his presentation. It was not a paper expected from any sophisticated man but a desperate dossier to soil someone's reputation. In the end, the Great Crocodile requested Tadpole's presentation and also wanted to question him about the presentation. Runo stopped the interrogation and promised to give the Great Crocodile a chance to make his rebuttal. Runo, instead, leaked the presentation to the press.

After the meeting, Tadpole met Runo briefly at the Presidential Palace to review their charges. Runo was happy with anything that negatively affected the Great Crocodile. The mood was different. Hopes were high that their target would surrender. They were giggling and smiled throughout the conversation.

"Well done, Tadpole. You nailed him."

"Thank you, Your Excellency. I always do my best."

"Do you think he is ours for dinner and ready for the platter?"

"First things first, I think we have delayed his plans to put me behind bars. Next, we accuse him of not attending your rallies to pile up the charges until he cannot breathe."

"My roommate should go for him at our next rally to finish him off. I will not allow him to make a rebuttal unless and until it's convenient for us."

"Your Excellency, you would have done me a big favour. If he does ask, he must give you his report before it is presented."

"He should buckle under pressure, Tadpole!"

"He shall lose his temper."

"You should give him a nudge while holding a trap. Any wrong turn should deliver spaghetti and bolognese immediately."

"Spaghetti bolognaise? My favourite."

"It's all yours, Tadpole."

The two went their separate ways, satisfied that they were

making progress to clear any hurdles that could affect the smooth flow of their lives. Great Crocodile was their major, if not their only, preoccupation.

At an annual business expo, Runo had to be the guest of honour to polish up his public image. He also wanted to downplay rumours that his health was failing. Runo delivered the keynote speech and toured many exhibitions. His company that Bullman had helped establish also participated in the event. On the awards, his company scooped everything on offer in its category. He presented all the awards to himself. He assumed this would give his company a formidable public reputation and exalt his business acumen. Instead, a video circulated on social media about how much of a tyrant he had become. The insinuation was that he was a shameless and sadistic dictator. Not a single newspaper carried the big awards story, feeling it was a sham.

Surprisingly, the Great Crocodile attended the next rally. He was the last senior official to arrive. When he entered the venue, everything was brought to a standstill. The disc jockey played *Mdhara vachauya* to everyone's applause and dance. For a moment, people forgot that the rally should have been about Runo. Even Runo, in his frail and crab-walking stance, managed to grab a post close to him and shake his almost skeletal body to the tune. All war veterans had been barred from attending the rally and all future rallies. A special police unit was put in place to prescreen all rally attendants to make sure that the war veterans would not cause trouble. At this rally, the war veterans were milling outside the venue after having been denied entry.

Once the song and dance were over, Novice took to the podium and took a swipe at the disc jockey and the Great Crocodile. Marujata had her turn, and she was in her usual vile and temperamental fury. She made a very incoherent but scornful speech, attacking the Great Crocodile and anyone who wanted to align with him. Marujata even dressed down some popular scribes for not covering her life-changing work and forced them to quit the profession. One prolific writer, Giorgio, was heckled by Marujata and his widely read weekly column was forcibly taken down. Runo also made sure that his company supplied all the refreshments for Party and government gatherings. Meanwhile, Runo was in his now normal comfortable position, dreaming of ruling the nation even from his grave. He was only startled when the security personnel woke him up to address the crowd.

That evening, Marujata confronted Runo before he could get lost in his sleep. She was restless, and getting to power was taking too long. An overnight change would have been the best solution for her.

"Others are so proud and are having anthems out of their totems like the Great Crocodile. We were forced to sing and dance to it and glorify him. Why can't you hire someone to do the same for you, if not better?"

"The one I use is a public taboo."

"All totems are taboo in one way or another. Just do it."

"No. I mean a public taboo. A sacred passage is not something to boast about in this nation's culture."

"Oh, shame, couldn't your father have adopted something better than a private totem? What shall you do, Runo?"

"He was destitute and had to take the first option. I can only ban the song and just fire the Great Crocodile."

"He has many allies and has more lives than a cat. You are failing at every turn to bury him."

Runo did not take it kindly, being reduced to a mere powerless and helpless man. His temper was roused, and he said, "If all else fails, I will do the unthinkable."

Marujata leapt into the air with joy. "You are such a darling old timer. If only you still had the energy, I would have rewarded you in kind."

"Let's be more progressive. I need someone who can cast that first stone, but I suppose Tadpole can do it or should find a suitable messenger."

"You know he can be sneaky and devious."

"I hold him below the belt always because of his Sodom roots, which is such a poisoned chalice. He will do whatever I want. Besides, he is from the same secret school as me and should serve my interests."

"If you feel comfortable, by all means, go ahead, old timer. I will see to it that he gets an extremely strong dose. However, be very careful with your Sodom poodles; one day people may begin to question why you associate with them."

"You seem to be forgetting something, roommate."

"What is it, old timer?"

"We now have a grandchild, and by the way, you can call me Sim's Grandpa, not old timer..."

"You are such an old timer."

"That was not the point. You must wait until I finish talking."

"Just say what's on your mind then."

"Sim needs a farm, or a few, and you must make arrangements for him."

The plan was set in motion, and at the next gathering Great Crocodile was hit by an invisible arrow that contaminated his bloodstream. These Nations, his wife and Fly Half rushed him for medical assistance. Eventually, they airlifted him out of the country for hospitalisation. Runo, Tadpole and Marujata breathed a sigh of relief and assumed that it was finally over.

Runo even said, "For the first time in my life, I can afford to drink as we celebrate the demise of the Great Great Great Crocodile. He has been a thorn in my flesh for nearly half a century."

That night, Runo had a wild party despite his frail state. He thanked the lord for finally empowering Marujata to take the Great Crocodile's life. Thanks were also given to Tadpole for masterminding the move.

Tadpole took to social media, mocking the Great Crocodile

for behaving like a child and eating baby refreshments. He made video clips of a Great Crocodile look-alike vomiting, being harassed and harangued by diarrhoea. All he got in return was a public rebuke.

The public went on to mention that the Great Crocodile was poisoned by refreshments from Runo's company. Sales nosedived, and Runo and his team were on the back foot again, defending themselves. They issued a public statement that only the Great Crocodile did not partake in the refreshments. It was alleged that he had eaten stale food while at home. The public was not convinced because no one at his home had suffered from the alleged source of poison. The Great Crocodile's sickness got unprecedented press coverage, which further infuriated his enemies. Instead of wishing him well in public, they were busy attacking him. At every function, be it a birthday, company anniversary or political gathering, the trio took turns attacking the Great Crocodile.

Tadpole was tasked with working on an obituary for the Great Crocodile. It pleased him very much, knowing that once the Great Crocodile was gone, his task would be much easier, pushing aside Marujata and her old timer. He could afford to enjoy his imminent win in advance. Giving thanks and praise for having a stooge and a dying old timer feeding from his hand was his daily bread. He could not have asked for a better gift.

It was a foregone conclusion that Tadpole was now counting the days, not only for the Great Crocodile, but for Runo as well. He could dream as the only true and supreme authority for the nation. It was going to be at his discretion to turn the nation into a Sodom or anything that pleased him. He wondered whether to burn the Great Crocodile's body in public or hang it to decompose in the bush or a public street. He also dreamt of tossing Runo's body into the sea, denying him his wish to receive the highest honour as the head of the armed insurrection. Destroying Runo's reputation had been easy to accomplish. Leading the nation with good memories of Runo was not ideal, and he had soiled his standing in preparation for taking over the reins. Knowing the veterans might give him a hard time, he pushed Runo for a quick resolution. Runo, in turn, directed Diesel to crush the veterans. Diesel issued a public statement denouncing any veteran claiming to be representing that section of the Party. New elections were announced, and Diesel hand-picked only Runo loyalists to participate.

Meanwhile, Marujata was also busy, assuming that what happened to the Great Crocodile could also happen to her old timer once her appointment was confirmed as Runo's deputy. In that case, she would be alone at the top. She would have Tadpole's life terminated so that she could enjoy the spoils of the nation by herself. At least she wanted some of her inner circle to share the spoils with her. Her son-in-law was in line to stand as a house of assembly member as well as her son and daughter. These were already in line to be confirmed for ministerial positions. In addition, her brothers were already serving as diplomats, an uncle as a Mines minister, one cousin as a Tourism minister and another as a Commerce minister. Consolidation was going to be easy for her. Furthermore, Runo's young brother was in charge of the National Roads Authority, another was Head of the Tobacco Board, a brother's son was a Deputy Chief of Police, his sister's husband led the Electricity Authority, a brother to Runo in charge of the football mother body, a nephew as Labour Minister and several other shadowy appointments.

Marujata could not believe that she was on the verge of achieving greatness and making history. The historical perspective amused her more. She had risen from the boss' assistant to a side chick, to concubine and later wife, finally landing the top job in the nation. It was her moment to shine, and she stood ready to thrust greatness upon herself. The plans to elevate her were, however, delayed as she had been involved in a diplomatic and domestic fiasco. She had pulverised a young woman, a friend of her son, with a cable. It became an international news headline, and she was quickly renamed Madam Cable. The bad publicity was not good for her name, and postponing her appointment to replace the ailing Great Crocodile was the only plausible option. Meanwhile, her son-in-law was poised to become a billionaire. The run-down and debt-ridden national airline was set to be liquidated, and a new project funded by the government was supposed to replace the airline. This new project was to be spearheaded by the son-in-law as the majority shareholder. While awaiting an opportune time for her appointment, she instructed law enforcement agents to evict a farmer so that baby Sim, her infant grandchild, could assume ownership.

Igi, Runo's premier money-spinning agent, trusted confidante and secret heir apparent, had amassed too much money and assets that he felt he had to be protected. This man had one of his wives on the Anti-Corruption board, and any investigation into his deals would be swept under the carpet. He saw an opportunity being created by Tadpole and Marujata's team. Once the Great Crocodile was gone, it meant the coast was clear for him. Igi knew that Runo trusted him with his life and, therefore, could manoeuvre his way to the top without any possibility of a backlash. Runo was going to appoint him instead of the weak-kneed Diesel. Besides, as the top Party leader, in the absence of Runo, his ascendancy to the top had few hurdles. It was going to be easy to expel Tadpole and Marujata as a humane gesture but not barring the possibility of eliminating Tadpole. He would then be alone at the top and even push aside Runo to claim top honours. The man deeply resented Tadpole, and at one point, he supported an opposition member of parliament who Termite was suing. In preparation for his grand move, Igi hired top international marksmen to help him clear the path to the top. If anyone became a stumbling block, he was not going to hesitate to eliminate them. He played his game with cards close to his chest and in secrecy.

Tadpole was also ready to roll into the sunset when it was announced that the Great Crocodile was going to land back in the nation, having miraculously recovered. His plans were scuttled. He had overlooked the fact that *kudambura mhashu makumbo hunge waibata.*

It was an unexpected turn of events. Runo summoned the doctors who had attended to the Great Crocodile to give him an account of his health and why he had survived. Marujata completely lost it, and she started mocking everyone, especially the Great Crocodile, for making an issue out of his sickness. Tadpole went berserk with his social media frenzy as a way of dealing with the stress of counting the chickens before they were hatched. Runo's camp was gripped by a publicly visible melancholic mood and panic. To clear his tattered image, he forced a written confession on behalf of the Great Crocodile, confirming that he was never poisoned neither did he partake of any refreshments from Runo's company. They signed the confession on his behalf and made it available to the public. Runo also pushed him to make his rebuttal against Tadpole at the next Party executive meeting. He had to visit the Great Crocodile and put more pressure before he could fully recover. Runo was pushed into the house in a wheelchair to speed up the talks.

"Great Crocodile, I know you survived by a whisker, but you must know we have some unfinished business," Runo showed no sympathy.

"Are you desperate that your mission was not successful?" the Great Crocodile answered calmly.

"I didn't do it. Stop spreading unfounded rumours, Great Crocodile," he burst with anger, triggering the wheelchair to speed towards and crash against a wall. He was shaken, and the Great Crocodile watched until Runo regained a little strength. Without saying a word, he gazed at Runo as he feebly pushed the wheelchair closer to him, and then he spoke.

"That is not what I asked you. Why are you talking about unfinished business instead of giving me time to fully recover?"

"You need to give me your rebuttal presentation so that I can consider when to slot you in."

"Do not worry yourself, Runo. You are too frail, and any further loss of weight could see you being blown away by the wind. See, the flesh is fast thinning away and separating from your bones, and you look like a withered body or dried mummy. I will present when I am strong." Great Crocodile felt humour was the best medicine.

"As the leader of this nation, I need to be in charge."

"You embarrass yourself, Great Grandpa Runo. In your wisdom or lack of it, how can you continue to send your puppy to bark at me? *Uri kutuma bofu kunomema hunza!*"

"I did no such thing, Great Crocodile. I couldn't stoop so low." He felt humbled.

"Then I don't see how you should be worried about my response to Tadpole if you had nothing to do with his accusations."

"This information is now a public record. You must defend yourself."

"You have started your stupid games again. When will you grow up?"

"Shall I take it that you are not going to respond?"

"Don't put words in my mouth, Runo. I will present the truth, not your frivolous allegations, when I am good and ready. It's time for you to buzz off if you have nothing else to say. There is a failing economy to attend to, yet you spend all your awake time working on me. You must be ashamed of what you have become, squandering all the goodwill you may have created."

A shameless Runo left without saying anything further.

The Great Crocodile met with his friends once again, but this time with an enlarged entourage. They agreed and mapped all the strategic positions to station their military equipment should Runo continue with his madness. Great Crocodile and his crew resolved strategically and stood ready to send any Runo loyalists in the force on vacation. Any negotiations with Runo were to be very hostile and never to allow him room to dictate terms.

Chapter 26

At the next rally, Great Crocodile made time to attend briefly and test his readiness for public gatherings. He again brought the house down at the rally because *Mdhara Vachauya* was played to acknowledge his presence. The Novice graced the stage later and took a swipe at the Great Crocodile. This young man tried to intimidate him, showing uncontrolled anger and told the crowd that there was only one Mdhara, His Excellency Runobvepi. His rented crowd applauded but never gave him a standing ovation. Marujata supported the Novice and went on to dispute any poisoning allegations as well as her refreshments having anything to do with it. She came short of chopping off his head in public. It was clear that she was unhappy that the man had survived.

Marujata's insanity must have peaked that day as she levelled serious allegations against anyone that displeased her. She named many people as traitors and supporters of the Great Crocodile, calling them to the podium, one by one. Her uncouth personality was on full display as she castrated powerful men, dressing them down in public. This had become a daily ritual and came as no surprise. She seriously lacked political legitimacy and hoped to make that up with borrowed power from Runo and her nervy, brash presence. She made some unrivalled violent gestures employing her infamous trademark phrase, *Stop it* warning, to intimidate all supporters of the Great Crocodile. At this rally, she also took a swipe at the press and those that called her names or presumed her to be a harlot that had an insatiable sexual appetite with a net of lovers, calling on them to, *Stop it*, forthwith. It was time for her to fight back. She declared that she was not a whore but a legitimately married woman with good morals, Runo's wife and first lady, not a harlot. The army, friends of the Great Crocodile, were not spared either as she threatened them and mocked them.

Marujata's assuming the bully, commandeering the unsophisticated, created a very negative quality of her to the public as it felt sorry for her, but she misunderstood it to be working in her favour. She overestimated her erotic power over Runo and irredeemable fondness for cash and borrowing Runo's robes as being equal to political legitimacy and power. Already, she was the laughingstock of the nation, a joke, but Tadpole could not care less about this fact because everything was working in his favour.

Finally, she absolved Tadpole and Bossy Boy of any wrongdoing and declared that they were innocent. Marujata even suggested that those accusing the two were guilty and needed to be punished. She assumed the role of mother of the nation with infinite power through her poisoned tongue, having the prerogative to arrest, prosecute, judge, punish and reward as she wished.

Runo, in his geriatric temperament, went off on a tangent from the objective of the address. He instead focused on the Great Crocodile and regurgitated all of Tadpole's allegations against him. His slow-aged tone took him longer to conclude his speech than anticipated. The speech ended without addressing the crowd and also due to physical exhaustion. It seemed a well-rehearsed show, and the public forgave him for the speech, assuming it was owing to old age and, therefore, was out of touch with reality.

After the rally, the singer of the Great Crocodile's theme

song had his life threatened, and he had to leave the nation in a huff. Marujata and Tadpole were determined to terminate his life.

Great Crocodile managed to spare a few moments to talk to Runo a day after the mindless road show. He went to Runo's office late in the afternoon to ensure he'd had enough sleep and knew any appointment at his Presidential Palace was not welcome. His eighteen-hour sleeping schedule was not appropriate for his job. It meant the country was on auto-pilot because the Commander-in-Chief was incapacitated.

"How is my dear leader, Runobvepi?"

"You don't have to be polite, Great Crocodile."

"Our children must learn from us. If we lose it, then we will have destroyed the future of our nation."

"Don't patronise me. I hope you are not looking for my sympathy."

"I don't believe it's necessary at this stage because the battle lines have been drawn."

"Sure. *Handidzori tsvimbo nokuti gudo rabata kumeso*," he remarked, engulfed in his delusions of grandeur and ready to raise his voice even higher.

"That is your nature, and you need great help to understand it before your death. It will be good for you if you could improve on certain things."

"What do you think you can offer to my statesmanship?" His eyes were wide open, showing anger.

"*Chidembo hachihwi kunhuwa kwacho*, but for how long do you have to continue with the cheating mode?"

"There is a thin line between politics and cheating, but I need specifics to answer you fully."

"Runo, you are spending millions yet again to buy off chiefs and secure a rural vote by default."

"You know their role is critical in safeguarding traditional values and keeping the communities together. It is a deserved privilege."

"The spirit of the privilege is twisted, and some of the chiefs are conveniently picked based on party lines."

"I do not know of any such thing. If it's happening, then certainly it is never my fault."

"Provided it sustains your stay in power, then you are not worried because there was no budget for the vehicles. We now have to go into debt to fulfil your need for power."

"Suit yourself, Great Crocodile. At least I have the power."

"Is that why you, your wife and your puppies are barking at me all the time? You cannot even stop abusing these churches to sustain your agenda."

"I have to be on my roommate's side. We are a family. The State and church must always work together. We cannot be a godless nation."

"Do you have to persecute me all the time for being successful at what I do?"

"What success, Great Crocodile, are you referring to?"

"The agricultural success which has helped your standing since the farm invasions. I knew you had set me up to fail so that you could have a solid reason to dispense with me. Now that the opposite happened, you are disappointed. Are you sure you only want non-performing money gangs and bootlickers around you?"

"That is a very serious allegation. Your presidential ambition shall be thwarted."

"Do it with a clear conscience, Runo."

"If I don't, what will you do? I can sack both you and your military friends and leave you languishing in the cold. Worse still, I could imprison you so that you feel the pain of trying to challenge my position."

"Must you always maintain a legacy of torture and imprisonment for aspiring leaders? Don't you suppose you could lose the plot in your anger, and the tables will be turned against you?"

"A military takeover will never be tolerated by the region

and the international community. I am safe from that threat."

"What if there is a hostile negotiation? *Vushe imhute, huno-parara zuva rabuda.* As you always say, it may be necessary to use other methods, not constitutional ones. Remember, *hakuna nenji risina kumusha kwaro.*"

"It's a matter of semantics, but the action remains illegal. Politics should always lead the gun, not the other way around. We should never bring that curse unto ourselves and remember that my rule is not about to end any time soon."

"It's just a piece of friendly advice because *chati homu chareva.* Forewarned is forearmed. I have always tried to appeal to your better nature only to realise that you don't have one," Great Crocodile realised that fear was the only solution since democracy and justice had become just words.

"I am invincible, Great Crocodile. Don't waste your time. Political manoeuvres are key in keeping one in power. I am a deal maker and this has kept me going. Economics is just a means, not an end in itself." He tried to threaten Great Crocodile.

"*Dzangove shungu dzomutana waxhwera padare kuramba nemhandire seane meno.* Remember, very recently, you read a speech for the wrong occasion when everyone in the nation was either watching or listening. It's time to give up. Sleeping an average of eighteen hours every day is no mean task."

"Stop insulting me. You are my subordinate," he stood up full of anger and quickly fell back in his chair, scrambling to balance himself.

"*Zvinonzi gore jena chirego penya unozotoregwa vushe nedema. Ziva kuti, chigere ibwe, muti unowa.* So don't say I didn't try. At your age, the power of wisdom must take precedence over concentrating all your power on the tongue like the pincers or its cousin, the pliers. *Zvinonzi, gombarume kudze soro, kukudza dumbu wonge wava chanana zvikurusei kubotsakufa rakaita sewe.* It's not plausible that your imperviousness to good advice can even be surgically corrected. Just like separating you from your seat of power, legally, it's a surgical impossibility."

The Great Crocodile left.

Runo felt that he was losing at every turn and, therefore, had a support mission to all neighbouring countries. He wanted the assurance that no palace coup was going to be tolerated and used this against the Great Crocodile. Runo had secret meetings with his former financiers and friends who had deserted him for Sabi. He assured them that if they worked with him, they could have all the land and mineral rights they could ever have wanted. For the public, he only appeared with the leader of the team members he had dined with. He got the backing and assurances he needed and immediately returned home. On his return, he sacked every professional executive member, or those who aligned with the Great Crocodile. All posts were filled by extremely incompetent or corrupt individuals who served Runo's interests. These were the same people who were his money-spinning conduits. His final solution was to have Marujata as his deputy to complete the power consolidation game and relieve the Great Crocodile of his post. A plan B was quickly put in place. That young man from Sabi's party, who used shoe polish to style his hair and had become Runo's close business associate and ally, was called in. They assured him that he would be financed to ascend to the top position of his party and, in return, should accommodate all of Runo's lieutenants if anything negative happened to Runo's grip on power. He was literarily anointed as a successor, and if things went Runo's way, he would be accommodated in the Great Revolutionary Party with a promise to rule in the not-so-distant future.

That concubine, spying on the Great Crocodile on Runo's behalf, was running scared of the political games at play. She had been mum on information and was contemplating fleeing the nation to save her life. Tadpole, knowing the Great Crocodile's schedule, arranged for her demise, hoping to pin all the evidence on him. When Great Crocodile sniffed on the plot, it was already too late to save her. What he managed to do was make a quick visit to a neighbouring country on a chartered plane to fulfil a diplomatic obligation. Tadpole's planned alibi fell apart, and he could not have the Great Crocodile behind bars as he had planned. She died for nothing, and Tadpole had to work hard to conceal any foul play on the death.

The Great Crocodile sued Tadpole first before presenting his rebuttal. Runo and Marujata worked hard to ensure the Great Crocodile excluded certain content from his presentation. They were afraid of the potential damage it could cause to their persons and the effects of the unintended consequences. Great Crocodile received support from the majority in the executive council. Runo went against the opinion of the majority.

The nation's public court of opinion was very much against Runo, and any minor negative on him was turned into a carnival celebration in secret and on social media. People were ready to march in the streets, and the mood was building up. Small but growing crowds could occasionally be heard singing.

The Great Crocodile took time to talk to his nemesis one day at his office yet again.

"I know I am the last person on earth you want to see, but when you die you must at least know the truth."

"What truth, Great Crocodile?"

"Do you hear them sing Great Grandpa? Can your broken-up ear bones hear a single word? They sing for your demise. They have had their Independence but are now clamouring for freedom. When we became independent, everyone celebrated, had high hopes and great expectations, and imagined a future marked by success and progress, but now all the hope is gone. Despair and hopelessness are the new normal because you promoted imported beliefs instead of uprooting them, you relaxed, got sidetracked, and barriers were erected when you wanted to have your way at a very late stage."

"They are wasting their time. I belong in this office."

"No, Runo, you are behind time. Make peace and do yourself a favour. Very soon, your puppies will be trapping themselves in a worse manner than you and Marujata have been."

"What do you mean, Great Crocodile? Are you threatening me?"

"I could never do that, but remember Marujata almost faced incarceration. You faced international public ridicule after being stripped of your short-lived honour. Imagine what is in store for your puppies."

"Don't you think the public hate them but love me."

"You could never be further from the truth. You could, however, only save yourself if you dissociate from them."

"What truth?"

"If anyone sacrifices his life to take out yours, there will be a stampede at his funeral and only a handful of family members at yours."

"You are only dramatising, Great Crocodile. There were lots of people attending our meet-the-people rallies. I am loved in this nation."

"A rented crowd does not count."

"Do you mean my crew has been fooling me all along?"

"Of course, Runo, they want to impress you. As we speak, some are holding night vigils to request your death."

"Do you suppose if I divorce my roommate, then I will be back in business since she is the one with my poisoned tongue?"

"It's a little too late for that, but you can be their hero again if you announce your retirement. There has been too much of a leadership backlog in this nation. One man for forty years is way too much, and the economic principles will be difficult to get right while democracy will be impossible to maintain with everyone clamouring for a chance to rule."

"Never, Great Crocodile. They love me. You only want to take my position."

"Let me subject you to a litmus test and a reality check at our congress this year, this coming month."

"What test?"

"Democratise our Party. You and me contesting for the top position in the Party as the press is fully aware of my intentions and the cold war between us. You can't continue kicking the can down the road."

"Aaah." Runo was surprised and upset. "You are testing my patience. By the end of the day tomorrow, you shall be jobless. Leave now before I call security to remove you."

The following day, Runo called for a press conference, had a letter drafted to relieve the Great Crocodile of his duties and hurriedly invited all provincial leaders to attend and support his move. The information secretary read the letter as assigned by Runo. Each provincial leader was asked to take the podium and denounce the Great Crocodile. Novice, too, came with his entourage chanting songs to denounce the Great Crocodile and gave a moving speech in support of Runo. Igi did not attend. He had instructions to capture the Great Crocodile and his team, dead or alive, with the assistance of some snipers.

All TV stations suspended their broadcasting schedules to focus on the press conference. The Great Crocodile's house was surrounded by a security detail, but he had already escaped to the army barracks just before Runo commenced the press conference. He then gave a signal to his peers and circulated a letter on social media that he would soon be the Nation's new leader and that no one should be despondent. His sacking was just a desperate attempt by a spent force to prolong his stay in power while oppressing the people.

A few hours after the press conference, towards the day's end, very few people left the city as masses gathered in the city square in support of the Great Crocodile. Fly Half and These Nations had joined the Great Crocodile in barracks to avoid capture by Runo. They called a press conference which was attended by many journalists. Runo instructed that all newspapers and TV stations should shy away from broadcasting the event. The footage was, therefore, only available on social media. It was, however, enough to give the crowds the impetus they needed. Shops were swamped by crowds purchasing candles and torches for use throughout the night.

By the time Runo returned to the Presidential Palace, it was already surrounded by the army, and he was captured. His life was spared to show compassion for a dying old man. Igi could not figure out what hit him. The army easily captured him after ruthlessly eliminating his snipers. TV stations were surrounded and taken over by the army the following morning. Checkpoints were mounted on all routes from and into the city. Novice, realising the folly of his actions, tried to escape and was captured on the outskirts of the city. Tadpole and his friends were captured at a checkpoint and faced incarceration. Runo had hoped the police would put up resistance and create a need for the international community to intervene. Law enforcement agents had no chance to resist. The Great Crocodile made sure the police armoury was sealed off with army tankers surrounding the depot. The crowds who had spent the night singing and marching around the city square erupted with joy at the announcement of the events of the night. The Great Crocodile had completed the most fast-tracked takeover of power in the history politics.

Shona Glossary

1. Dzinofura nzivani – Birds of a feather
2. Mazano marairanwa – Ideas are meant to be shared
3. Mbimbindoga akasya jira kumasese – People who forsake advice fall into calamity
4. Mapenzi anomwa muto – Greedy and selfish people
5. Wakadzidza Herę? – Are you educated?
6. Warova sechumi yepapa – Long time no see
7. Uchaona tsvuku inenge pondo – Trouble is on the way
8. Zvirahwe – Riddles
9. Ngano – Folk tales
10. Totenda maruva tadla chakata – We will only believe once accomplished/fulfilled
11. Kumisa pfambi hunge une mari – Bargaining power or wealth can facilitate some transactions
12. Mudzimu waro bonga – Good luck/fortune
13. Inga vari kuno vanoshura – Deliberate or false accusation
14. Poshi haagwigwi – Once can be forgiven
15. Makara asivonani – Sworn enemies
16. Mhumhi, Isingadli chakafa choga, Bonga Chihwa – Wild dog, only eats fresh meat, wild dog

17. Dhadha haridliwi musoro – No one eats a duck's head

18. Zhou mutupo pane vamwe – Taboo in public but not in private

19. Nzenza mumvuri – Some seemingly bad things are a necessity/a necessary evil

20. Ukaravidza chembere muto wegwaya – Some things are better left hidden

21. Miviri iri sei? – How is your health?

22. Ndiri njanji, ndakasimba somutandanda wehambautare – Strong like a train track or bicycle cross bar

23. Kukwira gomo hupoterera – Prepping

24. Musha mukadzi – A house becomes a home only when there is a wife around/a man is incomplete without a wife

25. Kugara ndichiridza ngoma nenyama – Having regular intimacy/sex

26. Baba angu Shumba! – My ancestors of the lion totem!

27. Zvatichaitigwa mashura – An omen is in the making

28. Inga gumbo retatu rinoparira – The penis can be a curse

29. Dzvetera matadza, Gona mashavi, bvupa muderere, bungu muridzo – A gorgeous woman

30. Watopera pfungwa – You are getting crazy/losing your mind

31. Chimurerekedzwa chindiro chine buri – A worthless person

32. Mupfuhwira rudo – A love potion is part of love

33. Mupfuhwira uroyi – A love potion is a form of witchcraft

34. Mvana ndoodzinochengeta – Single mothers make good wives

35. Ubuhle bendonda inkomo zayo – The beauty of a man is in his wealth

36. Harahwa ndoo dzinochengeta – Older men make good husbands

37. Harahwa ndoo dzinochengera – Older men never let you out of their sight

38. Tsenzi igara wadla/Uswa hwenyati/Gara wadla – Don't waste time/opportunity

39. Chirungurira chirwere – Don't keep problems to yourself

40. Ukasekerera mhashu – Nip problems in the bud

41. Atengeswa isipo – To be tricked/cheated

42. Chiri pamuchena chari pamutenure/Nhanga rekuzhira – A poor man's victory is short-lived

43. Kuraira kuuya kweshamhu kwakadana musimbwa – Teaching/training/advising can only be achieved through persuasion

44. Ura mapako – The womb is unpredictable. It can produce murderers, scoundrels, witches and thieves

45. Kubereka kokubvisa bundu muura – A birth being an act of removing impurities in the womb

46. Handipedzeri hoko padehwe reshindi – Not wasting time on trivial issues

47. Rakateya mapfumo seSoso – Setting traps all the time

48. Tichapedzerana – A threat

49. Nakirezvo mbudzi yatunga bere – Take advantage of an opportunity that presents itself

50. Kuramba nyama yechidembo hunge une yeshuro – To turn down an offer means one has better options/opportunities

51. Akarasha moyo achisiya ndove – A cold-hearted person (excreting the heart instead of the dirt)

52. Hapana chembwa Tenzi vavatira mutakura – If a leader loses, his followers suffer

53. Mafunga mafunga pavete nzuma ichifunga chakadla nyanga dzayo – Deep thinking/pondering

54. Mvura bvongodzeki ndoogarani – Only warring parties can make peace

55. Mucheri wembeva mutevedzi wemwena – Doing things by the book

56. Bhuru rasarira shure rasarira shamhu – Punishment is the reward for those not towing the line/not following the law

57. Ava mangongomera mupasha wapfura musoro – Being in deep trouble and there is no way out

58. Afa nemavanga enyora haachemwi – Self-inflicted harm

59. Rukova gwizi – Respect

60. Kutatarika humira – Any attempt is a good progress

61. Ashunya agwa – Any contribution must be appreciated

62. Atsinzina rega atsikwe – If you snooze you lose

63. Chikomo shata divi rime ritambire pwere – It's necessary to have a good side in every personality

64. Hatisvori chambere parwendo tisati tafamba nayo – Everyone deserves a chance

65. Kuiboba nekumuxhwe – To turn things upside down

66. Chinotaura ndechiri mumusungo chiri muriva chinoti denga rawa – There are no negotiations after a complete defeat

67. Lokhu la lokhu – This and that

68. Sakunatsa ndiye sakubaiwa – The good guy always suffers

69. Shiri yakangwara – Taking advantage of/Treat someone badly in order to get something good

70. Kudiridzira rugare nemisodzi yevamwe – Exploitation

71. Mununura ndakapinga/Zimhuhwa Riri mundove – Pretending to help while destroying

72. Kurumwa netsikidzi gara mumba – Weigh options before making a choice/Better the devil you know

73. Chaunoda chii pahuku yomweni – You are an uninvited and unsolicited meddler

74. Anebenzi ndeane rake – When you know the bad traits of someone, you will not be offended when they do bad things

75. Misodzi yebere – Crocodile tears

76. Muroyi munhu kubaiwa anochema – An evil person is still a human being

77. Panomera muxhwe panonyeredza – People who forsake advice fall into calamity

78. Chingoma chamusinzwi chakaguma nataisireva – People who forsake advice fall into calamity

79. Kutonga nedemo – Authoritarianism

80. Kudla chomuzvere hubata mwana – Let's all contribute to making a successful deal

81. Matanda manyoro mazungunutswa – Everything is worth a try

82. Chakataira pasi ndecho munhu wese – Dare to be different

83. Chakachenjedza ndechakatanga – Once bitten, twice shy

84. Ziita kamwe mimba yousikana – One successful attempt

85. Manyengedza pfungwa efodla kuzadza dama noutsi husingasviki kuguru – A false sense of achievement

86. Waniwa haachahli kufamba mudova – Facing problems head on

87. Zhira ine mhihwa ndoo ine vushe/Chitende chinorema ndoo chine mhodzi – The harder the option, the more the rewards

88. Kana rokwata roda kuibva – Darkest hour is always before dawn

89. Kudambura mhashu makumbo hunge waibata – Do not count chickens before they are hatched

90. Kutuma bofu kunomema hunza – The blind/ignorant cannot lead

91. Handidzori tsvimbo nokuti gudo rabata kumeso – Showing no mercy

92. Chidembo hachihwi kunhuwa kwacho – You don't see the log in your own eye

93. Vushe imhute – Power is temporary

94. Chati homu chareva – Forewarned is forearmed

95. Shungu dzomutana axhwera padare kuramba nemhandire seane meno – There comes a time to let go/retire to avoid falling into problems

96. Gore jena chirego penya unozotoregwa vushe nedema – Pride comes before a fall

97. Chigere ibwe muti unowa – Power is temporary

98. Gombarume kudze soro kukudza dumbu wenge chanana – Maturity and wisdom are a necessity

About Atmosphere Press

Founded in 2015, Atmosphere Press was built on the principles of Honesty, Transparency, Professionalism, Kindness, and Making Your Book Awesome. As an ethical and author-friendly hybrid press, we stay true to that founding mission today.

If you're a reader, enter our giveaway for a free book here:

SCAN TO ENTER
BOOK GIVEAWAY

If you're a writer, submit your manuscript for consideration here:

SCAN TO SUBMIT
MANUSCRIPT

And always feel free to visit Atmosphere Press and our authors online at atmospherepress.com. See you there soon!